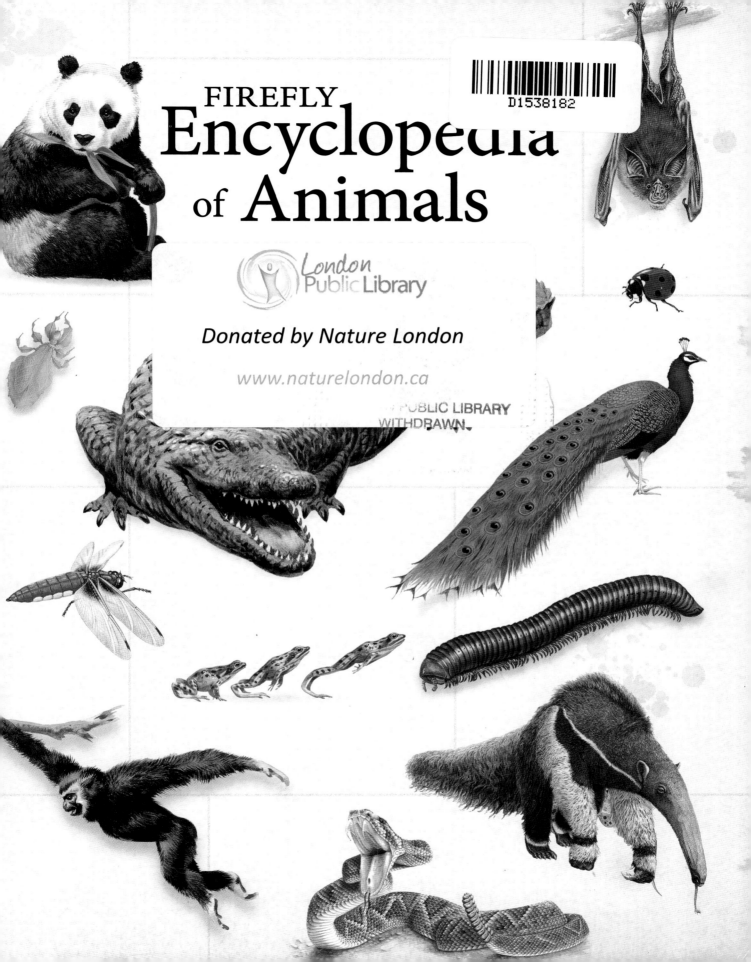

# FIREFLY
# Encyclopedia
## of Animals

# A FIREFLY BOOK

Published by Firefly Books Ltd. 2014
Copyright © 2014 Marshall Editions

First printing

**Publisher Cataloging-in-Publication Data (U.S.)**
A CIP record for this title is available from the Library of Congress

**Library and Archives Canada Cataloguing in Publication**
A CIP record for this title is available from Library and Archives Canada

Published in the United States by
Firefly Books (U.S.) Inc.
P.O. Box 1338, Ellicott Station
Buffalo, New York 14205

Published in Canada by
Firefly Books Ltd.
50 Staples Avenue, Unit 1
Richmond Hill, Ontario L4B 0A7

Created by Tall Tree Ltd.
Editors: Camilla Hallinan, Jon Richards
Designers: Marisa Renzullo, Malcolm Parchment
Art Director: Susi Martin
Publisher: Zeta Jones

Printed in China
by Toppan Leefung Printing Ltd

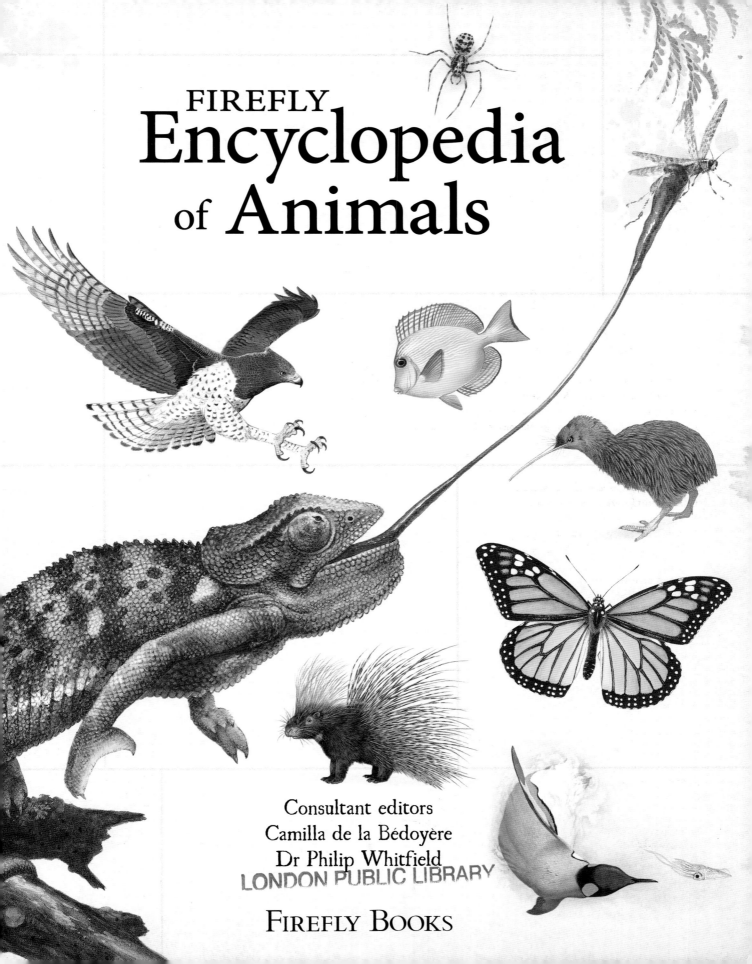

# FIREFLY
# Encyclopedia
## of Animals

Consultant editors
Camilla de la Bédoyère
Dr Philip Whitfield

FIREFLY BOOKS

# CONTENTS

## MAMMALS

## BIRDS

## REPTILES

# AMPHIBIANS

# FISH

# INSECTS, SPIDERS AND OTHER INVERTEBRATES

# MAMMALS

Human beings are just one of about 5,500 mammal species. Mammals come in all shapes and sizes and are found in almost every part of the world, from the frozen Arctic to the hottest deserts, densest forests and biggest oceans. There are many different kinds of mammal, each with its own way of life. The tiger, for example, hunts prey in the depths of the forest, while dolphins swim through the sea, moles burrow underground, bats fly through the air, horses gallop across the ground and monkeys swing through the trees.

# WHAT IS A MAMMAL?

Mammals are a diverse group of animals, but they all have certain things in common. They are warm-blooded, have lungs to breathe in air and a bony frame called a skeleton to support their bodies and protect their internal organs. Most also have relatively large brains, good senses and hair or fur.

## TYPES OF MAMMAL

Most mammals give birth to live young. In most mammals, known as eutherians, the babies grow inside the mother's womb. They are supplied with food and oxygen by a special organ called the placenta, and are well-developed when they are born. Marsupials are very undeveloped at birth and crawl into a special pouch where they can grow stronger in safety. Monotremes are unusual — they lay eggs instead of producing babies.

## MARSUPIAL

Baby wallaby feeding in pouch

Large head

Young wallaby clings to teat

Long face to make room for large flat teeth used for chewing plants

Young wallaby

Poorly developed legs

Powerful legs for bounding along fast

Furry pouch

Long thick tail for balance

Ring-tailed wallaby

Indian elephant

Mammals are warm-blooded animals — they can keep their body temperature constant, whatever the temperature of their surroundings. When they are too hot, many mammals sweat to cool down. Elephants cannot sweat, so they keep cool by staying in the shade, bathing in water and letting heat evaporate from their huge ears.

## SENSES

Mammals generally have well-developed senses of sight, hearing, smell, taste and touch. These senses help them to locate food, avoid predators, find a mate and much more. The sense organs are often found in the head, near the brain.

Acute hearing

Sharp eyes

Sensitive whiskers

Keen sense of smell

Female wild boar with young

# SUCKLING

A female mammal has mammary glands (also called breasts or udders) that produce milk, which the babies suck from teats. This is called suckling. The milk contains sugar, fat, proteins and vitamins, which the babies need to grow and stay healthy.

## MONOTREME

### Short-beaked echidna

Female carries egg in a groove on her belly

Coat of protective spines

Echidna has no teats — milk oozes from pores in skin

## EUTHERIAN MAMMAL

### Pileated gibbon

Long arms for swinging from tree to tree

Forward-pointing eyes to judge distances accurately

Fur covers skin

Five-toed feet

Short strong legs

Shoulders

Vertebrae

Skull

Hips

Jaws

Rib cage

Arms

Gorilla skeleton

Feet

Hands

# MAMMAL SKELETONS

Mammals are vertebrates, which means that their skeleton has a backbone made up of individual bones called vertebrae. A rib cage surrounds the heart and lungs, and a skull protects the brain. Some mammals have adapted parts of their skeletons to suit their particular lifestyle. Sea mammals, for example, have flippers instead of arms and legs.

### Blue whale skeleton

Vertebrae

Tail

Jaws

Shoulders

Skull

Flippers

Rib cage

Hips, but no hind limbs

# MONOTREMES AND MARSUPIALS

In most mammal species, the young develop inside their mother's body for a long time before they are born. But monotremes and marsupials are different. Like their reptile ancestors, monotremes lay eggs, but when they hatch, the young feed on their mother's milk. Marsupials give birth to very undeveloped babies: some are no bigger than a grain of rice, and all are hairless and blind. Once it is born, a young marsupial develops in a furry pouch on the underside of its mother's body.

## MONOTREMES

Monotremes consist of echidnas (or spiny anteaters) and platypuses. A female echidna lays a single, soft-shelled egg and puts it in a groove on her belly, where it is protected for seven to 10 days until it hatches. The platypus is one of the few venomous mammals: the male has a spur on each hind foot, for injecting venom into an enemy. A female platypus lays two or three eggs in a long tunnel; they take up to two weeks to hatch.

Size: body 17¾–30¼ in (45–77 cm); virtually no tail

Range: New Guinea

Habitat: tropical evergreen forest

### Long-nosed echidna
*Zaglossus bruijni*

Echidnas have long slender snouts. They have no teeth and weak jaws, so they lap up ants, termites and other small creatures with their sticky tongues and crush them against the roof of their mouths.

Size: body 13¾–19¾ in (35–50 cm); tail 3½ in (9 cm)

Range: Australia, Tasmania, southeast New Guinea

Habitat: deciduous and tropical evergreen forest, temperate grassland, desert

### Platypus
*Ornithorhynchus anatinus*

The platypus spends most of the day in a riverside burrow. At dawn and dusk it comes out to feed on the riverbed, using its sensitive bill to probe the mud for insects, worms, grubs, crayfish and frogs. Its bill is a skin-covered framework of bone.

Size: body 18 in (46 cm); tail 7 in (18 cm)

Range: Australia, Tasmania

Habitat: fresh water

### Short-nosed echidna
*Tachyglossus aculeatus*

The echidna's spiny coat protects it from attackers. When threatened, it either curls itself up into a ball or, if it is on soft soil, digs straight downward so that only its spines are visible.

# MARSUPIALS

The word marsupial means "pouched mammal." A tiny marsupial baby has to wriggle its way through its mother's fur to reach her pouch. Once inside, it latches on to a teat and drinks her milk. The pouch gives the baby a safe place in which it can grow and develop until it is ready to face the outside world. There are more than 335 marsupial species.

## Kowari
*Dasyuroides byrnei*

Size: body 6½–7 in (16.5–18 cm); tail 5–5½ in (13–14 cm)
Range: central Australia
Habitat: tropical grassland, desert

At home in grasslands and deserts, this small marsupial lives alone or in small groups in an underground burrow. At night, it hunts among the tussock grass for insects, lizards and small birds. Kowaris breed in winter and produce litters of five or six young. Due to overgrazing and loss of habitat, the kowari is now listed as vulnerable.

Size: body 10½–13 in (27–33 cm); tail 14¼–15¾ in (36–40 cm)
Range: Mexico, Central and South America
Habitat: fresh water

## Water opossum
*Chironectes minimus*

The water opossum is the only marsupial that lives in water. It emerges from its riverbank burrow to swim and search for fish, shellfish and other small water creatures, which it carries back to the bank to eat. It swims with its webbed hind feet, and steers with its long tail. Its oily fur repels water, keeping it dry.

## Brown bandicoot
*Isoodon obesulus*

The brown bandicoot hunts by following the scent of its prey. It feeds on worms, insect larvae and underground fungi. It will even eat scorpions, biting off their poisonous tails before consuming them. In areas of dense vegetation, it hides from predators such as eagles and foxes.

Size: body 11¾–13 in (30–33 cm); tail 3–7 in (7.5–18 cm)
Range: southern and eastern Australia, Tasmania
Habitat: deciduous forest, desert

Size: body 12¾–19¾ in (32.5–50 cm); tail 10–21 in (25.5–53.5 cm)
Range: southeast Canada, through USA to Central America
Habitat: deciduous and tropical evergreen forest, desert, inhabited areas and farmland

## Virginia opossum
*Didelphis virginiana*

This is the sole North American marsupial. It often scavenges for food in dumpsters and trash cans. To escape a predator, such as a dog, eagle or bobcat, the opossum may "play dead," lying on its side with its tongue hanging out and its eyes shut or staring into space. Thinking it is already dead, the predator may lose interest, giving the opossum vital seconds to make its escape.

**11**

## Koala
### *Phascolarctos cinereus*

The koala spends up to 18 hours each day asleep. The rest of the time it feeds on the leaves of eucalyptus trees. It has a long gut, which enables it to digest the tough leaves and deal with the leaves' poisonous chemicals. Special pouches in its cheeks store the leaves until it needs to eat them.

Size: body 23½–33½ in (60–85 cm); virtually no tail

Range: eastern Australia

Habitat: deciduous forest, tropical forest

Size: body 12½–22¾ in (32–58 cm); tail 9½–13¾ in (24–35 cm)

Range: Australia, Tasmania; introduced into New Zealand

Habitat: deciduous forest, tropical evergreen forest

## Common brush-tailed possum
### *Trichosurus vulpecula*

Like most possums, this one is nocturnal. In its natural woodland habitat, it feeds on flowers, leaves, fruit, insects and young birds. In populated areas, it makes its home on buildings and feeds on garbage. It breeds one young once or twice a year.

## Tasmanian devil
### *Sarcophilus harrisii*

About the size of a small dog, the Tasmanian devil moves slowly, but with cunning. Its keen sense of smell enables it to locate prey in the dark and take it by surprise. It feeds on reptiles, birds, fish and small mammals, and crushes the bones of its prey in its powerful jaws. Badly affected by disease, the species is now listed as endangered.

Size: body 20½–31½ in (52–80 cm); tail 9–11¾ in (23–30 cm)

Range: Tasmania

Habitat: deciduous forest, inhabited areas and farmland, coast

Size: body 27½–47 in (70–120 cm); virtually no tail

Range: eastern Australia, Tasmania

Habitat: deciduous forest, desert

## Coarse-haired wombat
### *Vombatus ursinus*

The wombat feeds on grass in forests and scrubland and can go without water for months. In summer, it shelters from the heat in a long deep burrow. The female gives birth to a single young, which stays in her pouch for three months. Then it forages with her for several months before leaving to live independently.

Size: body 9–13½ in (23–34 cm);
tail 5–6¾ in (13–17 cm)
Range: northeastern Australia
Habitat: tropical evergreen forest

Size: body 3¼–5¼ ft (1–1.6·
); tail 35½–43½ in
(90–110 cm)
Range: central Australia
Habitat: tropical
grassland, scrub, desert

## Musky rat-kangaroo
*Hypsiprymnodon moschatus*

This tiny kangaroo is unusual because it regularly gives birth to twins. Unlike other kangaroos, it prefers to move around on all fours like a rabbit. Both males and females produce a strong musky smell, but no one knows why they do this.

## Red kangaroo
*Macropus rufus*

The red kangaroo is the largest marsupial. It bounds along with huge leaps, on its back legs only, reaching speeds of up to 35 mph (56 km/h). It lives in Australia's hot, dry deserts and grassland. The female gives birth to a single baby called a joey, which emerges from her pouch after two months. If danger threatens, the joey dives back into her pouch.

## Bridled nail-tail wallaby
*Onychogalea fraenata*

The nail-tail gets its name because it has a small, fingerlike nail hidden in thick hair at the tip of its tail. It has a strange way of hopping, moving its arms in circles as it bounces along. Heavy grazing by sheep and cattle has destroyed much of the scrubland where it used to live and feed, and so this wallaby is now an endangered species.

Size: body 20½–31½ in (52–80 cm);
tail 16½–36½ in (42–93 cm)
Range: northeastern Australia
Habitat: tropical evergreen forest

## Lumholtz's tree kangaroo
*Dendrolagus lumholtzi*

The tree kangaroo spends most of its time high up in the forest trees, where it eats leaves and fruit. It can even sleep up there, crouched on a thick branch. This species is rarely seen because it is nocturnal and well-camouflaged in trees.

Size: body 17¾–26¼ in (45–67 cm);
tail 13–26 in (33–66 cm )
Range: parts of eastern Australia
Habitat: scrub and grassland

# ANTEATERS AND OTHER INSECT EATERS

Although these insect eaters are not all related to each other, they are perhaps the oddest-looking and most fascinating mammals of all. They include the armored armadillos, the aardvark with its piglike body, rabbitlike ears and kangaroolike tail, the anteaters with their incredibly long snouts, and the small furry moles, shrews and spiny tenrecs and hedgehogs.

## AARDVARKS, ARMADILLOS AND ANTEATERS

Anteaters and armadillos belong to a group of animals called xenarthrans—a group that also contains sloths. Anteaters lack teeth, but some armadillos have up to 100 small, peglike teeth. They do not need big biting teeth, because they feed on ants and termites, which they lick up with their tongues. Aardvarks have similar lifestyles to armadillos and anteaters, even though they are not closely related.

Size: body 17¾–19¾ in (45–50 cm); tail 9¾–15¾ in (25–40 cm)

Range: southern USA, Central and South America

Habitat: grassland, forest, scrub

### Nine-banded armadillo
*Dasypus novemcinctus*

When threatened, this armadillo rolls up into a ball so that its soft belly is protected and only its armor-plated back is exposed. It spends most of the day asleep in the safety of its burrow.

Size: body 3¼–5¼ ft (1–1.6 m); tail 17½–23½ in (44.5–60 cm)

Range: Africa: south of the Sahara

Habitat: tropical grassland

### Aardvark
*Orycteropus afer*

The aardvark feeds on termites at night, finding them with its long snout and long sticky tongue. During the day, it sleeps in its burrow, which it digs with its strong feet. The burrow may be long and complex, with many openings.

### Giant anteater
*Myrmecophaga tridactyla*

This anteater sniffs out ants' nests and termite mounds, breaks them open with its claws and thrusts its long sticky tongue inside. It is careful never to destroy a nest or eat all the ants, so it can return there to feed in the future.

Size: body 3¼–4 ft (1–1.2 m); tail 25½–35½ in (65–90 cm)

Range: Central and South America, down to northern Argentina

Habitat: tropical evergreen forest, tropical grassland, fresh water

# MOLES, TENRECS, SHREWS AND HEDGEHOGS

A number of smaller mammals, including moles, shrews, tenrecs and hedgehogs, feed almost exclusively on insects and other small invertebrates such as worms, centipedes, snails and spiders. Many of these mammals have long narrow snouts in order to reach into the small spaces where insects hide. They also have sharp teeth and claws. They have poor eyesight, but an excellent sense of smell.

Size: body 3¾–5 in (9.5–12.5 cm); tail 3¾–5½ in (9.5–14 cm)
Range: southern Africa
Habitat: temperate grassland, desert

## Short-eared elephant shrew
*Macroscelides proboscideus*

Elephant shrews get their name because of their extraordinary trunklike noses. They walk on all fours, but when they need to move fast, they hop along on their back legs like miniature kangaroos. They feed on termites, seeds, fruit and berries in the daytime, but shelter from the midday sun in burrows.

## Western European hedgehog
*Erinaceus europaeus*

The hedgehog roots around in hedgerows and undergrowth for small creatures to eat, making piglike grunts as it goes. If it is attacked, it curls itself up into a ball, so that its prickly coat deters predators. In cold climates, it hibernates through the winter.

Size: body 5¼–10½ in (13.5–27 cm); tail ½–2 in (1–5 cm)
Range: western Europe; introduced into New Zealand
Habitat: inhabited areas and farmland, deciduous forest, desert

## European mole
*Talpa europaea*

This small mammal spends almost its entire life underground, digging tunnels with its broad, spadelike front legs. It has poor eyesight, but good hearing. It feels its way around and finds worms and insects to eat by detecting the vibrations in the ground caused by their movements.

Size: body 6¼–7½ in (16–19 cm); virtually no tail
Range: Madagascar
Habitat: tropical forest

## Streaked tenrec
*Hemicentetes semispinosus*

The streaked tenrec is covered in protective spines. The female produces a litter of seven to 11 babies. If she feels threatened, she raises a small patch of spines on her back and vibrates them rapidly. This makes a clicking noise to warn her young of approaching danger.

Size: body 3½–6½ in (9–16.5 cm); tail 1¼–1½ in (3–4 cm)
Range: Europe to Central Asia
Habitat: inhabited areas and farmland, deciduous forest, grassland

# BATS

Bats are the only flying mammals. They power themselves through the air on smooth wings of skin, making sudden midair turns and twists. Most bats spend the day asleep, hanging upside down, out of reach of predators. At night, they launch themselves into the air to hunt for food. Some bats make high-pitched sounds that bounce, or echo, off nearby objects and are picked up by the bats' large ears. The bats use this echolocation to detect prey and avoid obstacles. Others, such as fruit bats, rely more on their sense of smell.

Size: body 2½–3¼ in (6.5–8.5 cm);
no tail; wingspan 9–11¾ in
(23–30 cm)

Range: India to Burma (Myanmar),
southern China, Malaysia

Habitat: tropical evergreen forest,
temperate grassland

## Spear-nosed bat
*Phyllostomus hastatus*

Size: body 4–5¼ in (10–13 cm);
tail 1 in (2.5 cm); wingspan
17¼–18½ in (44–47 cm)

Range: Central and northern
South America

Habitat: tropical evergreen forest

The spear-nosed bat will eat insects and fruit, but prefers the flesh of mice, birds and small bats. The spear-nosed bat, in turn, is preyed upon by false vampire bats. It has a broad, spear-shaped flap of skin sticking up from its nose. Huge flocks of this heavy-bodied bat like to shelter in buildings and caves. Flocks emerge at dusk to fly to their feeding grounds. The female gives birth to a single baby, once or twice a year.

## Greater false vampire bat
*Megaderma lyra*

The greater false vampire is one of the largest of all bats. It feeds largely on insects and spiders, but also on rodents, frogs, fish and even other bats. It roosts in caves in groups of three to 50 bats. Unlike true vampire bats, false vampire bats do not drink blood.

Size: body 1½–2 in (4–5 cm);
tail 1¼–1¾ in (3–4.5 cm);
wingspan 9–11 in (23–28 cm)

Range: northern Europe eastward
to China and Japan

Habitat: deciduous forest

## Common long-eared bat
*Plecotus auritus*

This bat's ears are nearly as long as its head and body combined. The bat uses its sensitive ears to detect the calls and movements of insect prey, and to find its way by echolocation. The long-eared bat hibernates in caves during winter. In summer, it roosts in colonies of 50–100 bats in buildings and trees, feeding at night mainly on moths.

Size: body
8-10 in (20-25 cm);
no tail; wingspan 5 ft (1.5 m)
Range: southern and Southeast Asia
Habitat: tropical forest, swamp

The largest wings of any bat belong to the greater fruit bat. By day, it roosts in trees in flocks of several thousand bats, taking flight at dusk to find juicy fruit to eat or sweet flower nectar to sip. Fruit trees are able to reproduce as their pollen, sticking onto the bat's fur, is moved from flower to flower. Fruit seeds it spits out or passes in its droppings take root and grow into new fruit trees.

# Indian flying fox
*Pteropus giganteus*

# Ghost bat
*Macroderma gigas*

The ghost bat, a type of false vampire bat, gets its name from the eery color of its pale fur at night. It feeds on mice, birds, geckos and other bats. By day, it roosts in caves, rocky clefts and old mine shafts. It is rare because quarrying (removing stone) has destroyed some of its major roosts.

Size: body 4½-5½ in (11.5-14 cm);
no tail; wingspan 15¾-23½ in
(40-60 cm)
Range: northern and western
tropical Australia
Habitat: tropical evergreen
forest, desert

Size: body 3-4¾ in (7-12 cm);
tail ½-1 in (1.5-2.5 cm);
wingspan 8-11 in (20-28 cm)
Range: Papua New Guinea and
Solomon Islands
Habitat: tropical evergreen forest,
inhabited areas, farmland

Size: body 4½-5 in (11-13 cm);
tail 1-1½in (2.5-4 cm);
wingspan 13-13½ in (33-35 cm)
Range: Europe, Asia, northern Africa
Habitat: inhabited areas, farmland,
deciduous forest, temperate
grassland

# Dobson's tube-nose bat
*Nyctimene major*

The scroll-shaped nostrils of this bat stick out on each side of its head. They probably help the bat to find ripe fruit, such as guavas, figs and even young coconuts. Using its sharp teeth, the bat chews the fruit to extract the juice.

# Greater horseshoe bat
*Rhinolophus ferrumequinum*

This bat feeds on beetles, swooping down to snatch them off the ground with pinpoint accuracy. It roosts in caves, trees and the roofs of old buildings. But as caves are explored, trees felled and buildings pulled down, the bat finds it harder to find suitable homes. It is now rare or extinct in some parts of northwestern Europe.

**17**

# VAMPIRE BATS

The only mammals to feed entirely on blood are vampire bats, which live in the tropical countries of Central and South America. The common vampire bat (*Desmodus rotundus*) preys on sleeping animals — usually cattle and horses — and sometimes even people. The two other vampire species, *Diaemus youngi* and *Diphylla ecaudata*, prey on large birds such as chickens. The common vampire feeds on its victim for about 30 minutes. The victim does not lose a dangerous amount of blood, but the bat's bite can spread disease and infection. Over the course of a year, a colony of 100 bats drinks a volume equal to the blood of 25 cows or 14,000 chickens.

The body of the common vampire bat is 3½ in (9 cm) long, and its wingspan is 7 in (18 cm). It has no tail, a snub-nose, and short pointed ears. It has fewer teeth than most bats, since it has no need to chew or grind up food.

## YOUNG BATS

At birth, a baby vampire bat is helpless, but its strong claws and hooked milk teeth allow it to cling tightly to its mother, even when she flies. At first, the young bat feeds entirely on her milk. Then she gradually introduces blood into its diet, feeding it a few drops at a time.

## FEEDING

A vampire bat lands on the ground close to its victim and then creeps toward it on all fours. A heat sensor on the end of its nose helps it to locate an area of skin where warm blood flows close to the surface. The bat bites into its victim with its razor-sharp teeth and laps up the blood that flows from the wound. The bat's saliva stops the blood from clotting.

Hoof

# ROOSTING BATS

The common vampire bat is a cave-dweller, clinging to cave roofs and roosting in total darkness in colonies of up to 1,000 bats, but usually nearer to 100. It is a wary bat and prefers to stalk its prey on dark or moonless nights.

# FALSE VAMPIRE BATS

These bats eat a range of prey from insects to other bats. They swoop silently down onto their victim and eat its flesh. In the past, people mistakenly thought it was drinking the victim's blood, and assumed it was a type of vampire bat. Zoologists now know that this is not true, which is why it is called a "false" vampire.

19

# PRIMATES

Humans, monkeys, apes, lorises, tarsiers and lemurs all belong to a group of about 233 species called primates. With relatively large brains, these mammals are intelligent and quick to learn new skills. Many have opposable thumbs, which means that their thumbs can move across their palms to press against their fingers, allowing them to grasp objects firmly. Some also have opposable big toes. Most primates live in trees, and they have forward-pointing eyes to help them judge the distances between branches.

| Size: body 5½–6¼ in (14–16 cm); tail 6–7¾ in (15–20 cm) |
| Range: South America: upper reaches of Amazon River area |
| Habitat: tropical evergreen forest |

## Pygmy marmoset
*Cebuella pygmaea*

One of the smallest of all the primates, the pygmy marmoset is often attacked by large birds, so it tries to keep out of sight. It moves either in short dashes or by creeping along very slowly, sometimes staying very still to avoid being spotted.

# LEMURS, AYE-AYES, LORISES, BUSHBABIES, TARSIERS, MARMOSETS AND TAMARINS

Lemurs, aye-ayes, bushbabies, lorises and tarsiers are found in parts of Africa and southern Asia. They have smaller brains than monkeys and apes, and their skeletons resemble those of small, tree-dwelling, shrewlike animals, which were probably the first primates to evolve. The fast-moving marmosets and tamarins of the South American rain forests often have colorful fur and unusual "hairstyles."

## Ring-tailed lemur
*Lemur catta*

The ring-tailed lemur climbs up to the tops of trees to bask in the early morning sunshine after a cold night. It marks out its territory with smelly secretions from scent glands.

| Size: body 17¾ in (45 cm); tail 21½ in (55 cm) |
| Range: Madagascar |
| Habitat: deciduous forest, tropical evergreen for... |

| Size: body 3¼–6¼ in (8.5–16 cm); tail 5¼–10½ in (13.5–27 cm) |
| Range: Southeast Asia: Sumatra and Borneo |
| Habitat: tropical evergreen forest, farmland |

## Western tarsier
*Tarsius bancanus*

The tarsier's large, batlike ears and huge eyes make it a ruthless nighttime hunter, but the eyeballs are too big to move in their sockets. To make up for this, the tarsier can turn its head right around.

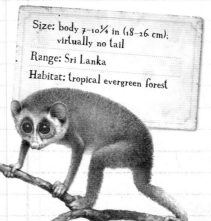

| Size: body 7–10¼ in (18–26 cm); virtually no tail |
| Range: Sri Lanka |
| Habitat: tropical evergreen forest |

## Slender loris
*Loris tardigradus*

The slender loris's opposable thumbs and big toes enable it to grip tightly onto branches as it creeps through the trees, grabbing insects, lizards, birds and eggs with both hands.

# Golden lion tamarin
*Leontopithecus rosalia*

This beautiful primate gets its name from the silky, lionlike mane that covers its head and shoulders. It lives in family groups and at night shelters in hollows in old trees. It is a nimble creature and leaps from branch to branch searching for insects, lizards and birds to eat.

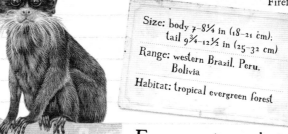

Size: body 7–8¼ in (18–21 cm);
tail 9¾–12½ in (25–32 cm)

Range: western Brazil, Peru, Bolivia

Habitat: tropical evergreen forest

# Emperor tamarin
*Saguinus imperator*

The emperor tamarin is easily recognized by its long drooping "moustache." Small troops of these tamarins dart through the trees looking for insects, fruit, tender leaves and flowers to eat. They also lap up tree sap and steal birds' eggs.

Size: body 10½–18½ in (27–47 cm);
tail 13–20½ in (33–52 cm)

Range: southern Africa

Habitat: tropical evergreen forest, temperate and tropical grassland

Size: body 7½–8¼ in (19–22 cm);
tail 10¼–13½ in (26–34 cm)

Range: southeastern Brazil

Habitat: tropical evergreen forest

# Greater bushbaby
*Otolemur crassicaudatus*

The bushbaby gets its name because its call sounds like a child crying. It eats plants but also preys on reptiles and birds, pouncing and killing its victims with one bite. A night hunter, the bushbaby's keen eyes can focus on prey in moonlight or starlight.

Size: body 14½–17½ in (36–44 cm);
tail 19¾–23½ in (50–60 cm)

Range: Madagascar

Habitat: tropical evergreen forest, deciduous forest

# Aye-aye
*Daubentonia madagascariensis*

The aye-aye is a nocturnal insect-eater. It taps on trees with its long middle finger, listens for the sound of insects moving under the bark, gnaws a hole and then uses the same finger to hook the insects out. Local tradition says that if you see this strange-looking animal you will have bad luck. Sadly it is often killed.

# OLD WORLD MONKEYS

The monkeys in Asia and Africa are known as Old World monkeys. They have close-set downward-pointing nostrils. On their buttocks are pads of hard skin that allow them to rest their weight on the bottoms comfortably while they sleep sitting upright. They tend to be larger than the New World monkeys of the Americas. Unlike the New World monkeys, they do not have prehensile (gripping) tails. Most Old World monkeys are active in the daytime and sleep at night. They have excellent eyesight, hearing and sense of smell.

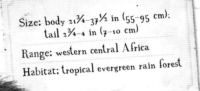

Size: body 21¾–37½ in (55–95 cm);
tail 2¾–4 in (7–10 cm)

Range: western central Africa

Habitat: tropical evergreen rain forest

## Mandrill
### Mandrillus sphinx

The forest-dwelling mandrill is unmistakable, with its flaming red nose and blue cheeks. The male mandrill is the largest of all monkeys. A female mandrill gives birth to a single baby, which she carries around with her, either on her back or clinging to her belly. Adults are bad tempered and aggressive and have even been known to attack humans.

## Diana monkey
### Cercopithecus diana

This elegant colorful monkey is an excellent climber and spends almost all its time high up in the trees of the rain forest. Troops of up to 30 monkeys live together, led by an old male. They feed mainly on plants, but also eat insects and the eggs and young of birds.

Size: body 15¾–22½ in (40–57 cm);
tail 19¾–29½ in (50–75 cm)

Range: west Africa

Habitat: tropical evergreen rain forest

## Japanese macaque
### Macaca fuscata

Japan's mountain forests are home to macaque monkeys, which are also known as snow monkeys. In cold winters, these monkeys warm themselves in volcanic springs, where water heated deep below ground bubbles up to the surface to form steaming pools. Macaques eat fruit, leaves, insects and small animals.

Size: body 19¾–29½ in (50–75 cm);
tail 2¾–4¾ in (7–12 cm)

Range: Japan

Habitat: tropical forest, marsh, high ground

Size: body 20¾–30 in (53–76 cm);
tail 21¾–30 in (55–76 cm)

Range: Southeast Asia: Borneo

Habitat: tropical evergreen
rain forest, fresh water

# Proboscis monkey
## *Nasalis larvatus*

The male proboscis monkey has a long fleshy nose, which straightens out when he makes his loud honking call. The nose probably acts like a loudspeaker, to warn other monkeys of danger. It also goes red or swells when he is angry or excited. The proboscis monkey lives in mangrove swamp jungle, where it climbs nimbly through the trees.

# Olive baboon
## *Papio anubis*

Orderly troops of up to 150 olive baboons move around Africa's savanna, eating leaves, shoots, seeds, roots, bark, fruit, insects, eggs and lizards. These large heavily built baboons also hunt small mammals such as young antelopes. They spend much of their time grooming each other's fur to keep it clean. They mainly live on the ground, but sleep at night in trees or on rocks.

Size: body up to 3¼ ft (1 m);
tail 17¾–29½ in (45–75 cm);

Range: western, central and
eastern Africa

Habitat: tropical grassland, tropical
evergreen forest

Size: body 18–27½ in
(46–70 cm); tail 16½–31½ in
(42–80 cm);

Range: western Africa

Habitat: tropical evergreen forest

# Red colobus
## *Procolobus badius*

This monkey lives in troops of 50 to 100 animals. The troop contains many small family groups, each consisting of a male and several females with their young. The red colobus makes spectacular leaps between the branches of trees as it searches for fruit, leaves and flowers to eat. Chimpanzees sometimes band together in hunting parties to prey on the red colobus.

Size: body 15¾–19¾ in (40–50 cm);
tail 17¾–21¾ in (45–55 cm)

Range: west Africa

Habitat: tropical evergreen
rain forest, fresh water

# Allen's swamp monkey
## *Allenpithecus nigroviridis*

This little-known monkey lives near rivers and in swamps. Though it eats mainly leaves and fruit, it also goes into the water to snatch crabs and even fish. It, in turn, is hunted by local people for meat and because it sometimes raids farmers' crops. It is now an endangered species.

# NEW WORLD MONKEYS

The monkeys that live in the lush rain forests of Central and South America are known as New World monkeys. Their long tails help them to balance when they are high off the ground. Many — such as the capuchin, howler and spider monkeys — have prehensile (gripping) tails, which they can wrap around branches and use like an extra limb. They have long fingers and strong feet that grip well, and are excellent runners and leapers. Unlike their Old World relatives, they have broad nostrils that open to the sides and no sitting pads on their buttocks.

Size: body 24 in (61 cm);
tail about 26¼ in
(67 cm)

Range: southeastern Brazil

Habitat: tropical evergreen forest

## Red howler
### *Alouatta seniculus*

Red howler monkeys live in the rain forest in troops of up to 30. Sometimes, all the males in a troop join together in a dawn chorus of howling that can be heard 1¾ miles (3 km) away, telling other monkeys to stay away from their territory. The male's large throat has a special chamber that amplifies its call.

Size: body 31½–35½ in
(80–90 cm); tail 31½–35½ in
(80–90 cm)

Range: South America

Habitat: tropical evergreen forest

## Woolly spider monkey
### *Brachyteles arachnoides*

This monkey moves around the rainforest by using its long arms and prehensile tail to swing from branch to branch. Its numbers are falling because its rain forest home is being destroyed, giving them little refuge from hunters who kill it for meat.

## Monk saki
### *Pithecia monachus*

The monk saki has long shaggy hair around its face and on its neck, and a thick bushy tail. This shy wary monkey lives high in the trees and never ventures down to the ground. It usually moves on all fours, but may sometimes walk upright on a large branch. It can make large leaps between branches. These monkeys spend their time in pairs or small family groups.

Size: body 11¾–15 in (30–38 cm);
tail 15–19¾ in (38–50 cm)

Range: South America: upper reaches of Amazon River area

Habitat: tropical evergreen forest

Size: body 13¾–19 in (35–48 cm);
tail 12¼–20 in (31–51 cm)

Range: South America: upper reaches of Amazon River area

Habitat: tropical evergreen forest

## White-fronted capuchin
### *Cebus albifrons*

This intelligent monkey is always picking up things, hoping they may be edible. It feeds on shoots, fruit, insects, young birds and birds' eggs. It soaks its hands and feet in urine and uses the scent to mark its territory as it moves through the trees.

# GIBBONS AND GREAT APES

Gorillas, chimpanzees and orangutans are called great apes. They are our closest living relatives. After humans, they are the most intelligent primates, but they are endangered, because of hunting and habitat loss. Gibbons are smaller, and are known as lesser apes. Apes live in family-based groups. They walk on all fours, using the knuckles of their hands rather than flat palms, but they can also walk upright, on their hind legs.

Size: height 4–5 ft (1.2–1.5 m); no tail

Range: Borneo

Habitat: tropical forest, swamp

## Bornean orangutan
### *Pongo pygmaeus*

After the gorilla, the orangutan is the second largest primate. It builds a platform of sticks to form a tree nest in which it sleeps, which may be a different one each night. A female orangutan gives birth to a single baby, which clings to her fur as she moves around in the treetops.

Size: body 16½–22¾ in (42–58 cm); no tail

Range: Southeast Asia

Habitat: tropical evergreen forest

Size: body 25¼–37 in (64–94 cm); height 4–5½ ft (1.2–1.7 m); no tail

Range: western and central Africa

Habitat: tropical forest, scrub, grassland

## Lar Gibbon
### *Hylobates lar*

The lar gibbon lives in trees and rarely descends to the ground. As it swings through the trees and runs upright along branches, it has to look out for weak or dead branches, because a fall from this height could be fatal. Lar gibbons live in small family groups, and are now an endangered species.

## Chimpanzee
### *Pan troglodytes*

The chimpanzee mainly eats plants, but occasionally insects and meat. It makes many noises, gestures and facial expressions. It has learned to use everyday objects as simple tools: stones, for example, are used to smash open nuts, wads of leaves to mop up drinking water and sticks to prise grubs out of rotten wood and extract ants and termites from their nests.

Size: height 4½–6 ft (1.4–1.8 m); no tail

Range: western central Africa

Habitat: tropical evergreen forest

## Western gorilla
### *Gorilla gorilla*

Gorillas spend most of their time on the ground. They feed on leaves, buds, stalks, berries, bark and fern. They live in troops of up to 30 animals, made up of a leading adult male, a few young males and several females and their young. Young gorillas travel on their mother's back until they are two or three years old.

# CARNIVORES

This group of flesh-eating mammals includes dogs, bears, raccoons, mustelids, mongooses, civets, hyenas and cats. Most carnivores have agile bodies and finely tuned senses of sight, hearing and smell, so they can find their prey before it detects them. The main difference, however, between carnivores and other mammals is that they have special teeth that can shear flesh from bone, the way scissors cut paper.

Size: body 4 ft (1.2 m):
tail about 11¾ in (30 cm)

Range: South America

Habitat: temperate grassland,
fresh water

## Maned wolf
### *Chrysocyon brachyurus*

The maned wolf is similar to the red fox in appearance, but with longer legs and a longer muzzle. A wary creature, the maned wolf lives in remote areas and hunts mainly at night. It preys on large rodents, birds, reptiles and frogs.

## DOGS

All domestic dogs are descended from wolves. Wolves and other wild dogs have long legs for chasing prey and sharp teeth for killing it. A dog's most developed sensory organ is its nose, which it uses to detect the scent of prey, find a mate, identify other animals and even tell whether they are afraid or relaxed.

## Bush dog
### *Speothos venaticus*

With its stocky legs, short tail, squat body and broad face, the bush dog looks more like a small bear than a dog. It inhabits grasslands and open forests, hunting in packs (family groups) during the day for rodents. It spends most of the night underground in a den.

Size: body 26 in (65 cm):
tail 6 in (15 cm)

Range: Central and South America

Habitat: tropical and temperate
forest, grassland, scrub

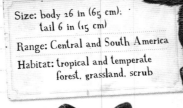

Size: body 31½–43½ in (80–110 cm):
tail 11¾–15¾ in (30.5–40 cm)

Range: Africa, south of the Sahara
to South Africa

Habitat: temperate grassland, desert,
high ground

## Hunting dog
### *Lycaon pictus*

These dogs hunt together as a pack. They chase a group of animals, such as wildebeest, split one from the fleeing herd and then move in for the kill. Once found across the African savanna, hunting dogs were shot by farmers protecting their cattle and now live in only a few scattered places.

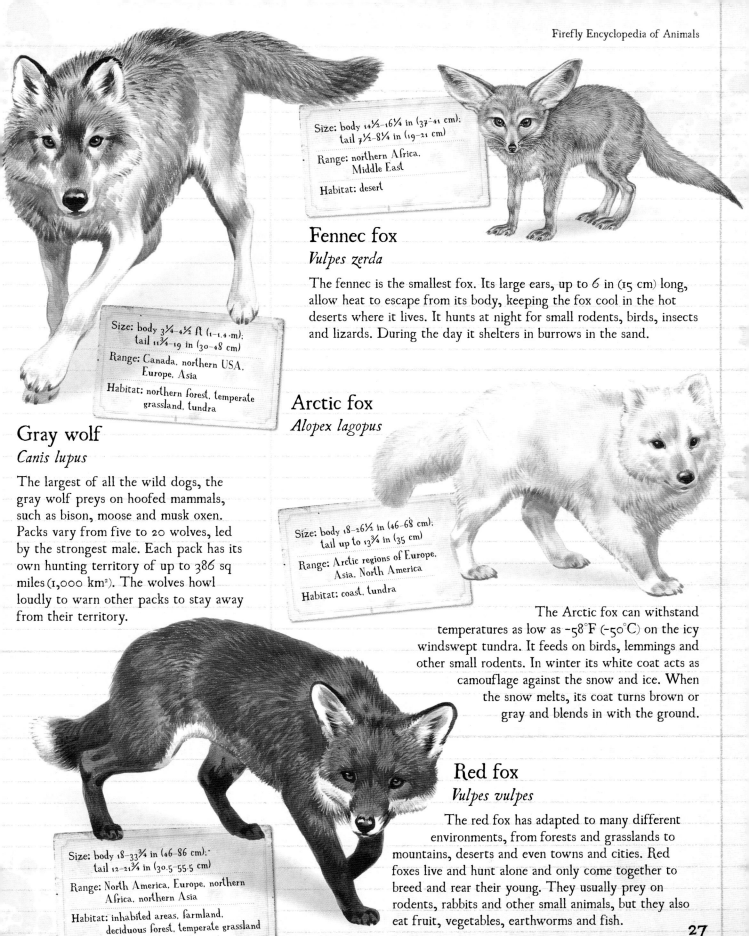

Size: body 14½–16¼ in (37–41 cm);
tail 7½–8¼ in (19–21 cm)

Range: northern Africa,
Middle East

Habitat: desert

## Fennec fox
*Vulpes zerda*

The fennec is the smallest fox. Its large ears, up to 6 in (15 cm) long, allow heat to escape from its body, keeping the fox cool in the hot deserts where it lives. It hunts at night for small rodents, birds, insects and lizards. During the day it shelters in burrows in the sand.

Size: body 3¼–4½ ft (1–1.4 m);
tail 11¾–19 in (30–48 cm)

Range: Canada, northern USA,
Europe, Asia

Habitat: northern forest, temperate
grassland, tundra

## Gray wolf
*Canis lupus*

The largest of all the wild dogs, the gray wolf preys on hoofed mammals, such as bison, moose and musk oxen. Packs vary from five to 20 wolves, led by the strongest male. Each pack has its own hunting territory of up to 386 sq miles (1,000 km²). The wolves howl loudly to warn other packs to stay away from their territory.

## Arctic fox
*Alopex lagopus*

Size: body 18–26½ in (46–68 cm);
tail up to 13¾ in (35 cm)

Range: Arctic regions of Europe,
Asia, North America

Habitat: coast, tundra

The Arctic fox can withstand temperatures as low as –58°F (–50°C) on the icy windswept tundra. It feeds on birds, lemmings and other small rodents. In winter its white coat acts as camouflage against the snow and ice. When the snow melts, its coat turns brown or gray and blends in with the ground.

## Red fox
*Vulpes vulpes*

The red fox has adapted to many different environments, from forests and grasslands to mountains, deserts and even towns and cities. Red foxes live and hunt alone and only come together to breed and rear their young. They usually prey on rodents, rabbits and other small animals, but they also eat fruit, vegetables, earthworms and fish.

Size: body 18–33¾ in (46–86 cm);
tail 12–21¾ in (30.5–55.5 cm)

Range: North America, Europe, northern
Africa, northern Asia

Habitat: inhabited areas, farmland,
deciduous forest, temperate grassland

**27**

# RACCOONS, BEARS AND PANDAS

Both the bear and raccoon families developed from doglike ancestors millions of years ago. Bears are the largest flesh-eating land mammals, but they will eat almost anything, including plants and insects. Raccoons — and their relatives the coatis and olingos — are long-tailed carnivores that like to spend much of their time in trees. There are two different types of panda: the giant pandas are classified with the bears and the red pandas are now classified in a family of their own.

Size: body 16–23½ in (41–60 cm);
tail 7¾–15¾ in (20–40 cm)

Range: southern Canada, USA,
Central America

Habitat: deciduous forest, temperate
grassland, tropical grassland

## Northern raccoon
*Procyon lotor*

The raccoon runs and climbs well, and swims if necessary. It is most active at night. As well as catching prey such as frogs, fish, mice and birds, it often raids trash cans, searching for edible items with its long sensitive fingers. It has a peculiar habit of washing food before eating it. Its thick fur keeps it warm during winter.

Size: body 20–25 in (51–63.5 cm);
tail 11–19 in (28–48.5 cm)

Range: Himalayas, from Nepal
to Burma (Myanmar),
southwestern China

Habitat: tropical evergreen forest

## Red panda
*Ailurus fulgens*

The red panda looks more like a raccoon than a giant panda. It sleeps during the day, curled up on a branch with its tail over its eyes or its head tucked into its chest. It feeds during the night, mainly on bamboo shoots, although it will also eat grass, roots, fruit, acorns, mice, birds and birds' eggs.

Size: body 17–26¼ in (43–67 cm);
tail 17–26¾ in (43–68 cm)

Range: tropical South America

Habitat: forest, mountain

## South American coati
*Nasua nasua*

With its long nose, the coati probes into holes and cracks in the ground, searching for insects, spiders and small animals to eat. Groups of up to 40 animals hunt both day and night, resting during the hottest part of the day. After mating, the female goes off alone to give birth to a litter of between two and seven young in a cave or a tree nest.

## Sun bear
### *Helarctos malayanus*

The sun bear spends the day sleeping and sunbathing. It searches for food at night, using its long tongue to lick honey out of bees' nests and termites from their mounds. With its curved claws it hooks fruit from branches and tears off tree bark to uncover tasty grubs.

## Polar bear
### *Ursus maritimus*

With a thick layer of fat beneath its skin to keep it warm, a polar bear is perfectly comfortable roaming across the Arctic ice in freezing temperatures. Cubs are born in dens dug by their mother in deep snow. They stay with her for about 28 months, learning how to hunt seals and fight.

## Brown bear
### *Ursus arctos*

Also known as the "grizzly," this bear mostly eats leaves, berries, fruit, nuts, roots and sometimes insects, rodents and fish. It also hunts large mammals such as moose and musk oxen. The bear may hide the dead prey under dirt and leaves until it is ready to consume it.

## Giant panda
### *Ailuropoda melanoleuca*

The giant panda has to feed for up to 15 hours each day to survive, during which time it consumes up to 44 lb (20 kg) of bamboo. The panda has a thumblike bone in its hands that allows it to grip its food. Unfortunately, there are only about 1,600 giant pandas left in the wild.

29

# MUSTELIDS, CIVETS AND MONGOOSES

All of these mammals are small- to medium-sized carnivores. Most of the mustelids, which include stoats, badgers, otters, skunks and wolverines, have a long supple body, short legs and a long tail. There are about 56 species of mustelid living throughout most of the world except Australia and Madagascar. The 34 or so species of civet are tree-dwelling hunters that are active at night. They live in southern Europe, Africa and Asia. About 34 species of mongooses live in Africa and Asia, and these are fast-moving ground dwellers.

## Eurasian otter
*Lutra lutra*

The slender-bodied otter moves fast both in water and on land. It uses its strong tail to push itself along in water and its short, thick fur keeps its skin warm and dry. Its nostrils and ears can be closed off when it is in water. The otter lives in a burrow in the riverbank. Rarely seen during the day, it comes out at night to find fish, frogs, voles and other water creatures to eat.

Size: body 21¾–31½ in (55–80 cm);
tail 11¾–19¾ in (30–50 cm)

Range: Europe, northern Africa, Asia

Habitat: fresh water, coast

Size: body 17–23½ in (43–60 cm);
tail 19–24½ in (48–62 cm)

Range: Central Africa

Habitat: tropical evergreen forest, tropical grassland, deciduous forest, inhabited areas, farmland

## African palm civet
*Nandinia binotata*

This civet has short legs and a long thick tail. It is a skilled climber and spends much of its life in trees, where it rests during the day. It usually hunts at night, catching insects and small creatures such as lizards and birds. It also eats many kinds of fruit and leaves. The female gives birth to litters of two or three young at any time of year.

## Sea otter
*Enhydra lutris*

This otter feeds on shellfish and uses rocks as tools to help it open the hard shells. The otter lies on its back in the water and places a rock on its chest. It bangs its prey against the rock until the shell breaks, revealing the soft flesh inside.

Size: body 3¼–4 ft (1–1.2 m);
tail 9¾–14¼ in (25–37 cm)

Range: north Pacific coast: Bering Sea and from Vancouver to California

Habitat: coast

Size: body 11–15 in (28–38 cm);
tail 7–9¾ in (18–25 cm)

Range: North America

Habitat: deciduous forest, temperate
grassland, inhabited areas,
farmland water

## Meerkat
### *Suricata suricatta*

Meerkats are a type of mongoose.
They are sociable animals and
several families may live together.
During the day, while most of
the group forages for food such
as insects, lizards, birds and
fruit, some meerkats watch out
for birds of prey. They give a
shrill call to alert the others
to any danger.

## Striped skunk
### *Mephitis mephitis*

Skunks are well known for the foul-smelling
fluid they spray when threatened. The fluid
comes from glands near the tail. The strong
smell makes it difficult for an enemy to breathe
and irritates its eyes. The striped skunk is
active at night, when it searches for food.

Size: body 9¾–11¾ in (25–30 cm);
tail 7½–9½ in (19–24 cm)

Range: southern Africa

Habitat: temperate grassland,
tropical grassland

Size: body 22–32 in (56–81 cm);
tail 4¼–7¾ in (11–20 cm)

Range: Europe, Asia

Habitat: deciduous forest,
temperate grassland

## Eurasian badger
### *Meles meles*

Families of Eurasian badgers live in huge burrows
called setts. These burrows have several
entrances and networks of underground
passages and chambers. Badgers are generally
active at night, coming out of the sett around
dusk. They eat large quantities of earthworms
as well as other small animals, plants, fruit and nuts.

Size: body 13¾ in (35 cm);
tail 9¾ in (25 cm)

Range: Middle East, Asia; introduced
into West Indies, Hawaii, Fiji

Habitat: tropical evergreen forest,
desert

## Indian mongoose
### *Herpestes javanicus*

The mongoose eats almost any food it can catch,
including snakes, scorpions and insects. It is popular
among humans because it hunts pests such as rats
and mice. As a result, the mongoose has been
introduced into areas outside its normal range.

# CATS AND HYENAS

Cats are ruthless hunters. Their strong legs enable them to catch their prey in a brief, rapid chase or with a lightning-quick pounce. They have bendy backbones that allow them to twist and turn easily when chasing prey. When they pounce, their claws extend and grip their victim's flesh, but when a cat is walking or running, the claws retract into the toes so they are not damaged. Most cats have coats patterned with spots or stripes to camouflage them as they stalk prey. There are 36 species of wild cat, from big cats such as lions and tigers, to smaller ones such as the lynx.

## Wild cat
*Felis silvestris*

The wild cat looks similar to a domestic cat, but it is larger and has a shorter, thicker tail. It is a good tree-climber, but stalks most of its prey on the ground, catching small rodents and birds.

Size: body 19¾–25½ in (50–65 cm);
tail 9¾–15 in (25–38 cm)
Range: Europe, Africa, Middle East,
India, Central Asia
Habitat: deciduous forest, temperate
grassland, tropical
grassland, high ground

Size: body 31½ in–4¼ ft
(80 cm–1.3 m);
tail 1½–3 in (4–8 cm)
Range: Europe, Asia
Habitat: northern forest

## Eurasian lynx
*Lynx lynx*

The lynx lives alone in forests and woodland and hunts hares, rabbits, rodents, small deer and birds such as grouse. The lynx has excellent eyesight — it can spot a mouse 250 ft (75 m) away.

## Striped hyena
*Hyaena hyaena*

Although hyenas have a doglike body, they are more closely related to cats. They specialize in feeding on carrion (dead animals) and the scraps left by big cats such as lions. They also prey on young sheep and goats, small mammals, birds, lizards, snakes and insects.

Size: body 3¼–4 ft (1–1.2 m);
tail 9¾–13¾ in (25–35 cm)
Range: northern and eastern Africa,
through Middle East to India
Habitat: temperate grassland, tropical
grassland, desert

## Jaguar
*Panthera onca*

The largest South American cat, the jaguar cannot run fast for very long, so it relies on getting close to its prey to make a successful kill. It is a good swimmer, and feeds on fish and turtles, as well as on deer and other land animals.

Size: body 5–6 ft
(1.5–1.8 m); tail 27½–36 in (70–91 cm)
Range: southern USA, Central and
South America
Habitat: deciduous forest, tropical
evergreen forest, tropical gras

## Leopard
*Panthera pardus*

Size: body 4¼–6¼ ft (1.3–1.9 m);
tail 3½–4½ ft (1.1–1.4 m)

Range: Africa, Middle East, southern
and Southeast Asia

Habitat: deciduous and tropical
evergreen forest, temperate and
tropical grassland, desert

The leopard hauls the bodies of large prey up into trees and out of reach of scavenging hyenas and jackals. Its stunning coat is dappled with spots to camouflage it among the leaves of the trees and the long grass below. It will sometimes leap straight out of a tree onto passing prey.

## Snow leopard
*Uncia uncia*

Size: body 4–5 ft (1.2–1.5 m);
tail about 36 in (91 cm)

Range: Himalayas in central Asia

Habitat: mountain forest,
high grassland

The solitary snow leopard feeds mainly on wild sheep and goats. Its broad, furry feet stop it sinking in the snow on high mountain slopes. It can make huge leaps between rocky crags, using its tail for balance.

## Cheetah
*Acinonyx jubatus*

Size: body 3½–4½ ft (1.1–1.4 m);
tail 25½–31½ in (65–80 cm)

Range: eastern and southern Africa,
parts of north Africa, Iran

Habitat: temperate grassland, tropical
grassland

The cheetah is the fastest land mammal, able to accelerate from 0–60 mph (0–96 km/h) in just three seconds. It has little stamina, so it will try to position itself as close as possible to its prey and catch it with an explosive burst of speed. If this attempt fails, it usually gives up.

## Lion
*Panthera leo*

Size: body 4½–6½ ft (1.4–2 m);
tail 26¼ in–39½ in (67–100 cm)

Range: Africa, south of the Sahara;
northwestern India

Habitat: tropical grassland

Lions live in family groups called prides. A pride normally contains up to three males, 15 females and their young. The females do most of the hunting, often stalking antelopes and zebras in pairs or larger groups. The male's role is to defend the pride's territory.

# TIGERS

The tiger is the biggest and strongest of all the wild cats. At the beginning of the 20th century, there were hundreds of thousands of tigers living throughout the forests of Asia. Hunting and the destruction of forests have had such a devastating effect on their numbers that there are now just 4,000 wild tigers left, mainly living in parts of India, China, Indonesia and Siberia. Tigers live alone, roaring loudly to tell other tigers to keep away from their territory, which they mark out with scent, droppings and scratches on tree trunks. They hunt large mammals, usually at night, and sometimes travel up to 12 miles (20 km) in search of food. As few as one in every ten hunts may be successful, so when they do make a kill they gorge themselves on as much meat as they can eat. Despite stories of "man-eating" tigers, they rarely attack humans.

## TIGER CUBS

Tigers are born in litters of between two and six cubs. They are blind for the first 10 days and their mother suckles the cubs for up to eight weeks. Not until they are about 18 months old do they hunt for themselves, and they stay with their mother for two to three years. The father takes no part in their rearing.

## HUNTING

At dusk, tigers set out to hunt buffalo, deer, wild pigs and other forest animals. They can only run fast for short distances, so they rely on their cunning and stealth to catch their prey. Their striped coat camouflages them against the background of trees and long grass, enabling them to sneak up on their victims without being seen. When they are close enough, they sprint forward and pounce on the unsuspecting animal.

Unlike domestic cats, tigers like to be near water, and (like this Bengal tiger) will take a dip to cool off on a hot day. They are good swimmers, and may cross rivers or swim between islands in search of their prey. Tigers can also be seen climbing trees occasionally.

# TIGER TYPES

A century ago, there were nine types, or subspecies, of tiger, but the Bali, Javan and Caspian tigers are now extinct. The Bengal tiger is the most numerous but it and the Siberian, South China, Indo-Chinese, Malayan and Sumatran tigers are all endangered. The largest of all is the Siberian tiger, weighing up to 847 lb (384 kg).

**Siberian tiger** Also known as the Amur tiger, this is one of the largest cats in history.

**Indo-Chinese tiger** It is thought that only 350 of these tigers survive.

**Caspian tiger** This tiger was last seen in the wild in the 1970s.

**Sumatran tiger** This is the smallest and darkest tiger, and is critically endangered.

# SEALS, WHALES AND DOLPHINS

**M**arine mammals are well adapted to life in the water, with sleek and streamlined bodies and paddle-shaped flippers. Under their skin, these marine mammals have a thick layer of fat called blubber to keep them warm. They spend much of their time underwater, often diving to great depths in search of food. But because they have lungs, and not gills like fish, they have to surface regularly to breathe air.

Size: 4½–6 ft (1.4–1.8 m)
Range: southern Pacific and Atlantic oceans
Habitat: coastal waters

## SEALS, SEA LIONS AND WALRUSES

**W**ith their torpedolike bodies, these marine mammals are skilful swimmers and divers. Their heart beat slows during dives, to enable them to stay underwater for long periods. Unlike whales and dolphins, they come ashore to have their babies. Seals and walruses swim by pushing themselves through the water with their hind flippers, but sea lions use their long front flippers.

### South American fur seal
*Arctocephalus australis*

This seal eats fish, squid, penguins and small marine creatures. The female gives birth to a single pup. She stays with it for 12 days, then goes off to sea to feed, returning regularly to suckle her young pup.

### Walrus
*Odobenus rosmarus*

Walruses live in the Arctic, where they feed on shellfish. They have sharp tusks which they use to drag themselves out of the water, and for fighting. Walruses are excellent swimmers, but on land they move with great difficulty.

Size: 7¼–11½ ft (2.2–3.5 m)
Range: Arctic Ocean, occasionally northern Atlantic Ocean
Habitat: coastal waters, polar

Size: 5½–7¼ ft (1.7–2.2 m)
Range: Pacific coasts, from Canada to Mexico
Habitat: coastal waters

### California sea lion
*Zalophus californianus*

This is the fastest swimmer of all the seals and sea lions, reaching speeds of 25 mph (40 km/h). It can also move fast on land by tucking its back flippers under its body. Huge colonies gather to breed on the rocky southwestern shores of the USA.

Size: 7¾–9¼ ft (2.4–2.8 m)

Range: northern Pacific Ocean

Habitat: coastal waters

## Harbor seal
### *Phoca vitulina*

Size: 4½–6 ft (1.4–1.8 m)

Range: north Atlantic and northern Pacific oceans

Habitat: polar, coastal waters

Like all seals, the harbor seal spends most of its life in water, coming to land only to mate and give birth. Harbor seal pups are well developed when they are born. They can swim from birth, and can dive for up to two minutes when just two or three days old. The harbor seal feeds on fish and squid.

## Steller sea lion
### *Eumetopias jubatus*

This is the largest of the sea lions. It catches fish, squid and octopus. A large male may even eat smaller seals. The beaches where it breeds can be so crowded that young pups are crushed. A seal mother often goes to sea to find food for herself and her pup. When she comes back, she calls to nearby pups, and then smells and touches them until she finds the one that belongs to her.

## Harp seal
### *Pagophilus groenlandicus*

The harp seal has a gray body with a black head and stripe across its back. In the breeding season, rival males fight over females. After mating, the females form groups on the ice to give birth. The pups grow rapidly as they feed on their mothers' nourishing, fat-rich milk.

Size: 5¼–6¼ ft (1.6–1.9 m)

Range: north Atlantic Ocean and Arctic Ocean

Habitat: polar

## Leopard seal
### *Hydrurga leptonyx*

The leopard seal is the fiercest hunter of all seals, with large, tooth-studded jaws for grasping prey and tearing it apart. The leopard seal preys on penguins by catching them underwater just as they launch themselves off the ice. It also hunts other smaller seals, as well as fish, squid and shellfish.

Size: 10–11½ ft (3–3.5 m)

Range: Southern Ocean

Habitat: coastal waters, polar

# ANTARCTIC SEALS

The world's coldest continent is Antarctica, most of which is permanently covered in thick ice. With wind speeds sometimes exceeding 200 mph (320 km/h) and temperatures plunging as low as –128°F (–89°C), few animals can survive. Even the surrounding seas freeze over, but they are rich in food and support many animals, including seals. There are six species of Antarctic seal: southern elephant, Ross, leopard, crabeater, Weddell and southern fur seals. The southern elephant seal is the world's largest seal, with males weighing up to 8,800 lb (4,000 kg). Born in late winter, by late spring seal pups are strong enough to find their own food in the Antarctic waters.

## CRABEATER SEAL

Surprisingly, crabeater seals do not eat crabs. They actually feed on small, shrimplike creatures called krill, which they filter from the water through their teeth. They detect nearby krill with their long, downward-curving whiskers. On land, crabeater seals can move as fast as 16 mph (25 km/h), but they are often attacked by killer whales.

## ELEPHANT SEAL

In the breeding season, a male southern elephant seal guards a group of 40–50 females, with whom he mates. If a rival male challenges him, he takes up a threatening pose and roars loudly. The skin bag on his nose inflates to amplify the sound. If the challenger does not back off, a bloody battle occurs. A female elephant seal gives birth to a single pup, which she suckles for about a month. During this period she herself does not eat but lives off the energy already stored in her blubber.

### Puppy fat

At birth, a Weddell seal pup weighs about 55 lb (25 kg) but it grows quickly, nourished by its mother's rich milk. It first enters the water when about six weeks old to start learning to find its own food.

# ROSS SEAL

The smallest of the Antarctic seals, the
Ross seal is uniformly gray along its
back and sides, and silvery-gray to white
underneath. It has a small head, needlelike
incisor teeth and long flippers. It feeds on
squid, fish and krill.

# WEDDELL SEAL

The Weddell seal makes longer, deeper dives than
any other seal, often reaching depths of 980–1,300 ft
(300–400 m) to feed on Antarctic cod. One Weddell
seal was recorded as diving to 2,000 ft (600 m) for
73 minutes. In summer, these large gentle seals spend
many hours asleep on the ice. In winter, they tend
to stay underwater to avoid the harsh conditions,
breathing through holes they make in the ice.

# WHALES, DOLPHINS AND PORPOISES

Whales are the largest sea mammals. There are two kinds of whale: toothed and baleen. Baleen whales have bristly plates in their mouths instead of teeth. When they feed, they take gulps of water. Baleen plates act like filters, so the water drains away but the fish, krill and plankton stay in the whale's mouth. Toothed whales can locate other sea creatures by echolocation. They send out high-pitched clicking sounds and detect the echoes as they bounce back from objects. Dolphins and porpoises are small-toothed whales. Whales swim with up-and-down strokes of their tails, using their flippers to steer.

Size: 6–7½ ft (1.8–2.3 m)
Range: northern Pacific Ocean
Habitat: coastal waters, oceanic

## Dall's porpoise
*Phocoenides dalli*

Dall's porpoise is larger and heavier than most porpoises, and inhabits deeper waters. It lives in groups of up to 15 porpoises. Schools of 100 or more porpoises may gather to migrate north in summer and south in winter. Mothers suckle their calves for as long as two years.

Size: 4½–6 ft (1.4–1.8 m)
Range: northern Atlantic and Pacific oceans, Black and Mediterranean Seas
Habitat: coastal waters, oceanic

## Harbor porpoise
*Phocoena phocoena*

These porpoises feed on fish such as herring and mackerel. They dive for up to six minutes when hunting prey, which they pinpoint using echolocation clicks. Before breeding, they perform long courtship rituals, caressing one another as they swim side by side. Calves are born 11 months after mating. While a mother suckles her calf, she lies on her side at the water's surface, so the calf can breathe easily.

## Killer whale
*Orcinus orca*

The largest of the dolphin family, the killer whale is a fierce hunter that feeds on fish, squid, sea lions, birds and even other whales. It sometimes snatches seals from the shore or tips them off floating ice into its mouth. It lives and hunts in traveling family groups of up to 40 animals.

Size: 23–32 ft (7–9.7 m)
Range: worldwide, especially cooler seas
Habitat: coastal waters, oceanic, polar

# Ganges dolphin
*Platanista gangetica*

One of only five species of freshwater dolphin, the Ganges dolphin lives in muddy rivers in India. It is blind and uses radarlike echolocation signals to find its prey of fish and shrimps.

Size: 5–8 ft (1.5–2.4 m)

Range: India: Ganges and Brahmaputra river systems

Habitat: fresh water

# Common dolphin
*Delphinus delphis*

Also known as the short-beaked dolphin, this mammal has pointed flippers, a curved dorsal fin and a long beak. It lives in groups of between 20 and 100 dolphins. Curious and playful, they are often seen swimming alongside ships, leaping and rolling in the water.

Size: 7–8½ ft (2.1–2.6 m)

Range: warm and tropical oceans worldwide

Habitat: coastal waters, oceanic

Size: 82–105 ft (25–32 m)

Range: all oceans

Habitat: oceanic

# Blue whale
*Balaenoptera musculus*

The world's largest mammal, the blue whale can weigh 145 tons and measure 105 ft (32 m). This giant feeds on huge quantities of tiny, shrimplike creatures called krill, consuming up to 4 tons each day in the summer. The blue whale is in danger of extinction, as there are only 10,000–25,000 left.

Size: 10–14 ft (3–4.2 m)

Range: warm and tropical oceans worldwide

Habitat: coastal waters, oceanic

# Atlantic bottle-nosed dolphin
*Tursiops truncatus*

The curving line of this dolphin's mouth makes it look as if it is always smiling. It feeds mainly on bottom-dwelling fish, and is a skilful echolocator, producing up to 1,000 clicking noises a second.

Size: 36–66 ft (11–20 m)
Range: all oceans
Habitat: oceanic, polar

# Sperm whale
## Physeter macrocephalus

The sperm whale has a huge head filled with a waxy substance called spermaceti. The spermaceti helps the whale to alter its buoyancy — its ability to float. This enables it to reach depths of more than 3,280 ft (1,000 m) in search of squid to eat.

Size: 13–20 ft (4–6.1 m)
Range: Arctic Ocean and subarctic waters
Habitat: coastal waters, oceanic

# White whale
## Delphinapterus leucas

White whales, also called belugas, often live together in small groups called pods. They communicate with a variety of sounds, such as whistles, clicks, clangs, twitters and moos. Polar bears prey on belugas that get trapped by the Arctic ice. In winter, big herds of belugas migrate south.

Size: 13–20 ft (4–6.1 m)
Range: high Arctic Ocean
Habitat: oceanic, polar

# Narwhal
## Monodon monoceros

The narwhal is related to the white whale, but has only two teeth. One of the male's teeth grows into a spiral tusk up to 8¾ ft (2.7 m) long, which sticks through its top lip. The tusk is probably used to impress females and fight rivals in the breeding season. Females sometimes have a short tusk.

# Cuvier's beaked whale
## Ziphius cavirostris

This whale dives deeper and for longer than any other mammal. A dive can extend to nearly 10,000 ft (3,000 m) and can last for more than two hours. A whale undertakes these long journeys in search of squid and fish.

Size: 21–23 ft (6.4–7 m)
Range: all oceans, temperate and tropical waters
Habitat: oceanic

Size: up to 10 ft (3 m)

Range: east African coast, Arabian Gulf, Indian Ocean, Red Sea to northern Australia

Habitat: coastal waters

# Dugong
*Dugong dugon*

Surprisingly, dugongs are related to elephants. The dugong is fleshy and streamlined, with a crescent-shaped tail. It is shy and solitary, spending much of its life on the seabed, feeding on seaweed and seagrass. A female dugong gives birth to a single baby in the water and helps it to the surface.

# Humpback whale
*Megaptera novaeangliae*

The humpback whale is famous for the amazingly complex songs it sings to keep in touch with other whales and to attract mates. It often sings for hours on end, only pausing to take a breath of air. These songs travel great distances through the water.

Size: 48–62½ ft (14.6–19 m)

Range: all oceans

Habitat: coastal waters, oceanic, polar

# Gray whale
*Eschrichtius robustus*

This whale stirs up the seabed with its snout and uses its baleen plates to filter tiny creatures to eat. It makes a round trip of 12,400 miles (20,000 km) between its summer feeding waters off Alaska and the warmer shallower waters off the coast of Mexico, where it breeds in winter.

Size: 40–50 ft (12.2–15.3 m)

Range: northeast and northwest Pacific Ocean

Habitat: coastal waters, oceanic

# Minke whale
*Balaenoptera acutorostrata*

The minke whale is a pint-sized relative of the humpback and blue whales. Like them, it has distinctive grooves along its throat. In polar regions, the minke feeds mainly on plankton, but in warmer waters it eats fish and squid as well.

Size: 26–33 ft (8–10 m)

Range: all oceans, temperate and polar waters

Habitat: coastal waters, oceanic

# ELEPHANTS

Weighing as much as 13,000 lb (5,900 kg) and standing up to 13 ft (4 m) tall at the shoulder, the elephant is the largest land mammal. There are three elephant species: two live in Africa, the other in India and Southeast Asia. An elephant's flexible trunk — a long nose fixed to its upper lip — contains up to 100,000 muscles, and is used for smelling, feeling, breathing, feeding and making loud trumpeting calls. The elephant uses its tusks for fighting, stripping bark off trees and digging for water. Elephants live on grassy plains and desert scrubland, and in river valleys and swamps. They can reach the age of 78. Females and young elephants live in family herds, while mature males roam alone.

A baby elephant does not need to forage for food, because it drinks its mother's milk for at least two years. Sometimes, other adult females in the herd also suckle it.

## SHOWERS AND MUD BATHS

As well as releasing heat through their large flappy ears, elephants also keep cool by giving themselves a shower. They suck up water with their trunks and spray it over their bodies. An elephant can reach every part of its body by swinging its trunk and blowing at just the right moment. Elephants sometimes wallow in mud, too, or throw dust over themselves, which coats their skin and protects them against insects and sunburn. It also stops moisture evaporating from their skin.

# THREE SPECIES

The African bush elephant is larger and heavier than its Asian cousin, with bigger, more rounded ears. It has two fingerlike projections on the end of its trunk, while the Asian has one. The African forest elephant is the smallest of the three species. Poachers are a major threat to African elephants, killing thousands every year for their ivory tusks.

African

Asian

# BIG APPETITE

An African elephant eats about 330 lb (150 kg) of grass, leaves, twigs, bark, roots and fruit every day. In order to consume such a large amount, it has to spend three-quarters of its time feeding.

# ELEPHANTS AT WORK

For thousands of years, humans have trained elephants to lift, push and drag heavy objects. In forestry work, Asian elephants are sometimes taught to use their tusks to raise heavy logs like a fork truck.

45

# HOOFED MAMMALS

Some mammals have toes that end in hard coverings called hooves. Hooves are made of keratin — the same substance as nails and claws. Long ago, all hoofed mammals had five toes. As they evolved, they lost the use of some toes to enable them to run faster. Hoofed mammals are classified according to whether their feet have an odd number (one or three) or an even number (two or four) of working toes.

Size: body 5½–6¼ ft (1.7–1.9 m); tail 6–8¼ in (15–21 cm)

Range: western Africa: Liberia, Ivory Coast, Sierra Leone, Guinea

Habitat: tropical evergreen forest, fresh water

## Pygmy hippopotamus
*Choeropsis liberiensis*

This small hippopotamus lives around swamps, but spends most of its time on dry land. This pygmy hippo is in severe danger of becoming extinct as its forest habitat is cut down. They are also at risk from hunters, who kill the animal for its meat.

Size: body 3½–4½ ft (1.1–1.4 m); tail 13¾–19¾ in (35–50 cm)

Range: central and southern Africa

Habitat: tropical grassland, desert

# PIGS, PECCARIES AND HIPPOPOTAMUSES

A pig is easily recognized by its long, muscular snout, which ends in a round, flat disk. The piglike peccary lives only in the Americas, while the hippo, the larger cousin of pigs and peccaries, is found in Africa. Pigs, peccaries and hippos are even-toed hoofed mammals, with four toes on their feet (peccaries have only three on their hind feet). They have simpler stomachs than other even-toed hoofed mammals.

## Warthog
*Phacochoerus africanus*

The warthog is not a pretty sight. It has long legs, curving tusks and a long, broad head with two pairs of large wartlike protruberances. It lives in small family groups on the African savanna and on treeless plains, where it feeds on short grasses and herbs. In the hottest part of the day, it shelters in its burrow, which is often the disused burrow of an aardvark. Its main enemies are lions and leopards.

## Collared peccary
*Pecari tajacu*

Size: body 29½–3½ in (75–90 cm);
tail ⅝–1¼ in (1.5–3 cm)

Range: southwest USA, Mexico, Central and South America

Habitat: deciduous forest, tropical evergreen forest, desert

A light neckband gives collared peccaries their name. They live in groups of up to 15 animals, marking their territory with scent produced by musk glands on their backs. They eat roots, herbs, grass, fruit, worms and insect larvae. They can run fast enough to escape from predators such as jaguars and pumas.

## Western bearded pig
*Sus barbatus*

Size: body 4–5 ft (1.2–1.5 m);
tail 7¾–11¾ in (20–30 cm)

Range: Malaysia, Sumatra, Borneo

Habitat: tropical evergreen forest

While some bearded pigs have bristles all over their snouts, others have a line of whiskers along their jaws and cheeks. The bearded pig lives in rain forests, but it is also found on beaches and around swamps. Fallen fruit, rats and insect larvae are this pig's main foods. It often follows monkeys to pick up any fruit that they might have dropped.

Size: body 3½–4¼ ft (1.1–1.3 m);
tail 6–7¾ in (15–20 cm)

Range: all continents except Antarctica

Habitat: deciduous and tropical forest, temperate and tropical grassland, inhabited areas, farmland

## Wild boar
*Sus scrofa*

The wild boar is the ancestor of the farmyard pig. With its long snout it roots around the woodland floor for plants and insects to eat. It also digs up bulbs and tubers. Young boars have stripey coats that blend in with the trees and hide them from predators.

Size: body 9¼–13¾ ft (2.8–4.2 m);
tail 13¾–19¾ in (35–50 cm)

Range: Africa, south of the Sahara

Habitat: fresh water, temperate grassland

## Hippopotamus
*Hippopotamus amphibius*

The hippo is one of the world's largest land mammals — only rhinos and elephants weigh more. It lives near rivers and lakes, and spends up to 16 hours each day in the water to keep cool. It emerges at sunset to graze on riverside plants and eat fallen fruit. It can swim well, but often prefers to walk along the river bottom.

# CAMELS

The camel family consists of the dromedary, the bactrian camel, the vicuña and the guanaco. They are cud-chewing animals, and their feet have just two toes on each foot. The desert-dwelling dromedary and bactrian camels have broad, flat pads under each foot to help them walk over the soft, sandy soil. Vicuñas and guanacos can breathe the thin air on high mountain pastures, and their thick, woolly coats enable them to endure the chilly temperatures at high altitude.

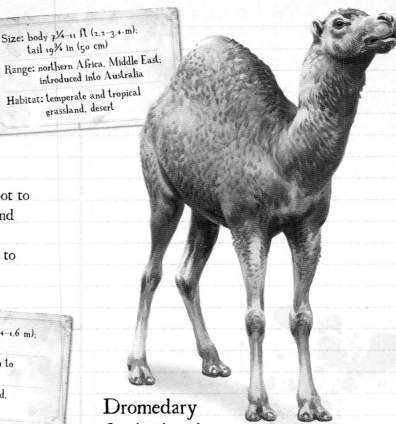

Size: body 7¼–11 ft (2.2–3.4 m);
tail 19¾ in (50 cm)

Range: northern Africa, Middle East;
introduced into Australia

Habitat: temperate and tropical
grassland, desert

## Vicuña
### Vicugna vicugna

Vicuñas are humpless camels. They live in small family herds in the Andes Mountains of South America, where they feed on grass and small plants. Each herd is guarded by an adult male. He warns the rest of the herd of danger by whistling loudly to them.

Size: body 4½–5¼ ft (1.4–1.6 m);
tail 6 in (15 cm)

Range: Andes, from Peru to
northern Chile

Habitat: tropical grassland,
high ground

## Dromedary
### Camelus dromedarius

Dromedaries are well suited to life in the desert. Their ears and nostrils can close to keep out sand, while their tough lips enable them to eat thorny desert plants without being injured. They use their humps to store fat, which their bodies break down into water and energy when food and drink become scarce.

Size: body about 3¼ ft (1 m);
tail 1½–2 in (4–5 cm)

Range: Himalayas to central
China

Habitat: deciduous forest,
high ground, desert

# DEER, GIRAFFES, PRONGHORNS AND BOVIDS

This group of even-toed hoofed animals all chew the cud, which means that they have complex stomachs. When they eat, they briefly chew leaves and grasses and swallow them. The animal then brings the partly digested food back up into its mouth and chews it properly. Giraffes, pronghorns and bovids (cattle, antelopes, sheep and goats) have horns on their heads, while deer have antlers. Horns are permanent growths, but antlers drop off and grow again each year.

## Alpine musk deer
### Moschus chrysogaster

A male musk deer has a scent gland which oozes a strong-smelling liquid called musk. The male uses this to send signals to females in the breeding season. The musk deer has a coat of long, thick, bristly hairs and two tusklike teeth. It feeds on lichens, shoots, buds, grass, moss and twigs.

Size: body 5¼–8 ft (1.6–2.5 m);
tail 4¾–9¾ in (12–25 cm)

Range: northern Africa, Europe, Asia,
North America; introduced
into New Zealand

Habitat: deciduous forest, high ground,
temperate grassland

# Red deer
## *Cervus elaphus*

Male and female red deer live in separate herds. The male's antlers drop off each spring, and are replaced by a new, larger set. In the breeding season, males use their antlers to fight each other for the right to mate with the females. The older males usually win.

Size: body 8–10 ft (2.5–3 m);
tail 2–4¾ in (5–12 cm)

Range: northernmost parts of Europe;
Asia, North America

Habitat: northern forest, fresh
water

# Moose
## *Alces alces*

The moose (also known as the elk) is the largest of all the deer species. It has massive antlers, a broad, overhanging muzzle and a flap of skin that dangles from its throat. In winter, the moose eats pine cones, and shovels away the snow with its hooves to find mosses and lichens too. It swims well, and in summer it will often wade into lakes and rivers to feed on water plants. Males bellow to attract the females.

Size: body 4–7¼ ft (1.2–2.2 m);
tail 4–8¼ in (10–21 cm)

Range: northern Europe, northern
Asia, Greenland, northern
North America

Habitat: northern forest, tundra

# Caribou
## *Rangifer tarandus*

The caribou, or reindeer, is the only deer species in which both males and females have antlers (it is usually only the males). The caribou feeds mainly on mosses, lichens and fungi in winter. In summer it travels north to feed on the rich grass and plants of the tundra, migrating up to 750 miles (1,200 km) each way. The females and young live in herds, but adult males often live alone.

Size: body 4–6½ ft (1.2–2 m);
tail 11¾–16½ ft
(30–40 cm)

Range: Democratic Republic of
Congo (Zaire)

Habitat: tropical evergreen forest

Size: body 10–13 ft (3–4 m); tail
35½–43½ cm (90–110 cm)

Range: Africa: south of the Sahara

Habitat: tropical grassland

## Giraffe
### *Giraffa camelopardalis*

The giraffe lives on
Africa's savanna. With its
amazingly long legs and
neck, it stands nearly 19½
ft (6 m) tall, making it the
tallest living mammal. Its
great height enables it to
feed on leaves and buds at
the tops of trees, and to
spot approaching danger.

## Okapi
### *Okapia johnstoni*

The African okapi feeds on the leaves and shoots of
rain forest trees. It pulls them off the branches with
its tongue, which is so long that the okapi can even use
it to clean its eyes and eyelids. Its leg stripes are a good
camouflage. It lives alone and
meets other okapis only in the
breeding season. Males have short
horns, like those of a giraffe.

## Pronghorn
### *Antilocarpa americana*

One of North America's fastest mammals, the pronghorn
can run at 50 mph (80 km/h). Both males and females
have horns with short,
forward-pointing prongs.
Pronghorns travel far in the
winter in search of food.

Size: body 3½–4¼ ft (1.1–1.3 m);
tail 4–6 in (10–15 cm)

Range: eastern South America,
south of the Amazon

Habitat: temperate grassland

Size: body 3¼–5 ft (1–1.15 m);
tail 3–4 in (7.5–10 cm)

Range: central Canada, west
USA, Mexico

Habitat: temperate grassland,
desert

## Pampas deer
### *Ozotoceros bezoarticus*

This deer lives among the tall grasses of the South
American grasslands—a habitat called 'pampas'. As the
pampas has been turned to farmland, this species has lost
much of its natural habitat. The pampas deer lives in
groups of up to six animals.

## Blue wildebeest
*Connochaetes taurinus*

In the dry season, huge herds of these large, cowlike antelopes walk very great distances across the African savanna in search of fresh grass and watering holes. Young wildebeest calves are born during the wet season, when the herds split up and food is more plentiful.

Size: body 8¼–10 ft (2.5–3 m);
tail 23½–35½ in (60–100 cm)

Range: India; Southeast Asia;
introduced into other places

Habitat: tropical grassland, tropical
evergreen forest, fresh water

Size: body 5½–7¾ ft (1.7–2.4 m);
tail 23½–35½ in
(60–100 cm)

Range: southern Africa

Habitat: tropical grassland

## Asian water buffalo
*Bubalus bubalis*

Water buffalo feed early and late in the day on grass and other vegetation growing near lakes and rivers. They spend much of the rest of the time wallowing in mud or submerged in the water, with only their muzzles showing. They use their long, curved horns to defend themselves against tigers.

## Wild yak
*Bos mutus*

Despite its size, the yak is surprisingly sure-footed as it grazes on remote mountain slopes. Its long, thick, ragged hair almost reaches to the ground. It also has a woolly undercoat to help protect it against freezing temperatures.

Size: body 5½–8¼ ft (1.7–2.5 m);
tail 17¾–25½ in (45–65 cm)

Range: central and west Africa

Habitat: deciduous forest, tropical
evergreen forest, high ground

Size: body up to 10½ ft
(3.25 m); tail 19¾–31½ in
(50–80 cm)

Range: Himalaya mountains of
central Asia

Habitat: high ground, tundra

## Bongo
*Tragelaphus eurycerus*

The shy, forest-dwelling bongo hides among the bushes and trees during the daytime. At dawn and dusk it comes out to feed on leaves, bark and fruit. When it runs, the bongo tilts its head so that its horns lie along its back, to prevent them catching on branches.

51

# HORSES AND TAPIRS

Along with rhinoceroses, horses and tapirs make up a group of odd-toed, hoofed mammals. Animals in the horse family, including zebras and asses, live in herds and feed mainly on grass. Their feet have only one toe with a single hoof on the end. This enables them to run fast. Tapirs are short stocky creatures with four toes on the front feet and three on the hind feet. Rhinoceroses have three toes on each foot, short legs, large heads and heavy bones.

Size: body 8 ft (2.5 m);
tail 2–4 in (5–10 cm)

Range: Southeast Asia: Indonesia, Malaysia, Burma, Thailand

Habitat: tropical evergreen forest, fresh water

## Malayan Tapir
### *Tapirus indicus*

The Malayan tapir is a shy, solitary animal that lives in humid swampy forests. It swims well and rushes into the water to hide when it feels threatened. The Malayan tapir prefers to feed on aquatic vegetation, but also eats the leaves, buds and fruit of some land plants.

Size: body 10–12 ft (3–3.6 m);
tail 23½–27½ in (60–70 cm)

Range: eastern and southern Africa

Habitat: tropical evergreen forest, tropical grassland, desert

## Black rhinoceros
### *Diceros bicornis*

The black rhino's hooklike upper lip helps it to grab leaves, buds and shoots from small trees and bushes. It has poor eyesight but good senses of hearing and smell. If it feels threatened, it will charge. Despite its bulk, it can reach a speed of 30 mph (48 km/h). This is one of five species of rhino, which are all endangered by the illegal trade in rhino horn.

# Przewalski's horse
*Equus ferus przewalskii*

This short sturdy horse is the ancestor of all modern horses. It was once common on the dry plains of Mongolia, where it grazed on grass and leaves. It had not been seen in the wild since 1968, but horses have been carefully bred and protected to create a small population that has been re-introduced to Mongolia, where it is living wild.

Size: body 6–6½ ft (1.8–2.6 m);
tail 35½ in (90 cm)

Range: Mongolia, western China

Habitat: temperate grassland

# Sumatran rhinoceros
*Dicerorhinus sumatrensis*

This is the smallest and hairiest of the rhinoceros family. There are only a few hundred wild Sumatran rhinos left. It is hunted for its horns, which are used in traditional medicine, and the forests where it lives are being chopped down.

Size: body 8–9¼ ft (2.5–2.8 m);
tail about 23½ in (60 cm)

Range: Southeast Asia: Sumatra,
Borneo, possibly Malaysia

Habitat: tropical evergreen forest,
fresh water

Size: body 8½ ft (2.6 m);
tail 27½–29½ in (70–75 cm)

Range: eastern Africa

Habitat: temperate grassland,
desert

# Grevy's zebra
*Equus grevyi*

Herds of grazing zebras roam Africa's savanna. Zebras need to drink frequently, so they spend most of their time near water holes. Grevy's zebra is the largest zebra — the others are the plains zebra and the mountain zebra — and each species has a different pattern of stripes. The stripes may confuse predators and help individuals to recognize each other.

# RODENTS AND RABBITS

Rodents are a large group of small- to medium-sized mammals, which include such groups as squirrels, rats and beavers. There are more than 2,000 species of rodent, found all over the world in every kind of habitat. Most feed on plants and they have a single pair of sharp incisor teeth, which allow them to chew through the toughest of food. Pikas, rabbits and hares are another successful group of plant-eating mammals called lagomorphs. They also have sharp incisors for chewing plant food.

## PIKAS, RABBITS AND HARES

Pikas are smaller than rabbits and have short rounded ears and no tail. There are about 30 species, most of which live in north and central Asia, although two species also live in North America. Rabbits and hares are common on every continent apart from Antarctica. There are about 60 species in all, and most of these fast-moving rabbits and hares have long narrow ears, small fluffy tails and well-developed back legs.

Size: body 7¾–9¾ in. (20–25 cm)

Range: northern Asia

Habitat: northern forest, high ground

### Northern pika
*Ochotona alpina*

The pika lives in family groups, which shelter in dens among rocks or tree roots. Grass and juicy plant stems are its main food. In summer it gathers extra food which it piles up in little haystacks to keep for the winter months. The pika can tunnel through snow to reach its food stores.

Size: body 14¼–20½ in (36–52 cm); tail 1–2 in (2.5–5 cm)

Range: Canada, Alaska, northern USA

Habitat: Northern forest, tundra, inhabited areas, farmland

### Snowshoe hare
*Lepus americanus*

The snowshoe hare is dark brown in summer but turns white in winter. Its light coat helps it to hide from enemies in its snowy home. Usually active at night and in the early morning, the snowshoe hare eats grass in summer and twigs and buds in winter.

### European rabbit
*Oryctolagus cuniculus*

Rabbits live in burrows which they dig near to one another. There may be a couple of hundred rabbits in a colony, called a warren. Grass and leafy plants are their main food, but they also eat grain and can damage young trees. Females have several litters a year.

Size: body 14¼–18 cm (36–46 cm); tail 1½–2¾ in (4–7 cm)

Range: Europe, northwest Africa; introduced into Australia, New Zealand, Chile

Habitat: inhabited areas, farmland, coast, deciduous forest, temperate grassland

# SQUIRRELS, BEAVERS, POCKET GOPHERS, POCKET MICE AND SPRINGHARES

These animals are all rodents. The squirrel family includes animals such as woodchucks, prairie dogs and chipmunks. Pocket gophers live in North America and spend most of their lives underground. Pocket mice are found in North and South America. Some live in dense forest, others bound across arid plains on long hind legs. The springhare can also leap like a kangaroo. Beavers spend much of their lives in water.

Size: body 17¾–24 in (45–61 cm);
tail 7–9¾ in (18–25 cm)
Range: North America
Habitat: deciduous forest, Northern forest, inhabited areas

## Woodchuck
*Marmota monax*

The woodchuck, or ground hog as it is sometimes known, eats plenty of plant food in summer and gets fat. At the first sign of frost it goes into its burrow and sleeps through the winter, living on its store of body fat.

## Black-tailed prairie dog
*Cynomys ludovicianus*

Prairie dogs live in huge underground burrows, called towns. A town may house several thousand animals. They come out during the day to feed on grass and other plants and warn each other of any danger with sharp doglike barks.

Size: body 4½–7 in (11.5–18 cm);
tail 4½–7 in (11.5–18 cm)
Range: India, Sri Lanka
Habitat: temperate grassland, deciduous forest, inhabited areas, farmland

## Indian palm squirrel
*Funambulus palmarum*

These active little squirrels leap about in palm trees during the day, feeding on palm nuts, flowers and buds. Rival males fight for females but after mating have nothing further to do with females or young. The females produce about three litters a year, each containing about three young.

Size: body 11–13 in (28–33 cm);
tail 3–4 in (7.5–10 cm)
Range: central USA
Habitat: temperate grassland

## European red squirrel
*Sciurus vulgaris*

Red squirrels use their sharp teeth to feed on conifer cones in winter, but in summer they also eat mushrooms and fruit. Where food is plentiful, females may have two litters of about three young a year. The young are born in a tree nest called a drey.

Size: body 7¾–9½ in (20–24 cm);
tail 6–7¾ in (15–20 cm)
Range: Europe, Asia
Habitat: deciduous forest

# Springhare
## *Pedetes capensis*

When alarmed or traveling a long way, the springhare bounces along on its long back legs like a kangaroo. When feeding, it moves on all fours. The springhare spends much of the day in its burrow and comes out at night to forage for bulbs, roots and grain as well as some insects.

Size: body 13¾–17 in (35–43 cm); tail 14¼–18½ in (36–47cm)

Range: southern Africa

Habitat: tropical grassland

# Plains pocket gopher
## *Geomys bursarius*

This gopher's name comes from its two deep fur-lined cheek pouches. These can be crammed full of food (mostly roots) to carry back to the nest. Gophers spend most of their lives underground in burrows, which they dig with their sharp front teeth and strong paws.

Size: body 7–9½ in (18–24 cm); tail 4–5 in (10–12.5 cm)

Range: central USA

Habitat: temperate grassland

Size: body 4¾–6½ in (12–16.5 cm); tail 7–7¾ in (18–20 cm)

Range: western USA

Habitat: temperate grassland, desert

# Desert kangaroo rat
## *Dipodomys deserti*

Kangaroo rats belong to the pocket mouse family. This desert species spends the day in a burrow and comes out at night to find food such as seeds. It is well adapted to dry areas and may live its whole life without ever drinking. It can carry food in cheek pouches.

# American beaver
## *Castor canadensis*

One of the largest rodents, the American beaver weighs up to 60 lb (27 kg). Beavers eat leaves, bark and twigs and always live near water. They build a dam across a stream with branches and mud, which creates a lake. A shelter, or lodge, is also made of branches and used to store food.

Size: body 28–39 in (70–100 cm); tail 8–12 in (20–30 cm)

Range: North America

Habitat: fresh water

# NEW WORLD RATS AND MICE

There are at least 430 species in this group of rodents, found in all kinds of habitats throughout the Americas. They adapt well to different conditions — fish-eating rats which live near rivers and lakes even have partially webbed feet. Most New World rats and mice are small — the largest, the giant water rat, measures 11¾ in (30 cm). Plant material is their main food, although some also feed on insects.

Size: body 4¾–8¾ in (12–22 cm);
tail 3¼–7 in (8–18 cm)

Range: Canada to Mexico

Habitat: deciduous forest,
northern forest, desert

## Deer mouse
*Peromyscus maniculatus*

Agile little mice, deer mice run and hop through grass and dense vegetation. They build nests underground or in tree holes and feed on insects as well as seeds, nuts and acorns. Young deer mice start to breed at only seven weeks old. They may have several litters a year, each containing up to nine young.

## Arizona cotton rat
*Sigmodon arizonae*

Cotton rats sometimes occur in such numbers that they are considered pests. They feed on plants and small insects but may also take the eggs and chicks of bobwhite quails as well as crayfish and crabs. The female has her first litter of up to 12 young when just 10 weeks old.

Size: body 5–7¾ in (12.5–20 cm);
tail 3–5 in (7.5–12.5 cm)

Range: USA

Habitat: temperate grassland,
deciduous forest, inhabited
areas, farmland

# HAMSTERS AND MOLE-RATS

Hamsters and mole-rats are both burrowing rodents. Hamsters are found from Europe across the Middle East to central Asia. There are about 18 species, all with a rounded body and short tail. They have large cheek pouches, which they use for carrying food back to the burrow. There are two groups of mole-rats: one group includes two species of East African mole-rats and four species of bamboo rats from Southeast Asia. All are plant-eating. The other group includes eight species, which all live in Africa. The most unusual is the virtually hairless naked mole-rat.

Size: body 8¾–11¾ in (22–30 cm);
tail 1¼–2¼ in (3–6 cm)

Range: western Europe, central Asia

Habitat: inhabited areas, farmland,
temperate grassland

## Common hamster
*Cricetus cricetus*

The hamster lives in a burrow with separate areas for sleeping and storing food. It feeds mainly on seeds, grain, roots, green plants and insect larvae. In late summer, it gathers extra food to store for the winter. From October to March or April, the hamster hibernates, waking from time to time to feed on its food stores.

# Naked mole-rat
*Heterocephalus glaber*

This little rodent has a lifestyle more like an insect than a mammal. It lives in a colony of up to 200 animals, ruled by one female, or queen. She is the only one to breed. Worker mole-rats dig burrows and gather food such as roots for the whole colony to eat. A few non-workers tend the queen.

Size: body 3¼–3½ in (8–9 cm); tail 1½ in (4 cm)

Range: eastern Africa

Habitat: tropical grassland, desert

Size: body 14½–19 in (36–48 cm); tail 4–6 in (10–15 cm)

Range: Southeast Asia

Habitat: tropical grassland

# Bamboo rat
*Rhizomys sumatrensis*

This rat has a heavy body, short legs and a short, almost hairless tail. Its front teeth are large and strong and it uses these and its claws for digging. It burrows underground near clumps of bamboo. Bamboo roots are its main food, but it also eats other plants, seeds and fruit.

# VLEI RATS, GERBILS, LEMMINGS AND VOLES

Africa's vlei rats do not always live near water or swampy areas, but they are all good swimmers. Lemmings and voles are plump-bodied rodents which live in North America and northern Europe and Asia. All feed mainly on plants and they usually live in large groups or colonies. There are about 120 species. Gerbils live in Africa and in central and western Asia. All are well adapted to desert conditions and are able to survive with very little water. Their long hind legs and feet help keep their bodies well away from hot sand.

# South African vlei rat
*Otomys irroratus*

This plump, active rat feeds on seeds, berries, shoots and grasses. It often goes into water and even dives to escape enemies — many larger creatures feed on these rats. It usually makes a nest of leaves and twigs above ground but may sometimes shelter in a burrow left by another animal.

Size: body 5–7¾ in (13–20 cm); tail 2–6¾ in (5–17 cm)

Range: southern Africa

Habitat: temperate grassland, fresh water

Size: body 5–6 in (13–15 cm); tail ¾ in (2 cm)

Range: Scandinavia

Habitat: temperate grassland, tundra

# Norway lemming
*Lemmus lemmus*

The Norway lemming is busy day and night, feeding on grass, leaves and moss. In winter it clears pathways under the snow so it can still run around foraging for food. Lemmings start to breed in spring under the snow and may produce as many as eight litters of six young each during the summer.

Size: body 6¼–7¾ in (16–20 cm);
tail 5–6¼ in (13–16 cm)

Range: Middle East and Asia

Habitat: desert

## Great gerbil
*Rhombomys opimus*

This gerbil manages to survive in the Gobi Desert, with its hot summers and icy winters. During the summer, it builds up stores of 130 lb (60 kg) or more of plant material in its burrow so that it has plenty of food for the winter months.

Size: body 3½–5 in (9–12.5 cm);
tail 1¼–2½ in (3.5–6.5 cm)

Range: North America

Habitat: deciduous forest, northern forest, temperate grassland, fresh water

## Meadow vole
*Microtus pennsylvanicus*

The meadow vole manages to live in many kinds of habitat. Grass, seeds, roots and bark are its main food and it moves along runways which it clears and keeps trimmed in the grass. It makes a nest on the ground or a burrow under the runways.

# OLD WORLD RATS AND MICE

This large group of almost 500 species of rodent contains some of the world's most common and widespread mammals. Rodents such as the brown rat and house mouse have adapted to life all over the world in many different kinds of conditions and will eat a wide range of foods. Many of this group are considered pests by humans because they damage grain and root crops as well as stored food. Some such as the brown rat also carry diseases such as salmonella.

## Brown rat
*Rattus norvegicus*

This rat is a serious pest. It has followed humans all over the world and lives wherever people settle. An extremely adaptable animal, it eats any scraps of waste food. It breeds all year round and produces about eight litters of eight to ten young each in a year.

Size: body 9¾–11¾ in (25–30 cm);
tail 9¾–12½ in (25–32 cm)

Range: worldwide

Habitat: inhabited areas, farmland, temperate grassland, fresh water

Size: body 3¼–5¼ in (8–13 cm);
tail 2¾–3¾ in (7–9.5 cm)

Range: Europe, Asia, northern Africa

Habitat: deciduous forest, northern forest, temperate grassland

## Wood mouse
*Apodemus sylvaticus*

The wood mouse is one of the most common small rodents in Europe. It comes out of its nest under the roots of trees in the evening and forages for seeds, insects and berries. The female usually produces young between April and November, but may breed through the winter if there is plenty of food.

# DORMICE AND JERBOAS

There are about 26 species of dormouse living in Africa, Europe and northern Asia. In the fall, most dormice eat extra food to build up reserves of fat in the body. They then hibernate — sleep through the winter — living on their fat but waking from time to time to feed on stored food. Jerboas are small rodents with long back legs used for jumping. There are 33 species of jerboa, living in North America, eastern Europe and Asia.

## Desert dormouse
*Selevinia betpakdalensis*

This dormouse is active at night, catching insects to eat. It also feeds on plants and makes stores of plant food for the winter months. It digs a burrow in which it shelters during the day, and it may also use it for hibernation.

Size: body 2¾–3¼ in (7–8.5 cm);
tail 2¾–3¾ in (7–9.5 cm)

Range: central Asia:
Kazakhstan

Habitat: desert

Size: body 3½–6 in (9–15 cm);
tail 6¼–8¾ in (16–22 cm)

Range: northern Asia

Habitat: temperate grassland,
desert

## Great jerboa
*Allactaga major*

This lively rodent leaps through the desert on its long back legs. At night, it searches for seeds and insects to eat, which it finds by combing through the sand with the long slender claws on its front feet. During the day the jerboa shelters in a burrow.

Size: body 7¾–15¾ in (20–40 cm);
no visible tail

Range: Peru to Argentina

Habitat: temperate grassland

## Montane guinea pig
*Cavia tschudii*

The wild guinea pig has a chunky body, short legs and small ears. It lives in family groups, which may join together to form colonies of up to 40 animals. At dawn and dusk, guinea pigs come out of their burrows to eat grass and leaves.

# PORCUPINES, CHINCHILLAS, GUINEA PIGS, CAPYBARA AND HUTIAS

These widely varied animals belong to small families of medium to large rodents. Porcupines have long sharp spines. There are two families: one in Africa and Asia, the other in North and South America. Chinchillas and guinea pigs are all ground-living rodents which live in South America, as does the capybara. Hutia live in the West Indies.

Size: body 8½–15 in (22–38 cm);
tail 3–6 in (7.5–15 cm)

Range: northern Chile

Habitat: high ground

## Common chinchilla
*Chinchilla lanigera*

With its large eyes, long ears and bushy tail, the chinchilla is an appealing animal. It lives in colonies of 100 or more and feeds on plants. It usually sits up to eat, holding its food in its front paws. Female chinchillas are larger than males. They breed in winter and have two litters of up to six young.

## Capybara
*Hydrochoerus hydrochaeris*

The largest rodent, the capybara spends much of its time in water and is an expert swimmer and diver. Its feet are partially webbed and when swimming only its eyes, ears and nostrils show above the water. It eats mainly plants, including water plants.

Size: body 3¼–4¼ ft (1–1.3 m)

Range: Colombia and Venezuela to Argentina

Habitat: flooded grassland, marsh, forest

## Bahamian hutia
*Geocapromys ingrahami*

The hutia feeds mostly on fruit and leaves, but it also eats some insects and small reptiles. It is a good climber and may search for food in trees. Active during the night, it shelters in a burrow or rock crevice at day.

Size: body 11¾–19¾ in (30–50 cm); tail 6–11¾ in (15–30)

Range: Caribbean: Bahamas

Habitat: tropical forest, scrub

## Tree porcupine
*Coendou prehensilis*

The body of the tree porcupine is covered with short, thick spines. Its tail is prehensile, which means it can grip easily, acting like an extra limb. Tree porcupines usually feed at night on leaves, plant stems and fruit.

Size: body 11¾–24 in (30–61 cm); tail 13–17¾ in (33–45 cm)

Range: Bolivia, Brazil, Venezuela

Habitat: tropical evergreen forest, tropical grassland

## Crested porcupine
*Hystrix cristata*

The spines on the back of this rodent are up to 12 in (30 cm) long. If threatened, it charges backward, driving these sharp spines, which detach easily, into its enemy. It feeds at night and shelters in its burrow by day.

Size: body 28–33 in (71–84 cm); tail up to 1 in (2.5 cm)

Range: northern Africa

Habitat: tropical evergreen forest, high ground

# WHY DO ZEBRAS HAVE STRIPES?

A zebra's stripes, the humps on a camel's back, the "fishing rod" on the head of an angler fish and the leaflike wings of an insect may seem extraordinary features, but they all make the animals that have them better able to survive in their environment. These types of features are called adaptations. They include the special markings or colors, known as camouflage, that allow creatures to hide from predators or prey. Other features help animals to survive in extreme conditions such as hot deserts or freezing polar lands.

Insect wings

## LEAF INSECT

Some insects look remarkably like the leaves of the trees and bushes they live among, and are very hard for their enemies to spot. The bright green, leaflike wings of this leaf insect have veinlike markings and edges which look as if they have been nibbled by other insects.

# BACTRIAN CAMEL

This is one of the biggest animals in the desert and it has special features to help it cope with life there. Wide flat feet stop it from sinking into soft sand. Large humps store fat to help it survive food shortages. When it gets the chance, the camel can drink a huge quantity of water at one go.

Angler fish

Glowing light

# ANGLER FISH

The long thin fin like a fishing rod on this deep-sea angler fish's head is topped with a special light that glows in the darkness. Other fish come near to investigate what could be a morsel of food. The angler opens its huge mouth and swallows the prey.

# ZEBRA

The bold black and white stripes of the zebra make the animal very obvious in the grasslands of Africa, but in a herd the mass of stripes makes it difficult for a predator to pick on one zebra to attack. Because the pattern of the stripes is slightly different in each individual, experts think that they enable the zebras to recognize their own family group. This helps keep them together and so safer from predators.

63

# BIRDS

There are about 10,200 species of birds, ranging in size from tiny hummingbirds to huge eagles and fast-running ostriches. Birds are among the most successful of all the world's animals, and have conquered air, land and water. They are found all over the world, including the icy lands of Antarctica and on the remotest islands. Despite their differences, all birds lay eggs. The baby bird is protected inside a hard-shelled egg, which is usually kept warm, or incubated, by the parents in a nest.

# WHAT IS A BIRD?

A typical bird has a strong but light body, two legs and a pair of wings. All birds are covered with feathers — and are the only creatures to have feathers. The feathers are made of keratin, a protein that also makes up the scales on reptiles and the hair and nails of humans and other mammals.

Yolk

Embryo (baby bird)

Growth region

Egg white (albumen)

A baby bird grows inside an egg. The yolk is its food supply and the egg white protects it from sudden movements or changes in temperature. The hard shell protects the whole structure.

Not all birds fly. The largest bird, the ostrich, is too heavy to take to the air. Instead it runs fast on its long legs.

Albatross

Swift

Hummingbird

Swallow

Hawk

Vulture

Pheasant

## WINGS

A bird's wings are shaped for different kinds of flight. The long broad wings of hawks and vultures allow these birds to soar for hours on air currents over land. The long wings of the albatross are suited to the different wind conditions over oceans. Agile fast-flying birds such as swifts and swallows have slender pointed wings. The hummingbird's wings can move in almost any direction, while the pheasant's wings are for slower flapping flight.

Primary flight feathers

Secondary flight feathers

Wing coverts (small feathers)

Beak

Eye

Breast

Tail feathers

Talons

Toes

## BIRD ANATOMY

Here is a powerful martial eagle poised to snatch its prey. Its strong wings keep its body in the air and its tail feathers are spread to help it steer during flight. Its strong talons are held ready to crush its prey, which it will then tear apart with its hooked beak. All birds have wings, beaks and claws that are shaped for their particular lifestyle.

# ALL TYPES OF FEET

Perching birds, such as crows, all have four-toed feet, three toes facing forward and one backward. Seabirds, such as the cormorant, have webbed feet. The ostrich's two-toed foot is suited to running and the eagle's strong toes and claws are used for killing prey.

Ostrich

Great cormorant

Harpy eagle

Carrion crow

Wings

## Feathers

Bristle feather

Filoplume

Contour feather

Flight feather

Feathers keep a bird warm and streamline its body. Colorful or specially shaped feathers, such as filoplumes and bristles, help to attract mates. The largest, strongest feathers are usually the flight and tail feathers. Softer contour feathers cover the body and down feathers beneath these add warmth.

Giant hummingbird

Warbler

# BEAKS

Beaks vary widely in shape depending on the bird's diet. The hummingbird probes long tubelike flowers to reach the nectar deep inside. The toucan reaches berries at the end of slender branches it is too heavy to sit on. Parrots crack open hard nuts, while finches feed on tough seeds. Warblers need thin sharp beaks to snatch insects. Birds of prey, such as eagles, use large hooked beaks to tear flesh. Waders such as the redshank probe sand for small prey. Most ducks crop grass at the water's edge and dabble in mud for plant seeds, but the merganser snatches slippery fish.

Toucan

Finch

Mallard duck

Red-breasted merganser

Common redshank

Parrot

# GAME BIRDS AND GROUND BIRDS

Not all birds are high fliers. Many spend most of their life on the ground, where they scratch around to find food. The ratites, or running birds, includes species such as the ostrich, rhea and emu. None of these birds can fly, because their wings are too small to be used for flight. The ratites feed on seeds, leaves and shoots. Game birds, too, spend most of their time on the ground, but they can fly when necessary and often roost in trees at night.

## GAME BIRDS

This large and varied group includes more than 260 different species – birds such as pheasants, grouse, guineafowl and malleefowl. Most have plump bodies and short strong legs. They are known as "game birds" because certain species have long been hunted and shot in some parts of the world. Pheasants and other game birds scratch around for seeds and berries. They usually make simple nests on the ground.

Size: male 7 ft (2.2 m) with train; female 34 in (86 cm)

Range: Pakistan, India, Nepal, Bhutan, Sri Lanka

Habitat: tropical evergreen forest, tropical and temperate grassland, inhabited areas, farmland

### Indian peafowl
*Pavo cristatus*

The male peafowl (peacock) is one of the most magnificent birds of all. It has colorful feathers, and it spreads its glittering train, adorned with "eyespot" markings, by raising the tail beneath. With his train fanned out, the male struts around to attract the female (peahen). She is plainer, with brown and green feathers and a small crest. In the wild, peafowl feed on seeds, berries, leaves and insects. They have been introduced into parks and gardens all over the world.

68

### California quail
*Callipepla californica*

These quail move and feed in flocks, eating leaves, berries, seeds and some insects. Both males and females have an unusual head plume, but only the male has black and white markings on the face.

Size: 9½–11 in (24–28 cm)

Range: western U.S.A., Chile, Argentina

Habitat: temperate grassland, farmland

### Temminck's tragopan
*Tragopan temminckii*

The favorite home of this beautiful bird is cool mountain forest. The male is striking and colorful, while the female has brownish feathers. At the start of the breeding season, the male bird courts the female by displaying his brilliant plumage. She lays three to six eggs. Tragopans eat seeds, buds, leaves, berries and insects.

Size: 25 in (64 cm)

Range: China, Southeast Asia

Habitat: tropical evergreen forest, high ground

# Ring-necked pheasant
## *Phasianus colchicus*

Pheasants came originally from Asia but have now been introduced into many other countries. The female is plainer than the male, with brown plumage. Wild pheasants eat seeds, buds and berries.

Size: male 30–35 in (76–89 cm); female 21–25¼ in (53–64 cm)

Range: China, east Asia; introduced to Europe and North America

Habitat: tropical evergreen grassland, temperate grassland, fresh water, farmland

# Red junglefowl
## *Gallus gallus*

The junglefowl is the ancestor of domestic chickens. The female is smaller than the colorful male and has brown and chestnut feathers. Junglefowl move in flocks of about 50 birds, searching for grain, grass, seeds and insects to eat. In the breeding season the female scrapes a shallow nest in the ground near a bush and lines it with leaves. She lays five or six eggs.

Size: 23½–27½ in (60–70 cm)

Range: Africa: Congo basin

Habitat: tropical evergreen forest

Size: male 25–29½ in (63–75 cm); female 16–18 in (40–45 cm)

Range: Southeast Asia

Habitat: farmland, deciduous forest, desert

# Congo peafowl
## *Afropavo congensis*

This shy, rare bird lives so deep in the African rain forest that scientists did not actually discover it until 1936. Even now, little is known about its life, but it is thought to roost in trees and feed mainly on grain and fruit.

Size: 13–15½ in (33–39 cm)

Range: Arctic and northernmost parts of Europe, Asia and North America

Habitat: tundra, high ground

# Rock ptarmigan
## *Lagopus muta*

In summer, the ptarmigan has mottled brown and gray feathers. But in winter, the ptarmigan molts and grows plumage that is pure white, except for its tail feathers. This white winter coat helps the ptarmigan hide from its enemies in its snowy Arctic home.

# Greater prairie chicken
## *Tympanuchus cupido*

Prairie chickens feed mainly on leaves, fruit and grain. In the summer they also catch insects, particularly grasshoppers. In the breeding season, male birds attract females by blowing out their orange neck pouches and raising their crests. They give booming calls and stamp their feet as they display. Females lay 10 to 12 eggs.

Size: 16½–18 in (42–46 cm)

Range: central U.S.A.

Habitat: farmland, temperate grassland

Size: 16–20 in (41–51 cm)

Range: northern Europe, northern Asia

Habitat: scrub, woodland, grassland

# Black grouse
## *Tetrao tetrix*

In spring, male black grouse perform a group display, called a lek, to attract female birds. Every morning they gather at a special place to dance, call and spread their beautiful tails before the watching females. The females mate with the best dancers and lay clutches of six to 11 eggs.

Size: 36–48 in (91–122 cm)

Range: U.S.A., Mexico

Habitat: forest, field, orchard, marsh

# Western capercaillie
## *Tetrao urogallus*

This magnificent turkeylike bird is the biggest of all the grouse. It feeds mainly on pine needles and pine seeds in winter. Its diet changes in summer, when it eats the leaves, stems and juicy fruit of cranberry, bilberry and other forest plants.

Size: male 34 in (86 cm); female 23 in (58 cm)

Range: northern Europe

Habitat: deciduous forest, northern forest

# Wild turkey
## *Meleagris gallopavo*

The wild turkey has a lighter, slimmer body and longer legs than domestic farm turkeys. It has bare skin on its head and neck. The turkey can fly well for short distances but finds most of its food on the ground. It eats seeds, nuts and berries and also catches small creatures such as insects and lizards.

# GROUND BIRDS

The long-legged running birds, such as ostriches, rheas, cassowaries and emus, live in dry grasslands and semidesert. They cannot fly and often have to travel far to find food so it is important for them to be fast runners. They also rely on running to escape from danger. Kiwis have shorter legs and move more slowly on the ground, and they cannot fly either. Groundliving birds from other families — such as the curassow, tinamou, great bustard and satin bowerbird — can fly, but spend most of their lives at ground level.

Size: 10½–13 in (27–33 cm)
Range: eastern Australia
Habitat: deciduous forest, tropical evergreen forest

## Satin bowerbird
*Ptilonorhynchus violaceus*

The male bowerbird builds a "bower" (chamber) on the ground to attract females. The bower is made of sticks and decorated with bright blue flowers and berries. If a female comes near, the male dances in his bower, flapping his wings and puffing up his feathers.

Size: 37 in (94 cm)
Range: Mexico to Ecuador
Habitat: tropical evergreen forest

## Great curassow
*Crax rubra*

The great curassow finds food, such as fruit and leaves, on the ground but flies up into the trees to roost. If in danger, it runs away rather than flies.

Size: 18 in (46 cm)
Range: South America
Habitat: tropical evergreen forest

Size: 27½ in (70 cm)
Range: New Zealand: North Island
Habitat: deciduous forest

## Brown kiwi
*Apteryx mantelli*

Using its long sensitive beak, the brown kiwi probes in the undergrowth for insects, worms and berries. Its keen senses of smell and hearing help it find food. Like other kiwis, this bird has tiny wings under its hairlike body feathers and cannot fly.

## Great tinamou
*Tinamus major*

Dense rain forest is the home of the great tinamou. This bird can fly but is weak and clumsy in the air. If in danger it usually remains still, relying on its brownish coloring to keep it hidden. It spends most of its time on the ground, eating berries, seeds and insects. Females lay up to 12 large greenish-blue or violet eggs that are among the most beautiful of all birds' eggs.

# Greater roadrunner
## *Geococcyx californianus*

True to its name, the greater roadrunner runs
at speeds of up to 12 mph (20 km/h) on its big,
strong feet. It can fly but does not often do so.
This speedy bird eats groundliving insects as well
as birds' eggs, lizards and even snakes.

Size: 27½ in (70 cm)
Range: South America
Habitat: tropical grassland

# Red-legged seriema
## *Cariama cristata*

The graceful seriema rarely
flies but runs fast to escape
from any danger. It kills snakes and lizards with its sharp
bill and also feeds on seeds, leaves and insects. The nest is
built in a tree and made from sticks. The female lays two
or three eggs which the pair take turns to incubate.

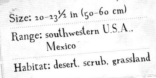

Size: 20–23½ in (50–60 cm)
Range: southwestern U.S.A.,
Mexico
Habitat: desert, scrub, grassland

# Ostrich
## *Struthio camelus*

The world's largest living
bird, the ostrich is too big
and heavy to fly. Instead
it runs fast and can reach
speeds of up to 43 mph
(70 km/h). Ostriches feed
on plants and seeds but also
catch small reptiles. Ostrich
eggs are larger than any other
bird's eggs. Each one weighs
about 3 lb (1.5 kg).

Size: 6–9 ft (1.75–2.75 m) tall
Range: Africa
Habitat: tropical grassland,
desert

Size: 5 ft (1.5 m) tall
Range: New Guinea,
northern Australia
Habitat: tropical evergreen forest

# Common cassowary
## *Casuarius casuarius*

The cassowary lives in the tropical rain forest and cannot fly.
It has a large horn casque on the top of its head. No-one is sure
if the bird uses this to push through dense undergrowth, or to
amplify the sound of its loud booming call. Males and females
look similar, but females are slightly larger and have brighter
plumage. They both have extremely strong legs with very
sharp-toed feet, which they use as weapons if attacked.

# Southern ground hornbill
## *Bucorvus leadbeateri*

Most hornbills live in trees, but this bird spends much of its life on the ground. It wanders around in pairs or family groups, searching for insects, reptiles and other small animals to eat.

Size: male up to 41 in (104 cm);
female 30 in (75 cm)

Range: parts of south and central
Europe, across Asia to Japan

Habitat: farmland, temperate
grassland

Size: 42 in (107 cm)

Range: parts of Africa
south of the equator

Habitat: tropical
grassland

# Great bustard
## *Otis tarda*

The great bustard is one of the world's heaviest flying birds. A large male weighs up to 40 lb (18 kg) but can still fly. Females are much lighter — up to 11 lb (5 kg) — and do not have bristly "whiskers." Great bustards move in flocks as they search for plants, seeds and insects to eat. They have strong legs and can run fast.

# Emu
## *Dromaius novaehollandiae*

The emu is the second largest bird in the world and, like the ostrich, it cannot fly. It runs at speeds of up to 30 mph (48 km/h) on its long legs as it looks for food in the Australian bush. Fruit, berries and insects are its main foods, and it also eats grass and other crops. The female lays 7 to 10 eggs, which the male keeps warm (incubates).

Size: 5 ft (1.5 m) tall

Range: Argentina, Bolivia, Brazil,
Paraguay, Uruguay

Habitat: tropical grassland

Size: 6½ ft (2 m) tall

Range: Australia

Habitat: deciduous
forest, desert

# Greater rhea
## *Rhea americana*

The largest birds in South America, greater rheas are fast runners but cannot fly. They usually live in groups of up to 30 birds. At breeding time the male rhea mates with several females. He makes a shallow nest on the ground and incubates all their eggs together.

73

# WADERS, WATERBIRDS, CRANES AND SEABIRDS

A huge variety of birds live in and around water. Wading birds, such as sandpipers, plovers and jacanas, spend much of their lives on seacoasts or by rivers and lakes farther inland. Waterbirds, such as herons, flamingos and ducks, spend more time actually in the water and many are excellent swimmers. Lakes, ponds, rivers and marshlands provide plenty of plant and animal foods and birds can nest among bankside reeds. Seabirds depend on the ocean for their food and many can swim and dive to perfection.

## WADERS

Most wading birds, or shorebirds, are small to medium-sized, ranging from the smallest plovers, only 6 in (15 cm) long, to curlews measuring almost 24 in (60 cm) in length. Wading birds usually feed on the ground and most are fast runners. Their beaks are various lengths and shapes for probing different depths in mud and sand looking for food. All are strong fliers, and many perform long migrations every year between winter feeding areas and the places where they lay eggs and rear young in spring and summer.

Size: 16½ in (42 cm)

Range: Europe, Asia

Habitat: coast, coastal waters, fresh water

### Pied avocet
*Recurvirostra avosetta*

The avocet has an unusual beak that curves upward. It catches insects and small water creatures by holding its long beak slightly open and sweeping it from side to side at the surface of mud or shallow water. In deeper water it dips its head below the surface to find food.

Size: 12 in (30 cm)

Range: Europe, Asia, west and north Africa

Habitat: farmland, temperate grassland, fresh water

Size: 11 in (28 cm)

Range: Europe, Asia, north Africa

Habitat: farmland, temperate grassland, fresh water, coast, coastal waters

### Lapwing
*Vanellus vanellus*

The lapwing is also known as the "pee-wit" because of the shrill call it makes during its display flight. A common bird in farmland and other open areas, it eats insects as well as worms, snails and some seeds.

### Redshank
*Tringa totanus*

This common bird lives near almost any kind of water. It breeds on moorland and marshes, but spends the winter on shores, mudflats, meadows and estuaries. Insects are its main food, but it also eats other small creatures such as crabs and snails. It lays its eggs in a grasslined nest on the ground.

# Northern jacana
## *Jacana spinosa*

The jacana is best known for its amazing feet. The toes and claws are very long so that the bird's weight is spread over a large area. This allows the jacana to walk on unsteady surfaces, such as floating lily pads, as it looks for food.

Size: 10 in (25 cm)

Range: Central America, West Indies

Habitat: fresh water

Size: 11–13 in (28–33 cm)

Range: northern Canada, Alaska

Habitat: coastal water

# Eskimo curlew
## *Numenius borealis*

Huge flocks of eskimo curlews used to migrate every year from the northern tundra to South America where they spent the winter months. Today, the bird is almost extinct because so many have been shot by hunters. Shooting is now banned, but it is probably too late to save the eskimo curlew.

# American golden plover
## *Pluvialis dominica*

The golden plover is a champion long-distance traveler. It breeds on the Arctic tundra of North America. After breeding, it flies about 8,000 miles (13,000 km) south to spend the winter months in South America. It feeds mainly on insects and other small creatures such as snails.

Size: 18 in (46 cm)

Range: Europe, coastal Africa, coastal Asia north of the equator

Habitat: farmland, coast, coastal water

Size: 9–11 in (23–28 cm)

Range: Arctic North America (summer); South America (winter)

Habitat: temperate grassland, fresh water, tundra

# Eurasian oystercatcher
## *Haematopus ostralegus*

The oystercatcher has a long, blunt beak that it uses to prize shellfish such as cockles and mussels off seashore rocks and to chisel open their hard shells. It also eats insects and worms, which it finds on farmland.

# American woodcock
## *Scolopax minor*

Although it is a kind of sandpiper, the American woodcock spends more time inland than other wading birds. It feeds mainly on earthworms, which it finds by probing the soil with its long beak. Females make their nests under trees or bushes and lay up to four eggs.

Size: 11 in (28 cm)

Range: North America, east of the Rockies

Habitat: temperate forest, farmland

# WATERBIRDS AND CRANES

Waterbirds such as egrets, storks, ibises and flamingos are all large birds with long necks and legs. They stand in water while feeding and take food with their beaks. Ducks, geese and swans swim on the water as they look for food, and some dive beneath the surface. Most have strong legs and webbed feet to help them swim. Other birds found in fresh water include cranes, grebes and divers, or loons. Cranes are long-legged birds that wade in shallow water to find food. Fast-swimming grebes and divers feed mainly on fish, which they chase and catch under the water with their pointed beaks.

Size: 17–20 in (43–51 cm)

Range: eastern Asia, China, Japan, introduced worldwide

Habitat: fresh water

## Mandarin duck
### *Aix galericulata*

The colorful mandarin duck is most active at dawn and dusk when it feeds on seeds, acorns and rice as well as insects, snails and small fish. Mated pairs stay together year after year. They perform elaborate courtship displays using the saillike feathers on their sides.

Size: 22–43½ in (56–110 cm)

Range: North America; introduced into Europe and New Zealand

Habitat: farmland, fresh water, tundra

## Canada goose
### *Branta canadensis*

This goose breeds in the north and migrates south in the fall. Birds use the same routes year after year and tend to return to their birthplace to breed. The female lays about five eggs in a shallow nest scraped on the ground. Her mate stays nearby while she incubates the eggs for 25 to 30 days. Canada geese feed on water and land plants.

Size: 21½–25½ in (55–65 cm)

Range: Central America, Africa, Europe, Asia, Australasia

Habitat: coast, fresh water

Size: 16–26 in (41–66 cm)

Range: Northern Hemisphere

Habitat: fresh water, inhabited areas, coast

## Mallard
### *Anas platyrhynchos*

The mallard is the ancestor of most domestic ducks. It has been introduced into Australia and New Zealand and can even live on ponds in city areas. It eats plants as well as insects and other small creatures and is often seen feeding tail-up in shallow water.

## Glossy ibis
### *Plegadis falcinellus*

The beautiful glossy ibis lives around lakes and marshes and eats insects and water creatures, which it picks from the mud with its long bill. It breeds in colonies, sometimes of thousands of birds. The female lays three or four eggs in a nest in a tree or reed bed. Both parents incubate the eggs and care for the young once they hatch.

# Common crane
## Grus grus

The common crane is famous for its dancing display. The birds walk in circles, bowing, bobbing and tossing small objects over their heads. Cranes nest on the ground or in shallow water. After breeding they fly south to spend the winter in northern Africa, India or Southeast Asia.

Size: 3½–4 ft (1.1–1.2 m)

Range: Europe, Asia

Habitat: farmland, temperate grassland, fresh water

# Sunbittern
## Eurypyga helias

In its courtship display, the sunbittern spreads its wings and fans its tail to reveal colorful feathers. It spends most of its life searching shallow water for prey, such as insects and fish, which it seizes in its sharp beak.

Size: 18 in (46 cm)

Range: southern Mexico to Bolivia and Brazil

Habitat: temperate grassland, fresh water

# Tundra swan
## Cygnus columbianus

This swan lays eggs and rears its young on the Arctic tundra. In the fall, it flies south, usually returning to the same place year after year. Tundra swans feed on plants in shallow water.

Size: 20 in (51 cm)

Range: Europe, Asia, Africa, Australia, New Zealand

Habitat: fresh water

Size: 3½–4½ ft (1.1–1.4 m)

Range: North America, northern Europe, Asia

Habitat: tundra, fresh water

# Great crested grebe
## Podiceps cristatus

This beautiful bird does not often fly and is rarely seen on land, where it moves awkwardly. Before mating, great crested grebes perform an elegant courtship dance on the water. During the dance they wag their heads and present one another with pieces of weed.

77

Size: 28–36 in (71–91 cm)

Range: Colombia, Venezuela

Habitat: fresh water

# Northern screamer
## *Chauna chavaria*

Although related to ducks and geese, the northern screamer does not have webbed feet and seldom swims in open water. It has a loud trumpeting call which it uses to warn others of danger. This noisy bird lives in the rivers and swamps of a small area of northern South America. It walks around over floating leaves, its long toes helping to spread its weight. Females lay four to six eggs in a nest made of plants.

Size: 35½–47 in (90–120 cm)

Range: worldwide except cold northerly places

Habitat: fresh water, coastal waters

# Red-throated diver
## *Gavia stellata*

This graceful bird has a slender beak and a red patch on its throat. It flies well and is an expert swimmer and diver. It feeds on fish, which it catches under water. It makes a variety of calls, including growling sounds and high-pitched wails. The female lays two eggs in a nest on the ground.

Size: 21–27¼ in (53–69 cm)

Range: North America, northern Asia, northern Europe

Habitat: fresh water, tundra, coastal waters

# Great egret
## *Casmerodius albus*

This egret, also known as the American egret, lives in marshy areas and eats fish, insects and other small creatures. It finds its food either by waiting in the water until it spots something or by slowly stalking its prey. In the breeding season adults have a mostly black beak. The rest of the year it is yellow. Breeding pairs make a nest in a tree or clump of reeds. The female lays two to five eggs and both parents take it in turns to incubate the clutch.

# Common eider
## *Somateria mollissima*

Like most ducks, the common eider lines her nest with downy feathers plucked from her breast. Eider down is particularly warm and soft. It has long been collected for making items such as duvets and sleeping bags. Eiders live mainly on shellfish and other small creatures.

Size: 22–28 in (56–71 cm)

Range: North Pole

Habitat: coast, coastal waters

## Limpkin
### *Aramus guarauna*

This long-legged waterbird uses its curved beak to probe for snails and mussels in muddy swamps. It also eats seeds, insects and even reptiles. It is called the limpkin because it seems to limp when it walks. Limpkins can fly but rarely do so and spend most of their lives on the ground.

Size: 23–28 in (59–71 cm)
Range: U.S.A., Mexico, Caribbean, Central America
Habitat: fresh water

Size: 4¼–4¾ ft (1.25–1.45 cm)
Range: southern Europe, parts of Asia and Africa
Habitat: fresh water, coast

## Greater flamingo
### *Phoenicopterus roseus*

The flamingo's long legs allow it to wade into deeper water than most other birds when looking for food. It feeds by sucking water and mud in at the front of its beak and then pumping it out again at the sides, where bristly plates trap small water creatures. The flamingo builds a nest of mud and lays one or two eggs.

## Whooping crane
### *Grus americana*

These cranes are very rare in the wild and are now strictly protected. To increase numbers, birds are being bred in captivity for release into the wild. Whooping cranes eat grain and plants as well as insects, frogs and other small animals.

Size: 4–4½ ft (1.2–1.4 m)
Range: northern Canada, southern USA
Habitat: temperate grassland, fresh water, coastal water

Size: 28–31 in (71–79 cm)
Range: Morocco
Habitat: desert, high ground, fresh water

## Hermit ibis
### *Geronticus eremita*

This peculiar, bald-headed bird used to be much more widespread, but it does not cope well with the changes in its habitat and food supply caused by farming. Last seen in Turkey in 1989, it now breeds only in Morocco, in a rather dry, rocky area where there is not much farming.

# SEABIRDS

Life at sea is harsh and demanding for birds. Many seabirds, such as albatrosses, terns and gannets, are powerful fliers. They cover long distances over the open ocean as they search for food. Some spend almost the whole year in the air, only coming to land to breed, lay eggs and raise their chicks. There are some seabirds, though, that cannot fly at all. Penguins are the best-known examples. They are expert swimmers and divers.

Size: 15½ in (39 cm)
Range: Antarctic coasts and South Atlantic islands, Chile, Argentina
Habitat: coast

## Snowy sheathbill
*Chionis albus*

These birds are eager scavengers of any food they can find. They haunt penguin colonies to seize eggs and chicks, and search the rubbish tips of Antarctic research stations. They also feed on fish and shellfish. They swim well and can fly, but spend most of their time on the ground.

Size: 32–40 in (80–100 cm)
Range: every continent except Antarctica and South America
Habitat: coast, fresh water

## Great cormorant
*Phalacrocorax carbo*

The cormorant swims by using its webbed feet to push itself along. It eats mainly fish and catches prey during underwater dives that may last a minute or more. The cormorant usually brings fish to the surface and tosses them in the air so they can be swallowed headfirst. The cormorant makes a nest in trees or on the ground. The female lays three or four eggs and both parents care for the chicks.

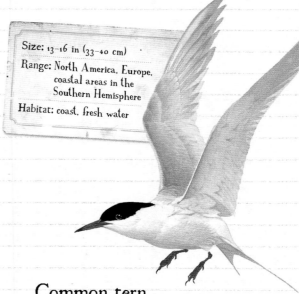

Size: 13–16 in (33–40 cm)
Range: North America, Europe, coastal areas in the Southern Hemisphere
Habitat: coast, fresh water

## Common tern
*Sterna hirundo*

A coastal bird, this tern feeds on shrimps and other small sea creatures. It catches its food by hovering above the sea until it spots something, then diving rapidly into the water to seize the prey in its sharp beak. Terns nest in large colonies on islands and cliffs. The female lays two or three eggs in a nest scraped in the ground.

# Great skua
## *Stercorarius skua*

A strong bird with a hooked bill, the great skua is a fierce hunter. It not only attacks other birds to steal their prey, but also kills and eats puffins, kittiwakes and gulls, and preys on their eggs and young. It also eats unwanted fish thrown overboard from fishing boats.

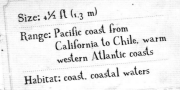

Size: 4½ ft (1.3 m)

Range: Pacific coast from California to Chile, warm western Atlantic coasts

Habitat: coast, coastal waters

# Brown pelican
## *Pelecanus occidentalis*

The brown pelican is the smallest pelican. It is a seabird and feeds by diving for fish, making high-speed plunges into the water from heights of more than 30 ft (9 m). Once in the water it opens its mouth and catches the fish in the pouch below its beak, then returns to the surface to eat. This bird lays two or three eggs in a nest on the ground.

Size: 20–22 in (51–56 cm)

Range: North Atlantic Ocean to the Equator, Mediterranean Sea

Habitat: coastal waters, oceanic

# Great black-backed gull
## *Larus marinus*

One of the largest gulls, this bird is a fierce hunter which spends more time at sea than other types of gull. It chases and kills other seabirds, such as puffins, and takes their eggs and young. It also eats fish and scavenges on waste. The young of these gulls have speckled brown feathers.

Size: 22–26 in (56–66 cm)

Range: most of Northern Hemisphere

Habitat: coastal water

# Herring gull
## *Larus argentatus*

The herring gull is the most common gull on North American and European sea coasts. It catches small fish, steals eggs and young from other birds and scavenges on waste. It also flies inland to find worms and other creatures on farmland. Herring gulls nest on cliffs, islands or beaches. They make nests of weeds and grass in a hollow in the ground or in a tree. The female lays two or three eggs which are cared for by both parents.

Size: 28–31 in (71–79 cm)

Range: Atlantic coasts of North America and Europe

Habitat: coast, temperate grassland, fresh water

Size: 34-40 in (87-100 cm)

Range: north Atlantic Ocean

Habitat: coast, coastal water

## Jackass penguin
### *Spheniscus demersus*

Also known as the African penguin, the jackass penguin lives in a warmer climate than most other penguins. It comes to land to breed and nests in a burrow or under rocks to avoid the hot African sun.

Size: 27 in (69 cm) tall

Range: coasts of southern Africa

Habitat: coast, coastal waters

## Northern gannet
### *Morus bassanus*

A sturdily built seabird with a strong beak, the northern gannet soars over the ocean, searching for fish and squid. When it spots prey, the gannet will plunge 100 ft (30 m) or more into the water to seize the catch and bring it to the surface.

## Red-tailed tropicbird
### *Phaethon rubricauda*

This elegant seabird is an expert in the air, but it moves awkwardly on land. It usually nests on ledges or cliffs in a position that allows for easy takeoff. Fish and squid are its main foods. Females lay a single egg on the ground. Both parents incubate the egg and care for the chick.

Size: 34-40 in (86-100 cm)

Range: Indian and Pacific oceans

Habitat: coast, oceanic

## Great frigatebird
### *Fregata minor*

This large seabird has a wingspan of more than 6 ft (1.8 m) and a big, hooked beak. It spends most of its life in the air and does not often land on the water. It catches food by snatching prey from the surface of the water or by threatening other seabirds until they drop their meals. Large colonies nest together on oceanic islands.

Size: 35½-40 in (90-100 cm) including tail

Range: Indian and Pacific oceans

Habitat: coast, oceanic

# Little penguin
## *Eudyptula minor*

The smallest of all the penguins, the little penguin lives around coasts and islands, looking for small fish and other food in shallow waters. It nests in a crevice or burrow. The female lays two eggs which both parents take turns to incubate for between 33 and 40 days.

Size: 3½–4½ ft (1.1–1.35 m)
Range: southern oceans
Habitat: coast, oceanic

# Wandering albatross
## *Diomedea exulans*

This seabird has the longest wingspan of any bird – up to 11 ft (3.4 m). It spends most of its life soaring over the open ocean, sometimes flying up to 300 miles (500 km) in a day.

Size: 16 in (40 cm) tall
Range: Australia, New Zealand
Habitat: coast, coastal waters

# Galápagos penguin
## *Spheniscus mendiculus*

This is the only penguin to live near the equator. The Galápagos Islands are bathed by a cool current, making the area suitable for a cold-loving penguin. The Galápagos penguin feeds mainly on small fish. It nests in small groups and females lay two eggs in a cave or a hole in volcanic rock.

Size: 11½–14 in (29–36 cm)
Range: North Atlantic and Arctic oceans
Habitat: coast, oceanic

Size: 20 in (50 cm) tall
Range: Galápagos Islands
Habitat: coast, coastal waters

# Atlantic puffin
## *Fratercula arctica*

This puffin uses its colorful beak to catch fish and can hold as many as a dozen fish at a time. An expert swimmer and diver, the puffin can also fly well. Its short legs are set well back on the body and it waddles clumsily when it comes to land to nest. The female puffin lays one egg, sometimes two, in an old burrow or in a hole it digs itself.

# PENGUINS

**P**enguins cannot fly but are better suited to life in the sea than any other bird. Expert swimmers and divers, they use their strong flippers to push themselves through the water. Most penguins live around the Antarctic and on islands near the Antarctic Circle and have to survive in freezing conditions. They have a dense covering of glossy waterproof feathers, which keep them both warm and dry. A thick layer of fat beneath the feathers also helps to keep out the cold. There are about 17 different kinds of penguin. The smallest is the little, or fairy, penguin, which measures about 15 in (40 cm). The biggest is the emperor penguin, which stands about 45 in (115 cm) high.

## TAKING CARE OF YOUNG

At the beginning of winter, the female emperor penguin lays one egg on land. Her partner then incubates the egg on his feet for about 64 days. When the chick hatches he keeps its warm on his feet, wrapped in a fold of skin.

## FRIENDLY BEHAVIOR

Penguins are sociable birds and usually live in huge colonies on land and in the sea. Penguins usually keep the same mate for several years. When a breeding pair meets, they rub their heads in greeting. They also preen each other's feathers.

## UNDERWATER HUNTER

The king penguin dives deep to catch prey and often plunges to 150 ft (45 m) or more. The deepest recorded dive is almost 1,050 ft (320 m). The penguin uses its webbed feet and tail for steering as it dives.

Fish is the main food for penguins, but they also catch squid and crustaceans. Smaller penguins such as gentoos and chinstraps catch much smaller prey as well, such as shrimplike krill.

Squid

Adélie penguins nest in large colonies around the Antarctic coasts. Eggs are laid in late November and incubated first by the male and then by the female for a total of 35 days.

# TOBOGGANING

Not at their best on land, penguins slip and slide as they waddle over the frozen ground. Often the birds lie down on their bellies and toboggan over the ice — an easier way to move. Once in the water, most penguins swim at speeds of 3–6 mph (5–10 km/h).

# OWLS AND BIRDS OF PREY

Most birds of prey hunt and kill other creatures to eat. They are among the most interesting of all birds and include species such as eagles, hawks and buzzards. This is a varied group of birds, ranging from tiny falcons to huge condors, but they all have features in common. These include keen vision, strong feet with sharp claws, and a hooked beak for tearing prey apart. Owls, too, kill other animals to eat but, unlike hawks and eagles, they usually hunt at night.

## OWLS

There are 202 or so kinds of owl found over most of the world, except on a few islands. Most look similar, with large, disklike faces and huge eyes. Typically, an owl sits on a branch watching and listening for the slightest movement of prey. When it hears something, it pinpoints the direction of the prey with its incredibly acute hearing before flying down to pounce. The edges of an owl's feathers are soft and fluffy — not hard like those of most birds. This cuts down the noise of flight so the hunter can fly almost silently in the darkness.

Size: 20½–25½ in (52–65 cm)
Range: Arctic to northern U.S.A., Europe and Asia
Habitat: coast, tundra, fresh water

### Long-eared owl
*Asio otus*

The tufts on the head of this owl are feathers not ears. But this bird does have excellent hearing, which helps it catch prey such as voles and mice. This owl lays its eggs in a nest abandoned by a bird such as a crow.

Size: 13–16 in (33–40 cm)
Range: North America, Europe, northwest Africa, Asia
Habitat: farmland, deciduous forest

### Barn owl
*Tyto alba*

The barn owl is easily recognized by its pale, heart-shaped face. During the day it roosts in a sheltered spot. At dusk it comes out to hunt for food, usually small creatures, such as rats and mice.

Size: 13½ in (34 cm)
Range: worldwide, except temperate Asia and many Pacific islands
Habitat: farmland, deciduous forest, temperate grassland

### Snowy owl
*Bubo scandiaca*

The snowy owl has long dense feathers right down to its toes to protect against the cold. It hunts by day as well as by night, for birds and for mammals such as mice, hares and lemmings. The female owl is bigger than the male and has dark markings on her mainly white feathers. She lays 4 to 15 eggs.

# BIRDS OF PREY

Birds of prey hunt in a variety of ways. Some, such as goshawks and sparrowhawks, live mainly in forests and woodlands. They move from one leafy perch to the next, ready to dash out to snatch their prey in a sudden attack. Others, such as buzzards and eagles, soar over open country, watching for victims. Not all birds of prey are killers. Vultures are scavengers — they eat carrion, the bodies of creatures that are already dead.

Size: 24–26 in (61–66 cm)

Range: Europe, Middle East, northern Africa

Habitat: deciduous forest, temperate grassland

## Red kite
*Milvus milvus*

This large bird of prey has long wings and a forked tail. It hunts in woodland and open country and often hovers briefly as it searches for prey, such as rats, birds and reptiles. Like vultures, it also eats carrion. The red kite nests in a tree and the female lays up to five eggs.

## Northern goshawk
*Accipiter gentilis*

A powerful, fast-moving hunter, the northern goshawk can catch creatures such as hares and pheasants. It flies through the forest, weaving in and out of trees as it chases prey. It kills its victims with its strong sharp talons and eats them on the ground.

Size: 20–26 in (51–66 cm)

Range: North America, Europe, northern Asia

Habitat: deciduous forest

Size: 3¼–3¾ ft (1.1–1.15 m)

Range: parts of Africa, Saudi Arabia, Yemen, Oman

Habitat: desert, high ground, tropical grassland

## Lappet-faced vulture
*Torgos tracheliotus*

Like all vultures, this bird feeds mostly on carrion. It has huge wings on which it soars long distances searching for food, and a powerful hooked beak, which cuts easily into the flesh of dead animals. This vulture lays one egg in a nest at the top of a tree.

Size: 18–24 in (46–61 cm)

Range: North and Central America, West Indies

Habitat: deciduous and tropical evergreen forest, desert, farmland

## Red-tailed hawk
*Buteo jamaicensis*

A powerful, aggressive bird, this hawk can live anywhere from forest to desert. It hunts other birds in the air or swoops down on rabbits, snakes and lizards from a high perch. It nests high in a tree or cactus plant. The female lays one to four eggs. Both parents take turns to incubate the eggs.

# Rough-legged hawk
## *Buteo lagopus*

The rough-legged hawk hovers over the tundra as it hunts for prey, such as lemmings and voles. It nests in the far north, laying up to four eggs in a nest of twigs made in a tree or on a rocky ledge. After the breeding season, this buzzard flies south for the winter.

Size: 20–23½ in (50–60 cm)

Range: North America, northern Europe and Asia

Habitat: tundra, temperate grassland, deciduous forest, high ground, fresh water

# Madagascar fish eagle
## *Haliaeetus vociferoides*

With a population of less than 120 breeding pairs, this fish eagle is one of the rarest of all birds. It usually hunts around shallow estuaries and coastal swamps where it plunges down to catch fish with its strong feet.

Size: 26¾–31 in (68–79 cm)

Range: western and southern Madagascar

Habitat: coast, coastal waters

# Bald eagle
## *Haliaeetus leucocephalus*

Once rare, the national bird of the United States is now thriving in many places. Fish is one of its main foods, and eagles gather around Alaskan rivers to catch exhausted salmon as they migrate up river. Made of sticks, the eagle's nest is one of the largest of all birds' nests.

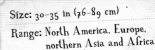

Size: 30–35 in (76–89 cm)

Range: North America, Europe, northern Asia and Africa

Habitat: northern forest, high ground, temperate grassland

# Golden eagle
## *Aquila chrysaetos*

The magnificent golden eagle has a hooked beak, extremely sharp eyesight and strong feet with long curved claws. When hunting, the eagle soars over land, searching for food. Once it spots prey, it dives down and kills its victim on the ground.

Size: 32–40 in (81–102 cm)

Range: North America

Habitat: coast, coastal waters, deciduous forest, tropical evergreen forest

# Osprey
## *Pandion haliaetus*

This bird of prey flies above water looking for fish to catch. When the bird catches sight of prey, it plunges down, holding its feet out to seize the fish. The soles of the osprey's feet are studded with small spines to help it grip its slippery catch.

Size: 20¾–24½ in (53–62 cm)

Range: almost worldwide

Habitat: coast, fresh water, farmland

# King vulture
## *Sarcoramphus papa*

With its brightly patterned bare-skinned head, the king vulture is one of the most colorful of all birds of prey. Although it may occasionally kill some prey for itself, it feeds mostly on carrion — animals that are already dead. The king vulture is one of the few birds that uses its sense of smell to find food.

Size: 31 in (79 cm)

Range: Mexico, Central and South America

Habitat: tropical grassland, tropical evergreen forest

# Secretary bird
## *Sagittarius serpentarius*

This long-legged bird spends much of its life on the ground where it may walk 20 miles (30 km) or so every day. It runs to catch prey such as small mammals, birds, insects and reptiles. Pairs make a nest of sticks and turf on top of a tree. The nest is lined with grass and leaves. The female lays two or three eggs.

Size: 5 ft (1.5 m) tall

Range: Africa, south of the Sahara

Habitat: tropical grassland

Size: 15–20 in (38–51 cm)

Range: almost worldwide

Habitat: coast, temperate grassland, tundra, high ground

# Peregrine falcon
## *Falco peregrinus*

One of the fastest flying of all birds, the peregrine is an expert hunter that preys on other birds. It makes a spectacular high-speed dive toward its prey, often a pigeon or a dove, and seizes it in midair. It kills the prey with its powerful talons and takes it to the ground to eat.

# EAGLES

**E**agles are large birds of prey with strong hooked beaks, sharp talons and big golden eyes. There are about 60 kinds of eagle living all over the world. Typically, a hunting eagle soars over the land for long periods, searching for food. With its keen eyesight, an eagle spots prey from a great distance, and then makes a rapid dive to the ground to seize and kill the animal with its talons. But some eagles hunt in a different way. Harpy eagles chase their prey through the trees and sea eagles seize fish from the water. Eagles usually build their nests in trees or on cliffs. The nests are made of sticks and branches and may be used year after year. All eagles look very similar, with black or gray feathers on the back and white on the belly.

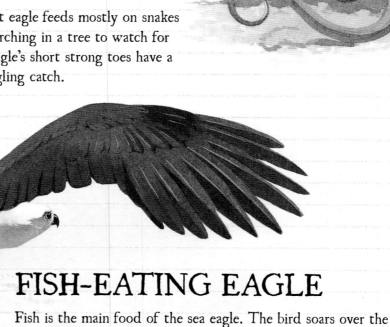

## A SNAKE HUNTER

Like other snake eagles, the crested serpent eagle feeds mostly on snakes and other reptiles. It generally hunts by perching in a tree to watch for prey, then dropping down on to it. The eagle's short strong toes have a rough surface that helps it to grip its wriggling catch.

## FISH-EATING EAGLE

Fish is the main food of the sea eagle. The bird soars over the ocean looking for prey. It then swoops down to the water surface to seize a fish in its talons. Sea eagles also catch other creatures and rob smaller birds of their prey. They may also dive repeatedly at swimming birds such as ducks until they are exhausted and easy to catch. There are several different types of sea eagle. The largest is the Steller's sea eagle which lives on Siberian coasts.

# RAIN FOREST EAGLE

The world's biggest and most powerful eagle, the harpy, lives in the South American rain forest. Instead of soaring high in the air, this eagle makes short flights from tree to tree, looking for prey. The harpy preys mostly on monkeys, sloths and tree porcupines. When it spots a victim, such as a monkey, the harpy chases it through the trees at high speed until it is close enough to catch the monkey in its strong talons.

# BIRDS OF THE TREES AND MASTERS OF THE AIR

One of the many advantages of flight is that it allows birds to fly up into trees. Up among the branches, they find havens from ground-living hunters, and safe places to roost and nest. Many birds also gather much of their food in trees. Pigeons and parrots feed mostly on seeds, nuts and fruits. Others, such as woodpeckers and cuckoos, eat insects. Some birds are more skilful fliers than others. Hummingbirds, for example, are true masters of the air and perform extraordinary aerial acrobatics. Swifts are so used to life in the air that they rarely, if ever, walk on land.

## Crested treeswift

*Hemiprocne coronata*

This swift catches insects in the air to eat. It makes a tiny cup-shaped nest from thin flakes of bark, glued together with spit. There is just room for one egg, which both parents take turns to incubate.

Size: 8 in (20.5 cm)

Range: Southeast Asia

Habitat: tropical evergreen forest

## Grey potoo

*Nyctibius griseus*

The potoo feeds by night, flying out from a perch to capture insects in its large beak. By day, it sits upright and very still on a broken branch or stump. With its head and beak pointing upward, the potoo looks like part of the tree and so is hidden from its enemies. It lays its single egg on top of a tree stump.

Size: 10¼ in (26 cm)

Range: Europe, Asia, northern Africa

Habitat: deciduous forest, tropical evergreen forest, temperate grassland, desert

Size: 16¼ in (41 cm)

Range: West Indies, Central America, tropical South America

Habitat: deciduous forest, tropical evergreen forest

## Nightjar

*Caprimulgus europaeus*

The nightjar becomes active at sunset, when it takes to the air to dart after moths and other night-flying insects. The nightjar's tiny beak opens very wide and is fringed with bristles that help it to trap its prey.

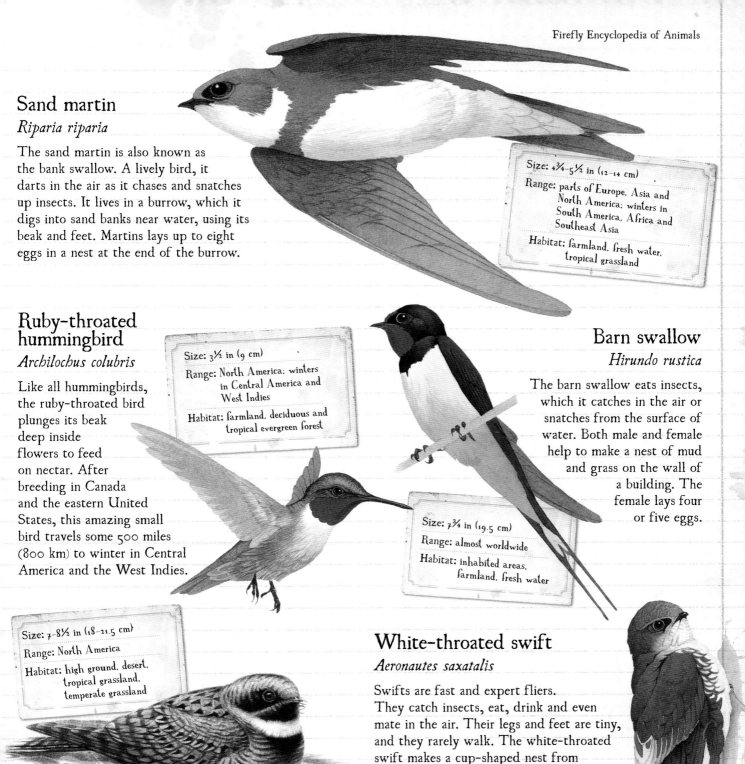

# Sand martin
## *Riparia riparia*

The sand martin is also known as the bank swallow. A lively bird, it darts in the air as it chases and snatches up insects. It lives in a burrow, which it digs into sand banks near water, using its beak and feet. Martins lays up to eight eggs in a nest at the end of the burrow.

Size: 4¾–5½ in (12–14 cm)
Range: parts of Europe, Asia and North America; winters in South America, Africa and Southeast Asia
Habitat: farmland, fresh water, tropical grassland

# Ruby-throated hummingbird
## *Archilochus colubris*

Like all hummingbirds, the ruby-throated bird plunges its beak deep inside flowers to feed on nectar. After breeding in Canada and the eastern United States, this amazing small bird travels some 500 miles (800 km) to winter in Central America and the West Indies.

Size: 3½ in (9 cm)
Range: North America; winters in Central America and West Indies
Habitat: farmland, deciduous and tropical evergreen forest

# Barn swallow
## *Hirundo rustica*

The barn swallow eats insects, which it catches in the air or snatches from the surface of water. Both male and female help to make a nest of mud and grass on the wall of a building. The female lays four or five eggs.

Size: 7¾ in (19.5 cm)
Range: almost worldwide
Habitat: inhabited areas, farmland, fresh water

Size: 7–8½ in (18–21.5 cm)
Range: North America
Habitat: high ground, desert, tropical grassland, temperate grassland

# White-throated swift
## *Aeronautes saxatalis*

Swifts are fast and expert fliers. They catch insects, eat, drink and even mate in the air. Their legs and feet are tiny, and they rarely walk. The white-throated swift makes a cup-shaped nest from feathers and grass, glued together with spit. The nest is built in a crack or crevice in a cliff or mountainside. The female lays four or five eggs.

# Poorwill
## *Phalaenoptilus nuttallii*

Named after its call, which sounds like "poor-will," this bird hunts insects at night. It is the only bird known to hibernate and each fall it finds a rock crevice in which to spend the winter. Its body temperature falls and heart and breathing rates slow down, so that it uses as little energy as possible.

Size: 6–7 in (15–18 cm)
Range: western USA, Central America
Habitat: high ground, desert

93

Size: 11 in (28 cm)

Range: Europe, Asia, Africa

Habitat: inhabited areas,
farmland, temperate
grassland, deciduous forest,
tropical evergreen forest

## Hoopoe
### *Upupa epops*

This bird catches insects and other small
creatures in trees and on the ground.
It makes a nest in a hole in a tree or wall
or on the ground. The female lays two to
nine eggs and is fed by her mate as she
incubates them for 16 to 19 days.

## Resplendent quetzal
### *Pharomachrus mocinno*

The beautiful male quetzal
has a train of long tail feathers
that wave and flutter as he
flies and performs courtship
displays. These feathers are
shed after each breeding
season and are then regrown.
The ancient Mayan and Aztec
peoples of Central America
and Mexico believed the
quetzal was a sacred bird, and
its feathers were highly prized.

Size: 9–11 in (23–28 cm)

Range: Mexico, Central and
South America

Habitat: tropical evergreen
forest, fresh water

## Rufous-tailed jacamar
### *Galbula ruficauda*

This brightly plumaged long-billed bird sits on a branch,
watching for insects. When it spots something, it darts after
the prey and snatches it up in midair. Then it flies to a perch
to eat it. The female jacamar digs a breeding tunnel in the
ground and lays two to four eggs. Both parents incubate the
eggs for 19 to 23 days and then feed and care for their young
until they can fly, at about three weeks old.

Size: 11¾ in (30 cm); tail
feathers 24 in (61 cm)

Range: Mexico, Central America

Habitat: tropical evergreen
forest, high ground

Size: 9 in (23 cm)

Range: Africa

Habitat: farmland,
tropical evergreen forest,
tropical grassland

## Double-toothed barbet
### *Lybius bidentatus*

This barbet has two sharp toothlike
structures on its beak. It perches in
trees and bushes, feeding on figs,
bananas and other fruits, and also
darts out to catch flying termites.

# Pileated woodpecker
## *Dryocopus pileatus*

Ants and termites are the main foods of this woodpecker. Clinging tightly to a tree trunk with its sharp claws, the bird hammers into the bark with its strong beak to find prey. It also feeds on fruit. The female bird lays four eggs in a tree hole nest.

Size: 23–29 in (58.5–73.5 cm)
Range: Indonesia, New Guinea, Biak and Yapen islands
Habitat: coast, fresh water, tropical evergreen forest

# Victoria crowned pigeon
## *Goura victoria*

The world's largest pigeon, the Victoria crowned pigeon has been hunted heavily and is now rare. This beautiful bird usually feeds on the ground, eating fallen fruit, seeds and berries. If disturbed, it flies off to perch in a tree.

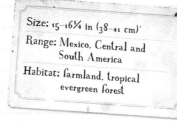

Size: 15–16¼ in (38–41 cm)
Range: Mexico, Central and South America
Habitat: farmland, tropical evergreen forest

# Blue-crowned motmot
## *Momotus momota*

This bird has an unusual tail which has two long central feathers with racquet-shaped tips. With its tail swinging from side to side like a pendulum, the motmot sits on a branch, watching for prey. It darts out from its perch to catch insects, spiders and lizards and returns to eat them.

Size: 15–19 in (38–48 cm)
Range: North America, Mexico
Habitat: deciduous forest

# Belted kingfisher
## *Megaceryle alcyon*

This kingfisher is an agile flier. It watches for prey from a tree overhanging a river or stream, then dives down to seize a fish or frog from the water. A breeding pair digs a long nesting tunnel in a riverbank. The female lays five to eight eggs in a nest made at the end of the tunnel.

Size: 11–14 in (28–35.5 cm)
Range: North America
Habitat: coast, fresh water

# Red-crested turaco
*Tauraco erythrolophus*

A fruit-eating bird, the red-crested turaco lives in trees and does not often come down to the ground. A poor flier, it runs, hops and climbs well among the branches. It also eats insects.

Size: 16 in (40.5 cm)

Range: Angola

Habitat: tropical evergreen forest

Size: 24 in (61 cm)

Range: South America: Amazon and Orinoco basins

Habitat: tropical evergreen forest

# Common cuckoo
*Cuculus canorus*

The cuckoo does not make a nest but lays her eggs in the nests of other birds. She usually lays eight to 12 eggs, all in different nests. The young cuckoos hatch in about 12 days and are bigger and stronger than the host's young, which they eject from the nest so they get all the food.

# Hoatzin
*Opisthocomus hoazin*

Although it lives in trees, the hoatzin is a poor flier. It clambers along branches, feeding on fruit, buds and leaves.

Size: 13 in (33 cm)

Range: Europe, northern Africa, Asia

Habitat: deciduous forest, temperate grassland

Size: 33½ in (26 cm)

Range: Mexico, Central America, northern South America

Habitat: tropical evergreen forest

Size: 1.5 m (5 feet)

Range: India, Southeast Asia

Habitat: tropical evergreen forest

# Scarlet macaw
*Ara macao*

These spectacular birds are usually seen in pairs or flocks of up to 20 birds. At sunrise the birds fly, screeching noisily, from their roost sites to feeding areas. There they feast on seeds, fruit and leaves high in the trees. At dusk they return to their roosts.

# Great hornbill
*Buceros bicornis*

This hornbill lives high in the rain forest, eating fruit and catching small animals. A female lays up to three eggs in a hole in a tree and she uses her own droppings to seal the entrance. A small slit is left for the male to pass food to the mother and her chicks. She stays walled up until the young are hatched and old enough to leave the nest.

## Toco toucan
### *Ramphastos toco*

Although the toucan's colorful beak is up to 7 in (18 cm)
long, it is not solid, so it is not as heavy as it looks.
The toucan feeds on fruit. It picks up food in the
tip of its bill, then tosses the morsel into its mouth.

Size: 24 in (61 cm)

Range: eastern South America

Habitat: tropical evergreen forest,
tropical grassland, farmland

## Rainbow lorikeet
### *Trichoglossus haematodus*

Screeching, chattering flocks of up to 100
lorikeets fly among the branches,
eating fruit, insects, pollen and
nectar. The brightly colored
feather patterns vary slightly
from bird to bird.

Size: 10¼ in (26 cm)

Range: Indonesia, New Guinea,
Australia

Habitat: inhabited areas, farmland,
deciduous and tropical
evergreen forest

## Budgerigar
### *Melopsittacus undulatus*

Best known as cage birds with many
color variations, these small
fast-moving parrots usually
have mainly green feathers
in the wild. Flocks of
budgerigars search the
ground for grass seeds.

Size: 7 in (18 cm)

Range: Australia; introduced
into USA

Habitat: farmland, desert,
forest, grassland, scrub

## Eclectus parrot
### *Eclectus roratus*

The male eclectus parrot has mostly
green feathers, while the female is bright
red with a blue belly. Both feed mainly on fruit, nuts,
flowers and nectar. They usually make a nest in a hole
high in a tree. The female lays two eggs and incubates
them for about 26 days.

Size: 13¾ in (35 cm)

Range: New Guinea,
northeast Australia

Habitat: tropical evergreen
forest

## Sulphur-crested cockatoo
### *Cacatua galerita*

This noisy parrot gathers
in huge flocks to feed on
seeds, fruits, palm hearts and
insects. In the breeding season
the cockatoos separate into
pairs or family groups. A pair
makes a nest in a tree
and both parents
incubate the two or
three eggs.

Size: 19¾ in (50 cm)

Range: Australia, New Zealand,
New Guinea, Indonesia, Palau

Habitat: tropical evergreen forest,
tropical grassland, farmland

97

# HUMMINGBIRDS

Beautiful hummingbirds are more agile in the air than any other group of birds. They are named after the humming sound made by the rapid beating of their wings. They hover in front of the flowers as they feed, and can fly upward, sideways, downward and even backward. They live only in the Americas, mostly in the warmest parts. They measure from just over 2 in (5 cm) to about 7 in (20 cm) long, but the tail feathers make up as much as half of this length. Females usually have duller plumage than males. The sweet nectar contained in flowers is the main food of hummingbirds. Most have long beaks, which they plunge deep into flowers to get to the nectar.

## A COLORFUL HUMMINGBIRD

The male crimson topaz has colorful plumage and long curving tail feathers. It takes nectar from a wide range of flowers and also catches insects. The female bird has mostly green feathers.

## WHITE-TIPPED SICKLEBILL

The long strongly curved beak of the white-tipped sicklebill is perfect for taking nectar from deep flowers such as heliconias.

## THE LONGEST BEAK

The sword-billed hummingbird has a longer beak than any other hummingbird. The beak allows the bird to reach nectar inside the deepest tube-shaped flowers. This bird also eats insects, which it catches in the air.

# COURTSHIP DISPLAY

This hummingbird, known as the marvellous spatuletail, has only four full-grown tail feathers, two of which have a long bare shaft ending in a broad wedge shape, or spatule. During courtship displays the male shows off these decorative feathers as he flies to and fro in front of the female.

Spatule

A male violet sabrewing hummingbird hovers on rapidly beating wings as he feeds on nectar from a ginger flower. Like many hummingbirds, this bird has shimmering feathers.

# THE SMALLEST BIRD

The bee hummingbird is the world's tiniest bird. The male is only about 2 in (5 cm) long, including its beak and tail. Females are about $^1/_5$ in (0.5 cm) longer.

# SONGBIRDS

About half of all the kinds of bird in the world are included in the group known as songbirds. There are more than 6,000 kinds, found all over the world except at the poles. Not all sing as sweetly as the lark or the nightingale, but the males of most species do sing sequences of musical notes when courting mates or defending their territory. Female singers are rare, apart from a few species such as song sparrows and robins. Songbirds are also called passerines, or perching birds, and have feet adapted for perching on trees and posts. Their feet have four toes — three that point forward and one backward — and are ideally shaped for holding on to twigs, reeds and even wires.

Size: 6½-7½ in (16.5-19 cm)

Range: North America: east of Rockies and into Central America

Habitat: inhabited areas, farmland, deciduous and tropical evergreen forest

## Eastern bluebird
*Sialia sialis*

The eastern bluebird feeds mainly on insects and berries. The male performs acrobatic flight displays to court his mate. Both birds then build a nest of grass and twigs in a hole in a tree. Eastern bluebirds lay between three to seven eggs. Both parents feed the young chicks for up to 20 days after they hatch.

Size: 6¼ in (16 cm)

Range: Europe, Asia, northern Africa: winters in tropical Africa

Habitat: farmland, deciduous forest, tropical evergreen forest

Size: 5½ in (14 cm)

Range: Europe, northern Africa, Asia

Habitat: inhabited areas, deciduous forest

## Nightingale
*Luscinia megarhynchos*

Best known for its beautiful song, the nightingale sings night and day. It eats insects such as ants and beetles, which it finds in undergrowth and on the ground. In summer, it also eats berries and fruit. The female makes a nest of leaves on or close to the ground and lays four or five eggs.

## Starling
*Sturnus vulgaris*

Starlings are common in both country and city areas and have been introduced into countries outside their natural range. Only a century ago, 60 birds were released in New York. Now, the starling is one of the most common birds in North America. Starlings eat insects, worms, snails, fruit, berries and seeds.

Size: 8½ in (21.5 cm)

Range: Europe, Asia: introduced almost worldwide

Habitat: inhabited areas, farmland, temperate grassland, deciduous forest

## European robin
*Erithacus rubecula*

In many areas the robin is a shy forest bird, but in Britain and parts of Europe it lives in gardens and is often quite tame. Insects, spiders, worms and snails are the robin's main food, but it also eats berries, small fruit and scraps of food put out by humans.

# American robin
## *Turdus migratorius*

This bird lives in urban areas and feeds on insects, earthworms, fruit and berries. In the breeding season, the male has a black head and tail and a reddish breast, while the female is duller, with a gray head and tail.

Size: 9–11 in (23–28 cm)

Range: North America, Mexico, West Indies

Habitat: inhabited areas, deciduous forest

# Northern cardinal
## *Cardinalis cardinalis*

Only the male cardinal has brilliant red plumage. The female is mainly brown, with a red beak. Cardinals eat foods such as insects, fruits, seeds and buds. They also visit bird feeders in gardens.

Size: 7¾–9 in (20–23 cm)

Range: North America, east and south of the Rockies; Mexico

Habitat: inhabited areas, deciduous forest, fresh water

Size: 4 in (10 cm)

Range: Trinidad, South America

Habitat: farmland, tropical evergreen forest

# Purple honeycreeper
## *Cyanerpes caeruleus*

Groups of purple honeycreepers feed on fruit, especially bananas, and insects in trees. They also perch by flowers and suck nectar from them with their long curved beaks. The female honeycreeper builds a neat cup-shaped nest in the fork of a tree or bush. She lays two eggs, which she incubates for 12 to 14 days.

# Winter wren
## *Troglodytes troglodytes*

The tiny northern wren has a plump body and a short tail, which it nearly always holds cocked up. Its main foods are insects and spiders, which it finds on low plants. In spring, the wren makes a nest in a hollow tree stump or among tree roots. The female lays five to eight eggs, which she incubates.

Size: 3¼ in (8 cm)

Range: North America, Europe, northern Africa, Asia

Habitat: inhabited areas, deciduous forest

Size: 9–11 in (23–28 cm)

Range: North America

Habitat: inhabited areas, deciduous forest

# Northern mockingbird
## *Mimus polyglottos*

One of the best-known American songbirds, the mockingbird is the state bird of five US states. The male sings night and day and often mimics other birds and sounds. Mockingbirds feed mainly on insects such as grasshoppers and beetles, and also eat spiders, snails, small reptiles and fruit. They lay three to six eggs at a time.

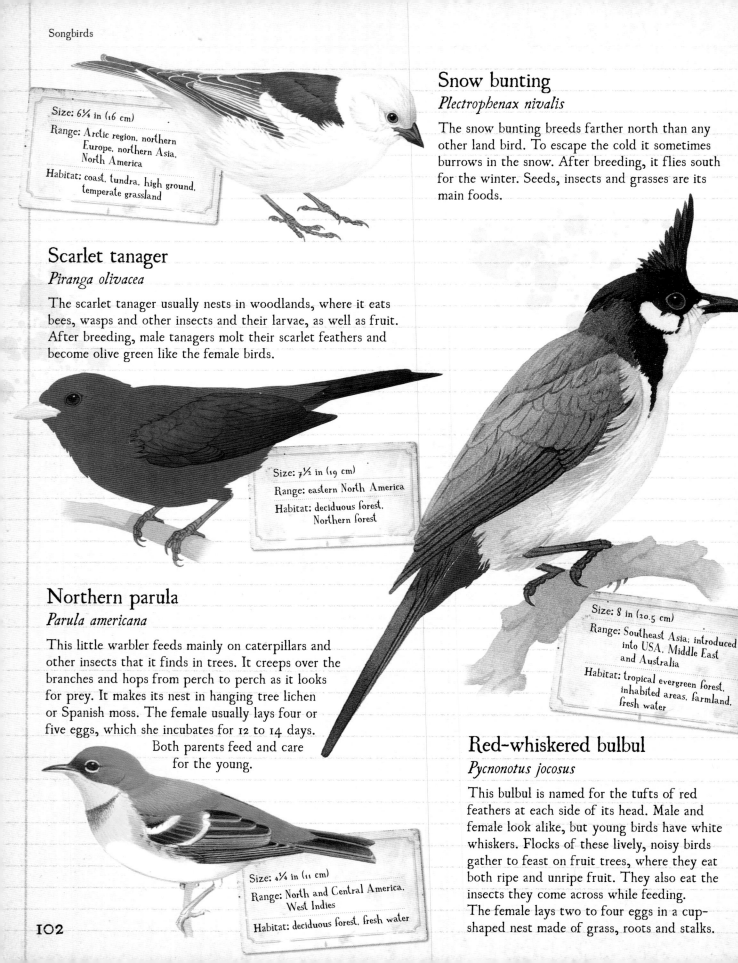

Size: 6¼ in (16 cm)

Range: Arctic region, northern Europe, northern Asia, North America

Habitat: coast, tundra, high ground, temperate grassland

# Snow bunting
*Plectrophenax nivalis*

The snow bunting breeds farther north than any other land bird. To escape the cold it sometimes burrows in the snow. After breeding, it flies south for the winter. Seeds, insects and grasses are its main foods.

# Scarlet tanager
*Piranga olivacea*

The scarlet tanager usually nests in woodlands, where it eats bees, wasps and other insects and their larvae, as well as fruit. After breeding, male tanagers molt their scarlet feathers and become olive green like the female birds.

Size: 7½ in (19 cm)

Range: eastern North America

Habitat: deciduous forest, Northern forest

# Northern parula
*Parula americana*

This little warbler feeds mainly on caterpillars and other insects that it finds in trees. It creeps over the branches and hops from perch to perch as it looks for prey. It makes its nest in hanging tree lichen or Spanish moss. The female usually lays four or five eggs, which she incubates for 12 to 14 days. Both parents feed and care for the young.

Size: 4¼ in (11 cm)

Range: North and Central America, West Indies

Habitat: deciduous forest, fresh water

Size: 8 in (20.5 cm)

Range: Southeast Asia; introduced into USA, Middle East and Australia

Habitat: tropical evergreen forest, inhabited areas, farmland, fresh water

# Red-whiskered bulbul
*Pycnonotus jocosus*

This bulbul is named for the tufts of red feathers at each side of its head. Male and female look alike, but young birds have white whiskers. Flocks of these lively, noisy birds gather to feast on fruit trees, where they eat both ripe and unripe fruit. They also eat the insects they come across while feeding.
The female lays two to four eggs in a cup-shaped nest made of grass, roots and stalks.

Size: 4 in (10 cm)

Range: Central and northwestern South America

Habitat: fresh water, tropical evergreen forest

## Pine grosbeak
### *Pinicola enucleator*

A type of finch, the pine grosbeak uses its heavy bill to crush the stones of fruit such as cherries and plums. It also eats seeds, buds and insects. A breeding pair makes a nest in a tree and the female lays four eggs.

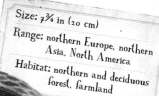

Size: 7¾ in (20 cm)

Range: northern Europe, northern Asia, North America

Habitat: northern and deciduous forest, farmland

## Torrent tyrannulet
### *Serpophaga cinerea*

This bird lives by fast-flowing streams. It often plucks insects from slippery rocks surrounded by foaming water, drenching itself in the process. A breeding pair makes a cup-shaped nest, usually hanging over water. The female lays two eggs. Both parents feed the young on insects.

Size: 8–9 in (20.5–23 cm)

Range: North America

Habitat: inhabited areas, farmland, temperate grassland, deciduous forest

## Eastern kingbird
### *Tyrannus tyrannus*

This noisy bird attacks anything that enters its territory, particularly larger birds. It eats many different types of insect, which it catches in the air or on the ground or scoops out of water. It also hovers in the air to pick berries from trees. The female lays three to five eggs.

Size: 4¾–6 in (12–15 cm)

Range: North America

Habitat: deciduous forest, northern forest, inhabited areas

Size: 14 in (35.5 cm) including bill

Range: northern South America

Habitat: tropical evergreen forest

## Long-billed woodcreeper
### *Nasica longirostris*

Using its long beak, this woodcreeper searches the leaves of rain forest plants for insects and spiders to eat. It also finds prey under the bark of trees. An expert climber, it uses its stiff tail for support as it clambers around trees. The female lays two eggs in a nest in a tree hole and incubates them for about 14 days.

## Black-capped chickadee
### *Parus atricapillus*

This little bird has a call which sounds like "chick-a-dee-dee-dee". It feeds on caterpillars and other insects as well as seeds and berries. The chickadee makes its nest in the soft wood of a dead tree, where it lays five to 10 eggs.

Size: 4 in (11.5 cm)

Range: Southeast Asia

Habitat: tropical evergeen
forest, tropical
grassland, farmland

# Crimson sunbird
## *Aethopyga siparaja*

This sunbird eats flower nectar as well as insects.
It hovers before tube-shaped flowers and reaches
into them with its long tongue. When feeding
from big blooms such as hibiscus, it pierces the
petals to get the nectar at the base.

Size: male 10–12 in (25.5–30.5 cm);
female 5½–6 in (14–15 cm)

Range: Africa

Habitat: high ground,
tropical grassland

# Red-tufted malachite sunbird
## *Nectarinia johnstoni*

This sunbird lives only on high mountain
slopes where it feeds on the nectar of
plants such as giant lobelias and protea
flowers. But its main food is insects, particularly
flies, which it catches in the air. Both male and
female have scarlet tufts at the sides of the breast,
but only the male has long central tail feathers.

Size: 11¾ in (30 cm)

Range: North America, Mexico

Habitat: inhabited areas, deciduous
forest, tropical evergreen
forest, northern forest

# American crow
## *Corvus brachyrhynchos*

This large, black bird eats almost anything it can find,
including insects, spiders, frogs and birds and their
eggs. It also scavenges on waste food. A nest of sticks
and twigs is made in a tree or bush. The female lays
three to six eggs in it.

# Blue jay
## *Cyanocitta cristata*

Noisy groups of blue jays are
a familiar sight in gardens. Seeds
and nuts are their main foods, and
they bury extra supplies to save for the
winter. Blue jays also eat insects and
even steal eggs and chicks from the
nests of other birds. A breeding pair
makes its nest in a tree or bush, and the
female lays two to six eggs.

Size: 17–20¾ in (43–53 cm)

Range: North America

Habitat: deciduous forest,
temperate grassland,
farmland, inhabited areas

Size: 5 in (13 cm)

Range: islands of Vanuatu, Samoa, Santa Cruz, Solomon, New Caledonia

Habitat: tropical evergreen forest, farmland, fresh water

# Wire-tailed manakin
## *Pipra filicauda*

Only the male manakin has dramatic black, red and yellow plumage, but both male and female have long wiry tail feathers. The male shows off his bright colors in courtship displays. These birds usually feed alone, searching for insects and fruit in forests and cocoa plantations.

Size: 4½ in (11.5 cm)

Range: northern South America

Habitat: tropical evergreen forest, farmland, fresh water

# Cardinal honeyeater
## *Myzomela cardinalis*

The cardinal honeyeater feeds by sipping nectar from flowers and picking insects from leaves. The female is duller than the colorful male. She has olive gray feathers with red patches. This bird's cup-shaped nest hangs from a forked branch, and the female lays two or three eggs.

Size: 6¼ in (16 cm)

Range: Europe, Asia, North America, northern Africa

Habitat: temperate grassland, desert, tundra, high ground

Size: 8 in (20.5 cm)

Range: Africa, south of the Sahara

Habitat: tropical grassland, farmland, fresh water

# Shore lark
## *Eremophila alpestris*

Only the male bird has black tufts of feathers on his head. He raises them during courtship displays or when defending territory. Shore larks eat seeds, buds, insects and other small creatures. A simple nest of plant stems, surrounded with pebbles, is made on the ground. The female lays four eggs.

# Yellow-throated longclaw
## *Macronyx croceus*

This bird gets its name from the back claw on each foot which is nearly 2 in (5 cm) long. It is often seen on farmland and feeds on insects which it often finds in grass. In the breeding season, the male makes a special courtship flight, and fans his tail and sings. The female lays three or four eggs in a nest hidden in long grass.

Size: 17¼–22½ in (44–57 cm)

Range: Europe, North Africa, Asia, North America

Habitat: inhabited areas, farmland, deciduous and northern forest, temperate grassland

# Black-billed magpie
## *Pica pica*

The magpie eats insects, spiders and snails but also snatches young birds from their nests. A breeding pair makes a large nest in a tree or bush. The female lays five to eight eggs and incubates them while the male keeps her supplied with food.

# BIRDS OF PARADISE

Birds of paradise are named for their beautiful plumage and are among the most spectacular of all birds. But only the males have the colorful and decorative head and tail feathers for which birds of paradise are famed. The females look quite different, with dull, usually brownish plumage. There are more than 40 species, ranging in size from about 5 to 42 in (13 to 107 cm) long. Most live in the rainforests of New Guinea, but a few birds of paradise are found in the nearby Moluccan Islands and the forests of northeast Australia. Fruit is their main food, but they also catch insects, spiders and occasionally frogs and lizards.

The striking colors and magnificent tail plumes of the greater bird of paradise are a spectacular sight as it perches on a branch in the rain forest.

Plume

## RIBBON-TAILED ASTRAPIA

The male ribbon-tailed bird has patches of shining green feathers around his head and long, ribbonlike tail feathers nearly 3¼ in (1 m) long. He twitches these tail feathers from side to side as he displays to females.

## KING OF SAXONY BIRD

Wirelike plumes, up to 19¾ in (50 cm) long, extend from the head of this bird. During courtship, these are held high while the bird bounds up and down, hissing loudly. As the female approaches, the male sweeps his long head feathers down in front of her. He follows her, and they mate.

# TAIL PLUMES

Wilson's bird of paradise has two coiled tail feathers. These are held at right angles to the body when the bird displays.

# A GROUP DISPLAY

Most birds of paradise display alone, but the Raggianas gather in groups. When females appear, the males hop around, flapping their wings and calling excitedly. Each then tries to outdo the others in showing off his glorious plumage. At the peak of the display, the birds make a series of high-pitched calls.

Size: 9½ in (24 cm)

Range: Europe, Asia, northwest Africa

Habitat: inhabited areas, decidous forest, tropical evergreen forest

Size: 6½ in (16.5 cm)

Range: Central and South America

Habitat: tropical evergreen forest

# Golden oriole
## *Oriolus oriolus*

Most of the golden oriole's life is spent high in the trees, feeding on insects and fruit with the help of its sharp beak. Its nest is like a tiny hammock made of grass and hung from a forked branch. Golden orioles lay three or four eggs.

# Royal flycatcher
## *Onychorhynchus coronatus*

This flycatcher has an amazing crest which normally lies flat but is opened and closed like a fan during courtship displays. Like all flycatchers, it feeds on insects which it snatches up in the air.

Size: 15 in (38 cm)

Range: northern South America

Habitat: tropical evergreen forest, fresh water

Size: 5 in (12.5 cm)

Range: Africa, south of the Sahara

Habitat: farmland, tropical grassland

# Cock-of-the-rock
## *Rupicola peruvianus*

In the breeding season, the brilliantly colored male cocks of the rock perform group displays, competing for the attention of the plainer females. They leap into the air, make noisy calls and flick their wings. These birds feed mainly on fruit.

# Red-billed quelea
## *Quelea quelea*

In huge flocks of thousands of birds, red-billed queleas move like clouds across the sky. They feed on grain crops and can destroy whole fields. Queleas breed in colonies and lay two or three eggs at a time, in a kidney-shaped nest which hangs from a branch and has a side entrance.

Size: 5¾ in (14.5 cm)

Range: Europe, Asia; introduced worldwide

Habitat: inhabited areas

# Superb lyrebird
## *Menura novaehollandiae*

Only the male lyrebird has a long lyre-shaped tail. In the breeding season, he displays to the female by spreading his tail feathers over himself and dancing. These birds rarely fly, but hop and flap up into trees to roost at night. They scratch on the ground to find insects to eat.

# House sparrow
## *Passer domesticus*

The house sparrow has been introduced worldwide and is an extremely common and adaptable bird. A few birds were taken to New York in 1850 and they have now spread all over North and South America. Seeds are the sparrow's main food, but it also eats insects and scraps put out by humans.

Size: male 31½–37½ in (80–95 cm); female 29¼–33 in (74–84 cm)

Range: southeast Australia

Habitat: tropical evergreen forest, deciduous forest

# Garnet pitta
## *Pitta granatina*

Both male and female garnet pittas have bright feathers, but young birds are a dull brown. This bird spends much of its time on the ground, catching ants, beetles and other insects. It also eats seeds and fruit and does fly short distances.

Size: 3½ in (9 cm)

Range: Australia, Indonesia

Habitat: deciduous forest, temperate grassland, farmland

Size: 6 in (15 cm)

Range: Malaysia, Sumatra, Borneo

Habitat: tropical evergreen forest, fresh water

# Zebra finch
## *Taeniopygia guttata*

Large flocks of zebra finches feed on seeds and insects in trees and on the ground. In dry areas these birds wait for rain before breeding. They make a domed nest low in a tree or bush and the female lays four to six eggs.

# HOW DO ANIMALS COMMUNICATE?

Almost all animals have some way of conveying information to others of their own kind. Many, such as birds, whales, dogs and monkeys, make a wide range of sounds, each with its own meaning. Other animals communicate by smell. They use scents to announce to others that they are ready to mate or that a particular area is their territory. Sight is also important. Courting lizards nod their heads in a special way and the positions of the ears of animals such as dogs and cats show when they are pleased, angry or frightened.

## ANTENNAE DETECTION

A male moth's antennae allow him to smell pheromones — chemicals given off by a female of his own kind — from more than half a mile (1 km) away. Silk moths live for just a few days, so they need to find a mate fast and lay eggs before they die.

The large feathery antennae of the male silk moth are especially sensitive.

## BARKS AND HOWLS

Like all wild dogs the coyote communicates with barks and yaps as well as by using its tail and ears to show its mood. The coyote's howl is a way of conveying information of ownership of a particular territory and warning off rival animals.

# SONG-FLIGHT

Warblers are well known for their songs. The zitting cisticola sings during its special song-flight to attract mates. It may go up to 100 ft (30 m) or more above the ground, circling over a wide area.

# FLASHING SIGNALS

Wingless female fireflies, called glow-worms, signal to males by making a series of flashes. Each species has a different sequence. The flashes are made by a combination of substances in the firefly's abdomen.

Male

# WAVING CLAW

One of the front claws of the male fiddler crab is much larger than the other and brightly colored. The male crab stands outside his burrow on the seashore and waves this claw to attract the attention of females. Each species of fiddler crab has a slightly different pattern of waves.

Female

The fiddler crab also uses his large front claw to fight off rival males and to dig the burrow where the female will lay her eggs.

# REPTILES

The first reptiles evolved from amphibians about 340 million years ago. In the form of dinosaurs, which first appeared about 230 million years ago, reptiles dominated life on Earth for 165 million years. Today there are more than 9,400 known species of reptiles, including such animals as sea-living turtles, predatory crocodiles, venomous snakes and fast-moving lizards. They live on all continents except Antarctica. Most hunt other animals to eat but there are some plant-eating turtles, tortoises and lizards.

# WHAT IS A REPTILE?

Reptiles are vertebrate animals — like mammals and birds, they have a backbone made up of small bones called vertebrae. Their bodies are covered in waterproof scales. Most reptiles live on land, but turtles and some snakes live in water, and crocodiles spend time in water and on land.

## TYPES OF REPTILE

Four groups of reptiles survive today. Turtles and tortoises have short broad bodies enclosed by a bony shell. Crocodiles and alligators are hunters and the largest living reptiles. The third group includes lizards and snakes. All snakes and most lizards are predators. The last group, the tuataras of New Zealand, has only two living species.

## TURTLES AND TORTOISES

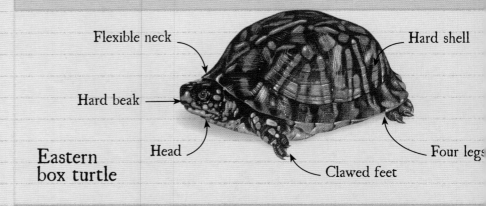

Flexible neck

Hard shell

Hard beak

Head

Four legs

Clawed feet

Eastern box turtle

## SNAKES

Legless body

Dark green whipsnake

Forked tongue

Yolk sac

Leathery shell

Embryo reptile

## EGG-LAYING REPTILES

Most reptiles lay eggs from which their young hatch, although some give birth to live young. The egg is protected by a tough shell. Inside is a yolk sac that provides food for the developing young, or embryo. The embryo grows inside the egg until it is ready to hatch out as a small version of the adult, able to live independently.

Some snakes, such as pythons, curl around their eggs to keep them warm.

# PREHISTORIC REPTILES

Although not the first reptiles, dinosaurs were the most successful, dominating the Earth for 165 million years. Like reptiles today, they had scale-covered skin and laid eggs. Many, such as *Lambeosaurus*, were plant eaters. Others, such as *Tyrannosaurus rex*, were fierce hunters.

*Lambeosaurus* with young

## LIZARDS

Race runner

Long tail

Ear openings

Slender body

Four legs

## TUATARAS

Crest on back

Large head

Tuatara

Four legs

## CROCODILES AND ALLIGATORS

Long tail

Bony plates on body

Four-toed back feet

Nostrils

Long jaws

Five-toed front feet

Nile crocodile

Nile crocodile skeleton

Vertebrae

Sharp teeth

Tailbones

Ribs

Four legs

Jawbones

A long spine and a strong tail help the crocodile to move efficiently in the water. Its legs are short but strong, and it has long jaws studded with many sharp teeth.

Most reptiles, such as turtles, simply lay their eggs in a safe place and leave them to hatch by themselves.

# COLD-BLOODED

Reptiles are cold-blooded and need the sun's warmth to be active. As a result, most live in warm climates. Reptiles usually switch between basking in the sun to gain heat and moving to shade or burrows to cool down.

Green iguana

# CROCODILES, ALLIGATORS, TURTLES AND TORTOISES

All of these kinds of reptile are armored, but in different ways. A typical turtle or tortoise has a hard shell that protects its soft body. Crocodiles and alligators are covered with hard scales and have thickened bony plates on the back for extra protection. The turtle group includes freshwater turtles and terrapins, sea turtles, and land tortoises. The crocodile group includes three families: crocodiles, alligators and caimans, and the gharial.

## CROCODILES AND ALLIGATORS

There are 14 species of crocodiles, eight species of alligators and caimans, and one species of gharial. All are powerful creatures that live on land and in water and hunt a range of other animals. They live in tropical and subtropical areas. Males and females generally look alike, but males tend to grow larger. Both crocodiles and alligators have a pair of large teeth near the front of the lower jaw for grasping prey. In crocodiles, these teeth fit into notches in the upper jaw and can be seen when the jaw is closed. In alligators and caimans, the large teeth fit into bony pits in the upper jaw and cannot be seen when the mouth is closed.

Size: 23 ft (7 m)
Range: India and Nepal
Habitat: fresh water

### Gharial
*Gavialis gangeticus*

The gavial has long jaws studded with about 100 small teeth — ideal equipment for seizing fish and frogs under the water. The most aquatic of all the crocodiles, it moves awkwardly on land and rarely leaves the water. The female hauls herself out onto the shore where she lays 35 to 60 eggs at night in a pit that she digs with her back feet. She stays nearby while the eggs incubate for as long as 94 days. Hunted for its skin, the gharial is now endangered — fewer than 200 survive in the wild.

Size: up to 18 ft (5.5 m)
Range: southeastern U.S.A.
Habitat: coast, fresh water

### American alligator
*Alligator mississippiensis*

At one time American alligators came close to extinction because hunters killed so many for their skins. Conservation efforts to protect the species have been very successful, and it is no longer endangered. These alligators usually mate in spring. The female lays about 50 eggs in a mound of leaves and other plant material and then guards the nest while the eggs incubate. The young stay with their mother for up to two years.

# Mugger crocodile
## *Crocodylus palustris*

The mugger is a powerful crocodile with a broad heavy snout. Adults can catch large mammals, such as deer and buffalo, but also feed on frogs, snakes and turtles. Young muggers eat insects and other small creatures. In the breeding season, the female lays ten to 35 eggs in a hole in the riverbank. She may lay a second clutch later in the season.

> Size: up to 13 ft (4 m)
> Range: India
> Habitat: fresh water

# Spectacled caiman
## *Caiman crocodilus*

> Size: 5–6½ ft (1.5–2 m)
> Range: Venezuela to southern Amazon basin
> Habitat: fresh water, coastal waters

This caiman is extremely adaptable and readily moves into watery habitats made by humans, such as reservoirs and cattle ponds. Smaller caimans feed mostly on insects, crabs and other invertebrates. Larger animals eat fish and and water snails. In the breeding season, the female makes a nest of earth and leaves and lays up to 40 eggs. In some areas, numbers of this caiman have fallen because so many have been hunted and killed for their skins.

# Saltwater crocodile
## *Crocodylus porosus*

This is one of the largest and most dangerous of all crocodiles. It has been known to attack humans. It spends much of its life in the sea, catching fish, but it also preys on land animals such as monkeys, cattle and buffalo. The female comes to land to lay up to 80 eggs in a mound of plant material.

> Size: 27 ft (9 m)
> Range: southern India, Indonesia, northern Australia
> Habitat: coast, tropical evergreen forest, coastal waters, fresh water

> Size: 5 ft (1.5 m)
> Range: West Africa south of the Sahara
> Habitat: fresh water

# West African dwarf crocodile
## *Osteolaemus tetraspis*

This small crocodile has become rare in recent years because of changes to the rivers and lakes it inhabits and because of increased hunting. A slow-moving and not very dangerous animal, it is easy to kill or catch. Little is known about this crocodile's life, but it is thought to be active at night, when it feeds on crabs, frogs and fish. The female lays 11 to 17 eggs in a mound of leaves and other plant material.

# NILE CROCODILES

Unlike most reptiles, the female Nile crocodile is a devoted parent. After mating, the female digs a pit near the river with her back legs and lays 16 to 80 eggs. She covers the nest with soil, then both parents stay close by to guard it while the eggs incubate for six to eight weeks. The female does not leave the nest area even to find food during this time. When they are about to hatch, the baby crocodiles call out to their mother from inside their shells. She uncovers the nest so that the young can get out. The mother may continue to care for her young until they are six months old. By then they are about 18 inches (45 cm) long and can find food for themselves.

Nile crocodiles are found along most of the Nile River, and in rivers and lakes all over tropical and southern Africa.

## THE CROCODILE'S NEST

The nest is usually made near water on a sandy beach or riverbank and is 8–18 inches (20–45 cm) deep. Once she has dug the nest burrow, the female lies over it and deposits her eggs inside.

## BEGINNING LIFE

When ready to hatch, the young crocodiles are very sensitive to any movements on the earth above them. When they hear their mother's footsteps they call out. Once she has uncovered the nest, each hatchling uses the sharp egg tooth on its jaw to chip its way out of its shell. The mother may help to pull the babies free.

# PROTECTION

Once the hatchlings are out of the eggs
they must find shelter from the many
predators waiting to catch them.
The mother picks the babies up, a
few at a time, and carries them to
a safe nursery site. She does not
close her mouth, and the tiny
crocodiles look like prisoners behind the bars
of her big sharp teeth. She releases her babies
in a quiet pool and defends them fiercely.

# FIERCE HUNTER

The Nile crocodile is a wily hunter. It lurks
in the water, often with only its eyes and
nostrils above the surface, waiting for prey
to come to the riverbank to drink. The
crocodile then seizes its prey, drags it
into the water and drowns it.

# TURTLES AND TORTOISES

There are more than 300 species of turtle and tortoise. Typically, they have a hard shell to protect the soft body. The shell is in two parts — the carapace on the back and the plastron underneath. The ribs and most of the vertebrae are attached to the shell, and most turtles and tortoises can pull their head inside the shell for protection. Turtles and tortoises have hard beaks instead of teeth for tearing off pieces of food. All turtles and tortoises lay eggs. Most bury them in sand or earth and leave the hatchlings to make their own way out.

Size: 24–30 in (61–76 cm)
Range: northern South America
Habitat: fresh water

## Arrau river turtle
*Podocnemis expansa*

This is the largest of the turtles known as sidenecks — a sideneck retracts it head by moving it sideways into the shell. Females gather in huge numbers on sandbanks to lay their eggs. When the young hatch, they must make their own way to the water.

Size: 22¾ in (58 cm)
Range: Bangladesh, Cambodia, India, Indonesia, Malaysia
Habitat: coast, fresh water

## River terrapin
*Batagur baska*

A large plant-eating turtle, the river terrapin, or batagur, lives in salt water as well as in rivers. It nests on sandbanks, so it is easy for people to catch and dig up its eggs for food. In Malaysia, to save the river terrapin, eggs are taken to hatcheries where young turtles are kept safe in pools until they are two years old.

Size: 5–9 in (12.5–23 cm)
Range: eastern Canada, northeastern to midwestern U.S.A.
Habitat: deciduous forest, temperate grassland, fresh water

## Wood turtle
*Glyptemys insculpta*

This rough-shelled turtle stays near water, but spends most of its life on land. It is a good climber and feeds on fruit, worms and insects. In May or June females lay six to eight eggs. These may hatch before the fall, but the eggs of turtles in northern areas usually do not hatch until the next spring.

## Yellow-bellied slider turtle
*Trachemys scripta*

This pond slider rarely moves far from water and often basks on a floating log. Young pond sliders feed mainly on insects, tadpoles, and other small invertebrate animals, but as they grow they also eat plants. In summer, the female pond slider lays up to three clutches of four to 23 eggs each.

Size: 5–11¾ in (13–30 cm)
Range: U.S.A., Central America to Brazil; introduced to Europe, Africa and Asia
Habitat: fresh water

# Galápagos giant tortoise
## *Chelonoides nigra*

Size: up to 4 ft (1.2 m)

Range: Galápagos Islands

Habitat: tropical evergreen forest, desert

This huge tortoise may weigh more than 475 pounds (215 kg) — males are usually larger than females. It lives on land and feeds on almost any plants it can find. Some have a shell that curves up behind the head, allowing the tortoise to reach higher plants. The female digs a pit with her back feet and lays four to ten eggs. She covers the eggs with soil and leaves them to incubate. The young dig themselves out of the pit when they hatch.

# Pancake tortoise
## *Malacohersus tornieri*

Size: 6 in (15 cm)

Range: Kenya, Tanzania; introduced to Zimbabwe

Habitat: desert

This remarkable tortoise has a soft flexible shell. If in danger, it crawls into a rocky crevice and breathes in lots of air. Its body expands so much that it becomes stuck tight in the hole and very difficult to pull out. But this does not protect the animal from people, who catch large numbers for the pet trade.

# Spur-thighed tortoise
## *Testudo graeca*

Also known as the Greek tortoise, this rare reptile has lost much of its native habitat, which has been built upon or turned into farmland. Millions of these tortoises have been captured and sold as pets, which further damaged the wild population. This species is now regarded as vulnerable to the risk of extinction.

Size: 6 in (15 cm)

Range: Northern Africa, southeastern and southwestern Europe, Middle East

Habitat: inhabited areas, farmland deciduous forest, temperate grassland, high ground

# Eroded hingeback tortoise
## *Kinixys erosa*

Size: 13 in (33 cm)

Range: western and central Africa

Habitat: tropical evergreen forest, fresh water

This tortoise eats some small animals but feeds mainly on plants and spends much of its life hiding among plant debris. Its shell is unique. A hinge allows the rear of the shell to be lowered to protect the animal's hindquarters if it is attacked. Young tortoises do not have a hinge — it develops as they grow.

## Matamata
### *Chelus fimbriatus*

The irregular shape of this turtle keeps it well hidden while it lies among leaves and other debris on the riverbed. Fleshy flaps at the sides of the head wave in water and may attract small fish. When a fish comes close, the turtle opens its large mouth and water rushes in, taking the fish with it. The turtle closes its mouth, leaving only a slit for the water to flow out.

Size: 16¼ in (41 cm)

Range: northern South America

Habitat: fresh water

## Hawksbill
### *Eretmochelys imbricata*

Hawksbills have long been hunted for their beautiful shells as well as for their eggs. There are now strict controls on hunting, but numbers are still low. The hawksbill has an unusual diet. As well as eating mollusks and crustaceans, it feeds on sponges. Many of these contain poisons but they do not seem to affect the turtles.

Size: 30–36 in (76–91 cm)

Range: tropical Atlantic, Pacific, and Indian oceans; Caribbean Sea

Habitat: coastal waters, coral reef

## Murray River turtle
### *Emydura macquarii*

The shape of the Murray River turtle's shell changes as it develops. Newly hatched young have almost circular shells. As they grow, the shell becomes widest at the back, and adult shells are almost oval. An active turtle, it feeds on frogs, tadpoles and plants. In summer, the female lays between 10 and 15 eggs in a hole dug in the riverbank. The eggs hatch after about 10 or 11 weeks.

Size: 11¾ in (30 cm)

Range: southeastern Australia

Habitat: fresh water

## Leatherback
### *Dermochelys coriacea*

The world's largest turtle, the leatherback weighs about 800 lb (360 kg). Its shell is not covered with hard plates like those of other turtles but made of a thick leathery material. It has weak scissorlike jaws and feeds mostly on jellyfish. Leatherbacks travel long distances between the areas where they feed and their nesting sites. Most breed only every other year. Newly hatched young have small scales on their shells and skin, but these soon disappear.

Size: 5 ft (1.5 m)

Range: temperate and tropical waters worldwide

Habitat: oceanic, coastal waters

Size: 3–5 in (8–13 cm)
Range: North America
Habitat: fresh water

## Common musk turtle
*Sternotherus odoratus*

Also known as the stinkpot, this turtle oozes a strong-smelling fluid from special glands if attacked. It eats insects and mollusks but also feeds on carrion (creatures that are already dead) and small amounts of fish and plants. It rarely strays far from the water.

Size: 6–18 in (15–46 cm)
Range: North America
Habitat: fresh water

## Spiny softshell
*Apalone spinifera*

Softshell turtles have rounded bendy shells with no hard plates. They can move fast on land and in water but spend most of their lives in water. The spiny softshell feeds on insects, crayfish and some fish and plants. It breeds in summer, when the female lays about 20 eggs.

## Loggerhead turtle
*Caretta caretta*

The loggerhead has a chunky head, which may be as much as 10 in (25 cm) wide, and powerful jaws. It can crush even hard-shelled prey such as clams, but it also eats jellyfish and plants. Its heavy shell is very thick at the back, which may protect it from attack by sharks. Loggerheads usually breed every other year and lay several clutches of about 100 eggs each.

Size: 30–40 in (75–102 cm)
Range: temperate and tropical waters worldwide
Habitat: oceanic, coastal waters

## Green turtle
*Chelonia mydas*

This turtle spends most of its life in water. It may travel huge distances to lay its eggs on the beach where it was born. The female drags herself on to the sand where she digs a pit and lays 100 or more eggs. She covers them with sand and returns to the sea. When the young hatch they must struggle down to the sea.

Size: 3¼–4 ft (1–1.25 m)
Range: temperate and tropical waters worldwide
Habitat: oceanic

## Alligator snapping turtle
*Macrochelys temminckii*

This turtle can weigh up to 200 lb (90 kg). It has a lumpy shell that makes it hard to see as it lies on the river bed, watching for prey. It waits with its large mouth open to show a pink fleshy flap on its lower jaw. Passing fish come to try this "bait" and are quickly swallowed or sliced in half by the turtle's strong jaws.

Size: 14–26 in (36–66 cm)
Range: southeastern U.S.A.
Habitat: fresh water

# LIZARDS AND SNAKES

Lizards and snakes belong to a large group of reptiles, all of which have a body covered with scales. There are at least 5,500 kinds of lizards living over most of the world except the far north and Antarctica. Most live on land or in trees, but the marine iguana spends much of its time in the sea. There are about 3,400 kinds of snakes. Like lizards, they live mainly in warmer parts of the world and there are none in the far north or Antarctica. Most snakes live on land, but there are some freshwater and marine species. Tuataras are a separate group.

## LIZARDS

Lizards are the largest group of living reptiles. They range from tiny geckos only five-eighths of an inch (1.6 cm) long to the huge Komodo dragon which measures up to 10 ft (3 m). A typical lizard has four legs, but there are some legless species and others, such as the skinks and snake lizards, that have extremely small limbs. Most have ear openings and movable eyelids. In general, lizards lay eggs in a hole or a safe place under a rock and give them no further attention. But a few types keep their eggs inside their bodies until the young are quite well grown. They hatch almost as soon as the eggs are laid.

Size: 11–16½ in (28–42 cm)

Range: southwestern U.S.A. and Mexico

Habitat: desert

### Chuckwalla
*Sauromalus ater*

This plump lizard lies among rocks at night and comes out in the morning to bask in the sun and warm its body. A plant eater, it spends the day feeding on leaves, buds and flowers. If in danger, it hides in a rock crevice and puffs its body up with air so it is almost impossible to move.

### Leaf-tailed gecko
*Uroplatus fimbriatus*

Size: 8 in (2.50 cm)

Range: Madagascar

Habitat: tropical evergreen forest

The spotted pattern on the body of this gecko blends well with tree bark and helps keep it hidden as it lies pressed against a tree trunk. It is usually active at night when it catches insects to eat. After eating, it cleans itself, licking over its whole body with its tongue.

Size: 5 in (12.5 cm)

Range: southwestern Africa: Namib Desert

Habitat: desert

### Web-footed gecko
*Pachydactylus rangei*

This rare desert-living gecko has webbed feet that act like snowshoes to help it run over soft sand. It also uses its feet for burrowing into the sand to hide from enemies or the burning sun. It sits in the burrow with its head facing the entrance, waiting to pounce on insects such as termites.

# Arabian toad-headed agama

*Phrynocephalus arabicus*

A burrowing lizard, this agama digs tunnels for shelter or buries itself in the sand. If alarmed, it takes up a defensive position to warn off the enemy — it lifts its tail high, rolls it up and then unrolls it again.

Size: up to 5 in (13 cm)
Range: Middle East
Habitat: desert

# Common iguana

*Iguana iguana*

A tree-living lizard, the iguana also swims well. It has sharp teeth and claws and defends itself fiercely when attacked. In the fall it lays 28 to 40 eggs in a hole in the ground, where they incubate for three months. The newly hatched young are about 7¾ inches (20 cm) long.

Size: 3¼–6½ ft (1–2 m)
Range: northern and central South America; introduced into U.S.A.
Habitat: tropical evergreen forest, fresh water

Size: up to 25½ in (65 cm)
Range: New Zealand
Habitat: deciduous forest, temperate grassland

# Tuatara

*Sphenodon punctatus*

There are only two kinds of tuatara and although they may look like lizards they actually form their own separate group. The tuatara lives on the ground and shelters in burrows. It eats insects and other small invertebrates as well as small birds and lizards.

# Rhinoceros iguana

*Cyclura cornuta*

This lizard, which gets its name from the pointed scales on its snout, is found only on Hispaniola and its small neighbor, Mona Island. It lives among thorn bushes and cacti and feeds mainly on plants, worms and mice. Its survival is threatened by the various animals, such as pigs, dogs, cats and mongooses, that have been brought to the islands. They eat its eggs and young.

Size: up to 4 ft (1.2 m)
Range: West Indies
Habitat: desert

Size: 4–5 ft (1.2–1.5 m)
Range: Galápagos Islands
Habitat: coast, coastal waters

# Marine iguana

*Amblyrhynchus cristatus*

The marine iguana is the only lizard that spends most of its life in the sea, swimming and diving as it searches for seaweed, its main food. When in the water, the iguana uses its powerful tail to push itself along. It has to come to the surface to breathe, but when it dives, its heart rate slows so that its body uses less oxygen.

125

# Granite night lizard
## *Xantusia henshawi*

This lizard is most active at night or warm winter days. It feeds on spiders, scorpions, insects and eggs. It does not lay eggs itself, but gives birth to one or two live young, which grow inside the mother's body and receive all the nourishment they need from her.

# Green anole
## *Anolis carolinensis*

The anole's long-toed feet help it climb in trees, where it searches for insects and spiders to eat. The male anole has a flap of pink skin on his throat, which he fans in a display to attract females. After mating, the female lays one egg on the ground among leaves or rocks every two weeks during the breeding season. The eggs hatch in five to seven weeks.

Size: 4¾–7¾ in (12–20 cm)

Range: southern U.S.A.

Habitat: inhabited areas, farmland, deciduous forest, temperate and tropical grassland

Size: 2–2¾ in (5–7 cm)

Range: southwestern U.S.A. to Mexico

Habitat: desert, scrub

# Gila monster
## *Heloderma suspectum*

This is one of just a few poisonous lizards. Its venom is made in glands in the lower jaw. When the Gila bites its prey, venom flows into the wound. Birds, mice and other lizards are its main prey. If food is scarce, the Gila can live off fat reserves stored in its tail.

Size: 17¾–24 in (45–60 cm)

Range: southwestern U.S.A., Mexico

Habitat: desert

# Ground lizard
## *Ameiva spp.*

Size: 2½–20 in (6–50 cm)

Range: Caribbean, Mexico, Central and South America

Habitat: forest, grassland, beach

# Centralian blue-tongued skink
## *Tiliqua multifasciata*

Skinks have plump bodies, with short necks and legs, and many species have short tails, too. They spend most of their time hiding in burrows, but they emerge to hunt and eat insects and other invertebrates, or even small lizards and rodents.

Size: up to 15 in (41 cm)

Range: central and western Australia

Habitat: desert, scrub

Ground lizards, or ameivas, are also called jungle runners because they dart around, looking for insects and other bugs. Their colors vary greatly, from dull grey or brown to blues and greens, usually with spots and stripes. Young ground lizards often look different to their parents.

Size: 10 ft (3 m)

Range: islands of Komodo, Flores, Pintja, and Padar, east of Java

Habitat: tropical grassland, deciduous forest

Size: 13½–21¼ in (35–54 cm)

Range: parts of Europe and Asia, northwestern Africa

Habitat: inhabited areas, farmland, temperate grassland, desert

## Slow worm
### *Anguis fragilis*

The slow worm is a smooth long-bodied lizard with no visible legs. It moves like a snake but can shed its tail if seized by an enemy. After spending the night under rocks or logs, it comes out in the morning to hunt for prey such as slugs, worms and insects.

## Komodo dragon
### *Varanus komodoensis*

This is the world's heaviest lizard and is strong enough to kill deer, wild boar and pigs. It has a heavy body, a long thick tail, strong legs with talonlike claws — and a venomous bite. Despite its bulk, it is a good climber and moves surprisingly fast. It also swims well and is often found near water.

Size: 26 in (66 cm) including tail

Range: Australia and New Guinea

Habitat: deciduous forest, tropical evergreen forest

## Frilled lizard
### *Chlamydosaurus kingii*

This lizard has a collar of skin, which normally lies in folds around its neck. But if disturbed, the lizard's collar stands up like a frill, making it look larger and more frightening than it really is. It eats insects and other creatures that it finds in trees and on the ground.

Size: 15¾ in (40 cm)

Range: South Africa

Habitat: temperate grassland

## Transvaal snake lizard
### *Chamaesaura aenea*

With snakelike movements of its long body, this lizard streaks through the grass in search of insects to eat. Its tiny legs are often held off the ground as it moves. The female's two to four eggs develop inside her body. The young break from their shells as they are laid.

Size: 6½–13¾ in (16.5–35 cm)

Range: U.S.A.; Mexico

Habitat: temperate grassland, deciduous forest, desert

## Great plains skink
### *Plestidon obsoletus*

This lizard is unusual in that the female guards her eggs carefully while they incubate and turns them regularly to make sure they warm evenly. She also helps the young to wriggle free of their shells, and then cares for them for about ten days.

# CHAMELEONS

The amazing chameleon has a tongue like a mobile flypaper, which it shoots out to catch prey such as insects. There are more than 150 species of these tree-living lizards. Most live in Africa and Madagascar, but there are few kinds of chameleon in Asia and one in Europe. A typical chameleon has a flattened body, large eyes and a strong tail that can be used to grip branches tightly. Most chameleons are between 6 and 11¾ in (15 and 30 cm) long, but one Madagascan species grows to 31½ in (80 cm). The color of its skin helps it to stay hidden from predators and prey — but that color can suddenly change.

## CHANGING COLOR

A chameleon can lighten or darken its skin to help lower or raise its body temperature, or to signal to other members of its species. In the breeding season, when two males compete for territory or for females, the dominant male displays bright coloration while the loser becomes a darker shade of green and hides away.

## CATCHING PREY

Once the chameleon is near enough to its prey, it judges its position with its superb eyesight and takes aim. Shooting out its tongue, which may be as long as its body, the chameleon traps the insect on the sticky pad at the tongue's tip and returns it to its mouth. This all happens in less than one-twentieth of a second.

# FLAP-NECKED CHAMELEON

This reptile has flaps of skin at the back of its head, which it can extend to threaten a rival of its own species. It spends nearly all its life in trees and only comes down to move to another tree or to lay eggs.

# JACKSON'S CHAMELEON

The male of this species has three large horns on his head. On the females, the horns are either tiny or absent. The dull green color of this chameleon's skin keeps it camouflaged on lichen-covered tree bark.

# MELLER'S CHAMELEON

The bold markings on this chameleon make it extremely hard to see as it sits motionless on a branch, watching for prey. Meller's chameleon grows up to 22¾ inches (58 cm) long.

Unlike most chameleons, the tiny dwarf chameleon spends its life on the ground and cannot grip with its tail. It looks like the dead leaves it hides among on the forest floor. It even has lines on its body that resemble the veins of a leaf.

# SNAKES

Snakes have long bodies and no limbs. Even though they have no legs, snakes can still move fast. They wriggle along the ground with wavelike movements of the body, and pointed scales on the underside of the belly help them grip. Snakes range in size from 4 in (10 cm) to about 30 ft (9 m). They all have a long forked tongue, but they do not have ear openings or movable eyelids. All snakes hunt other animals for food. Some, such as boas, wrap victims in their strong body coils and squeeze them to death. Others, such as vipers, have a venomous bite.

Size: 7–15 in (18–38 cm)
Range: southwestern U.S.A.
Habitat: temperate grasslands, desert

## Western blind snake
*Rena humilis*

A smooth round-bodied reptile, the western blind snake has a blunt head and tail. It lives where there is sandy or gravelly soil and spends much of its time below ground. It eats ants and termites, which it finds by smell, and its body is so slender that it can slide into their nests.

Size: 17–20 ft (5–6 m)
Range: India, Southeast Asia, Indonesia
Habitat: tropical evergreen forest, fresh water

## Indian python
*Python molurus*

One of the largest snakes in the world, the Indian python basks in the sun by day or rests in a cave or other shelter. At night, it prowls around, searching for prey such as birds, small deer and boar, or waits near a water hole where animals are sure to come. It stalks close to its prey, then grasps it in its body coils and crushes it to death.

## Anaconda
*Eunectes murinus*

One of the longest of all snakes, the anaconda spends much of its life in slow-moving water, watching for prey. When an animal comes to the water's edge to drink, the anaconda seizes the victim in its coils. Female anacondas produce up to 40 live young, each 20 in (66 cm) long.

## Boa constrictor
*Boa constrictor*

The boa constrictor kills prey, such as birds and mammals, by wrapping the victim in the strong coils of its body until it is suffocated or crushed to death. The boa spends most of its life on the ground, but it does climb trees and can grip branches with its tail.

Size: up to 18 ft (5.5 m)
Range: South America
Habitat: tropical evergreen forest, desert, inhabited areas, farmland, fresh water

Size: 30 ft (9 m)
Range: South America
Habitat: fresh water

# Gopher snake
*Pituophis catenifer*

This large snake is a good climber and burrower. It feeds mostly on mice, small birds and lizards, all of which it kills with its powerful body coils — the victim is squeezed until it suffocates. Gopher snakes mate in spring and the female lays up to 24 eggs in a burrow or under a log. The young hatch in 9 to 11 weeks.

Size: 4–8¼ ft (1.2–2.5 m)

Range: southwestern Canada, USA, Mexico

Habitat: deciduous forest, temperate grassland, desert

Size: up to 6½ ft (2 m)

Range: central to southern Africa

Habitat: tropical grassland

# Boomslang
*Dispholidus typus*

The active tree-living boomslang is one of the most venomous snakes in Africa. Its poison flows from special glands on to large grooved teeth in the mouth and then enters the victim's body as the snake chews. The snake normally uses its venomous bite on prey such as lizards, frogs and birds but it can even kill humans. It rarely attacks unless disturbed.

# Grass snake
*Natrix natrix*

The grass snake is a strong swimmer. It hunts fish and frogs in woodland rivers as well as mice on land. It is one of the commonest snakes in Europe. In the breeding season, the male courts the female before mating by rubbing his chin over her body. She lays 30 to 40 eggs in a warm spot.

Size: up to 4 ft (1.2 m); occasionally up to 6½ ft (2 m)

Range: from Europe to Mongolia, and northwestern Africa

Habitat: temperate grassland, fresh water

Size: 11¾–19¾ in (30–50 cm)

Range: Indonesia, Malaysia, Singapore

Habitat: fresh water

# Spotted water snake
*Enhydris punctata*

Able to move swiftly both in water and on land, this snake preys on creatures such as fish and frogs. Its small eyes face upward and its nostrils are also on the upper surface of the head. Pads of skin close off the nostrils completely when the snake dives underwater. It is mildly venomous.

## Bluebanded sea snake
*Hydrophis cyanocinctus*

This snake spends all its life in the sea. Its body is slightly flattened and its paddle-shaped tail helps it push itself through the water. It breathes air but can stay under water for up to two hours. Like all sea snakes, it eats fish and has a venomous bite.

Size: 6½ ft (2 m)
Range: Indian and Pacific oceans
Habitat: coastal waters

## Eastern green mamba
*Dendroaspis angusticeps*

The slender fast-moving mamba spends much of its life in trees, where it hunts birds and lizards. It has a strong venom. In the breeding season males take part in ritual fights for females. They wrap their bodies around one another and threaten each other with their heads.

Size: up to 4 ft (1.2 m)
Range: from Burma to Malaysia and the Philippines
Habitat: tropical evergreen forest

## Paradise tree snake
*Chrysopelea paradisi*

This snake is an excellent climber and spends much of its life in trees. Also known as the flying snake, it can launch itself into the air and glide 65 ft (20 m) or more from tree to tree in the rain forest. It does not have much control over its "flight" and cannot glide upward or steer.

Size: 6½ ft (2 m)
Range: eastern and southern Africa
Habitat: tropical evergreen forest

## Sidewinder
*Crotalus cerastes*

This venomous snake hides under a bush or in a burrow during the day and comes out at night to hunt for mice, rats and lizards. A desert dweller, the sidewinder has a special way of moving over sand. It presses its tail down, throws the rest of its body to one side, then moves its tail up and repeats the action, moving sideways over the sand.

Size: 17–32¼ in (43–82 cm)
Range: southwestern U.S.A. and Mexico
Habitat: desert, high ground

# Eastern diamondback rattlesnake
## *Crotalus adamanteus*

This is the most dangerous snake in North America, with venom that attacks its victims' blood cells. Like all rattlesnakes it makes a rattling sound with a series of hard hollow rings of skin at the end of the tail. Each ring was once the tip of the tail, and a new one is left behind each time the snake sheds its skin.

# Indian cobra
## *Naja naja*

This large, very venomous cobra feeds on mice, lizards and frogs. It can attack or defend itself from a distance by "spitting" out jets of venom. This can cause severe pain if it reaches the eyes of mammals. To threaten enemies the cobra raises the front of its body and spreads the ribs and loose skin at its neck to form a hood shape. Eyelike markings on the hood confuse the enemy further.

# Gaboon viper
## *Bitis gaponica*

The patterns on the Gaboon viper's body help keep it hidden as it lies among dead leaves on the forest floor. It hunts at night, preying on mice, frogs and birds. Its fangs are up to 2 in (5 cm) long, the longest of any viper, and it has powerful venom. The female viper gives birth to litters of up to 30 live young.

# Saw-scaled viper
## *Echis carinatus*

This snake is one of about 11 species of saw-scaled, or carpet, snakes, which are mostly small and slender. Carpet snakes are found in Asia and Africa. They are deadly reptiles because they are common in places where people live, and their venom is strong and acts quickly.

# AMPHIBIANS

Amphibians were the first vertebrate animals to live on land. They evolved from fish about 370 million years ago, and today's 6,500 species still spend part of their lives in water. Many also mate and lay their eggs in water. The eggs hatch into water-living larvae that have fins and gills. As they grow, they lose their gills and develop legs and lungs, so that they are able to live on land. Some amphibians such as mudpuppies spend their whole lives in water and keep their feathery gills.

# WHAT IS AN AMPHIBIAN?

Amphibians are cold-blooded vertebrates. They cannot control their body temperature and must gain heat by basking in the sun.

Though most have lungs, amphibians gain most of the oxygen they need through their skin. The skin is not scaly and must be kept moist.

## TYPES OF AMPHIBIAN

Caecilians are the least well known of all the amphibians. These wormlike creatures have long rounded bodies and no legs. They live in burrows and are rarely seen above ground. A typical salamander has a long body and tail and four legs. Although similar to lizards in shape, it does not have scaly skin, claws or ear openings on the outside of the body. Frogs and toads have much shorter bodies than salamanders, and no tails. The well-developed back legs are used for jumping on land and swimming in water.

## CAECILIAN

Long body

Eye covered with skin

São Tomé caecilian

## SALAMANDERS AND NEWTS

Eyes

Long body

Four legs

Tail

Dusky salamander

## FROGS AND TOADS

Backbone    Frog skeleton

Hip bones

Thigh bones

Skull

Calf bones

Foot bones ___                ___ Ankle bones

A frog has a short backbone and a rigid hip that helps keep the back straight for jumping. The long muscular rear legs provide power for the jump. The frog has no ribs.

Common frog

Short body

Large eyes

Smaller front legs

Strong back legs

Long toes

136

# LEAPING FROG

On land, the frog crouches with its long legs folded. The foot, calf and thigh are all about the same length. As the frog leaps, its legs unfold to push it into the air. When stretched out, the frog's back legs are usually longer than its body.

Getting ready to land

Back legs fully stretched

Taking off

# BEWARE OF BRIGHT COLORS

Many amphibians have extremely brightly colored and patterned skins. This is usually a warning to potential predators that the amphibian's skin contains nasty-tasting secretions. These can cause severe irritation in mammals and some even contain poisons that can kill. The South American false-eyed frog has large eyelike markings on its rear. If attacked, it displays these to fool its enemy into thinking it is larger than it really is.

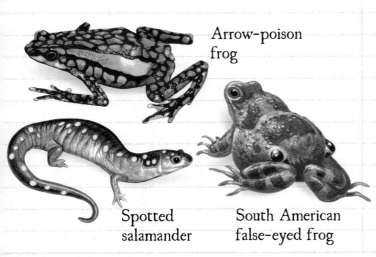

Arrow-poison frog

Spotted salamander

South American false-eyed frog

Mature frog

Ten weeks old

Five weeks old

Eggs

Lungs develop

Gills

Back legs grow

Two days old

Twelve days old

# FROM EGG TO ADULT

This is the life cycle of a typical frog. The eggs, which have a protective jellylike coating, are laid in water. They hatch into tadpoles, which have a tail and feathery gills. As each tadpole grows, it develops legs and lungs, and the gills disappear. Finally, when it has grown into a miniature version of the adult, the tadpole loses its tail. Not all frogs follow this same cycle. Some keep their developing eggs inside their body and produce live young.

# PREHISTORIC AMPHIBIANS

*Ichthyostega*

Amphibians such as *Ichthyostega* were the first known land animals. *Ichthyostega* was a strongly built creature with four legs. Like its fish ancestors, it had a tail fin and bony scales on its belly and tail.

# NEWTS AND SALAMANDERS

There are about 600 species of newts and salamanders divided into 9 groups, or families. Sirens, congo eels, olms and mudpuppies are all long-bodied water-living amphibians with small, almost useless legs. Many of these creatures keep their feathery gills throughout their adult lives, although most amphibians only have gills when they are larvae.

The lungless salamanders are the largest group of living salamanders. With no lungs, they obtain all their oxygen through their moist skin. There are several other groups of salamanders, most of which have sturdy bodies and well-developed legs. The newt family includes water- and land-living newts, but most stay near water.

Size: 18–45 in (45–115 cm)
Range: eastern U.S.A.
Habitat: fresh water

## Two-toed congo eel
*Amphiuma means*

The congo eel has a long body and tiny legs that are almost useless for walking. It usually comes out at night to hunt in water for creatures such as crayfish and frogs. During the day, it may hide in a burrow that it digs in the mud or takes over from another creature. Congo eels mate in water and the female lays about 200 eggs in a beadlike string. She curls around the eggs and protects them until they hatch.

## California slender salamander
*Batrachoseps attenuatus*

True to its name, this salamander has a long, slim body and tail. Its legs and feet are tiny, with four toes on each foot. It generally lives on land and moves by wriggling its body rather than by using its legs. During the day it hides among damp plants, coming out at night to hunt for creatures such as worms and spiders.

Size: 3–5½ in (7.5–14 cm)
Range: western U.S.A.: Oregon, California
Habitat: northern forest, deciduous forest, high ground

Size: 8–12 in (20–30 cm)
Range: Balkan Peninsula and Italy
Habitat: fresh water

## Olm
*Proteus anguinus*

This strange salamander has a long body and red feathery gills. Its tail is flattened and it has small, weak legs. It is almost blind and lives in total darkness in underground streams and lakes. There it rummages in the mud to find food such as worms and small crustaceans. Animal collectors have taken so many of these fascinating creatures from the wild that new areas where they have been found are kept secret.

# Mudpuppy
*Necturus maculosus*

The mudpuppy spends all its life in water, so even adults have large feathery gills. It hunts worms, crayfish and insects at night. In the breeding season the female lays up to 190 eggs, each of which is stuck separately to a log or rock.

Size: 7¾–17 in (20–43 cm)

Range: southern Canada and U.S.A.

Habitat: fresh water

Size: 3¾–7 in (9.5–18 cm)

Range: eastern U.S.A.

Habitat: temperate grassland, fresh water

# Red salamander
*Pseudotriton ruber*

The brilliantly colored red salamander has a stout body and a short tail and legs. It spends much of its time on land but usually stays near water. Earthworms, insects and smaller salamanders are its main foods. After courting and mating, the female salamander lays between 50 and 100 eggs. The larvae hatch about two months later but do not become adults until they are about two years old.

Size: 3½–5¼ in (9–13.5 cm)

Range: U.S.A.: San Marcos, Texas

Habitat: fresh water

# Texas blind salamander
*Eurycea rathbuni*

This salamander lives in water in underground caves. It has a pale body, tiny eyes and red feathery gills that it keeps throughout life. These salamanders eat cave-dwelling invertebrates that feed on the droppings left by the bats that roost in the caves.

Size: 19¾–39½ in (50–97.5 cm)

Range: U.S.A.

Habitat: fresh water

# Greater siren
*Siren lacertina*

The siren has a long, eel-like body and tiny front legs with four toes on each foot. It has no back legs and swims by fishlike movements of its body. During the day, it hides under rocks or burrows into the muddy riverbed. At night, it catches snails, insect larvae and fish.

# Spotted salamander
*Ambystoma maculatum*

Spotted salamanders spend most of their time well out of sight, burrowing through damp soil, but every spring they gather in crowds around pools to mate and lay eggs in the water. Sadly, this spectacle no longer occurs in many areas because acid rain has polluted breeding pools.

Size: 6–9½ in (15–24 cm)

Range: southeast Canada, eastern U.S.A.

Habitat: deciduous forest, fresh water

# Tiger salamander
*Ambystoma tigrinum*

Size: 6–15¾ in (15–40 cm)

Range: North America, Mexico

Habitat: temperate grassland, high ground, deciduous forest, fresh water

The world's largest land-living salamander, the tiger salamander, has a stout body, broad head and small eyes. It lives near water and often hides among leaves or in an abandoned burrow. It feeds on earthworms, insects, mice and even other small amphibians.

Size: 12 in (30 cm)

Range: North America: west coast

Habitat: fresh water

# Pacific giant salamander
*Dicamptodon ensatus*

Most salamanders are silent but this species can make a low-pitched cry. Adults live on land where they hide under logs and rocks. They are usually active at night when they feed on snails, slugs, insects and other small creatures. In spring the female lays about 100 eggs on a branch in water.

# Fire salamander
*Salamandra salamandra*

Bright markings warn that this salamander's body is covered with an unpleasant-tasting slime. This puts off most hunters that might otherwise try to catch it. Although it spends most of its life on land, it usually stays near water and prefers moist areas. Fire salamanders mate on land. The eggs then develop inside the female's body and about 10 months later she gives birth to up to 50 live young in water.

Size: 6–12 in (15–30 cm)

Range: central and southern Europe; north Africa; Middle East

Habitat: fresh water, deciduous forest

# Axolotl
## *Ambystoma mexicanum*

This unusual amphibian is now rare because so many have been collected for the pet trade and predatory fish have been introduced into the lake where it lives. Many axolotls remain as larvae with feathery gills all their lives.

Size: up to 11½ in (29 cm)
Range: Mexico: Lake Xochimilco
Habitat: fresh water

# Great crested newt
## *Triturus cristatus*

Size: 4–5½ in (10–14 cm)
Range: parts of Europe
Habitat: deciduous forest, fresh water

A large rough-skinned newt, the male develops a jagged crest on his back in the breeding season. Females are often larger than males, but they do not develop crests. Great crested newts feed on small invertebrates, small fish and other amphibians and their eggs.

# South American caecilian
## *Siphonops annulatus*

Size: 13¾ in (35 cm)
Range: South America, east of the Andes
Habitat: tropical forest, shrub, grassland, farmland

Caecilians are not salamanders but belong to a separate group of blind burrowing amphibians. This caecilian has a short thick body and spends most of its life underground, where it feeds on earthworms.

# Eastern newt
## *Notophthalmus viridescens*

Size: 2½–5½ in (6.5–14 cm)
Range: eastern North America
Habitat: fresh water, forest

This newt breeds in early spring. The female lays up to 400 eggs on water plants and larvae hatch two months later. After a few months of feeding and growing, the larvae turn into sub-adults called red efts, shown here. They leave the water and spend up to three years on land, feeding on insects.

Size: 12–29¼ in (30.5–74 cm)
Range: eastern U.S.A.
Habitat: fresh water

# Hellbender
## *Cryptobranchus alleganiensis*

Despite its fierce name, this large salamander is a harmless creature that hides under rocks in the water during the day. At night it comes out to hunt crayfish, snails and worms, which it finds by smell and touch rather than sight. In the fall, the female lays up to 450 eggs in a hollow made by the male on the stream bed.

# FROGS AND TOADS

There are more than 5,850 species of frogs and toads. All are very similar in appearance whatever their lifestyle. Typically, an adult frog or toad has long back legs, webbed toes and no tail. The skin is smooth or warty but always moist. Like all amphibians, frogs and toads are at home both on land and in fresh water and can swim, hop and even climb trees. Most feed on small creatures such as slugs, snails and insects, which they catch with their long sticky tongues.

Frogs and toads usually breed in water, laying eggs that hatch into tailed, swimming young known as tadpoles. The tadpoles live in water, breathing through feathery gills at the sides of the head and eating plants. As the tadpoles grow they lose their gills and tail and grow legs. Some weeks after hatching, they develop into tiny frogs.

Size: up to 1¼ in (3 cm)
Range: northern South America
Habitat: tropical evergreen forest

## Glass frog
*Sachatamia albomaculata*

This delicate little yellow-flecked glass frog lives in small trees and bushes, usually near running water. It has sticky disks on its toes that help it grip when climbing. The female lays her eggs in clusters on the underside of leaves overhanging water. When the tadpoles hatch they drop into the water below, where they complete their development.

Size: up to 2½ in (6 cm)
Range: northeastern South Africa
Habitat: forest, grassland, fresh water

## Natal ghost frog
*Hadromophryne natalensis*

This frog lives in fast-flowing mountain streams. The female lays her eggs in a pool or on wet gravel. Once hatched, the tadpoles move into the streams where they hold on to stones with their suckerlike mouths to stop themselves being swept away.

## African clawed toad
*Xenopus laevis*

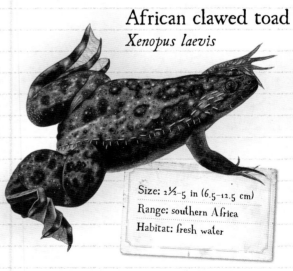

Size: 2½–5 in (6.5–12.5 cm)
Range: southern Africa
Habitat: fresh water

## Western spadefoot
*Spea hammondii*

An expert burrower, the western spadefoot toad has a hard spike on each back foot that helps it dig. It spends the day in its burrow and comes out at night to feed. The spadefoot waits for rain to fall before mating. Its eggs are laid in a rain-pool, hatching just three to four days later.

Size: 1¼–2½ in (3.5–6.5 cm)
Range: western U.S.A.
Habitat: temperate grassland, deciduous forest

This toad moves as fast in the water as any fish and is even able to swim backward. It uses the claws on its front feet to dig in the mud around pools and streams for food and eats any creatures it can find, even its own tadpoles. The toads mate in water, the male making a soft buzzing sound underwater to attract the female. The eggs are attached to water plants and hatch after seven days.

# Midwife toad
### Alytes obstetricans

The midwife toad hides by day under logs or in cracks in walls. At night it feeds on insects and other small creatures. It has unusual breeding habits. After the female has laid her eggs, the male takes them and carries them on his back while they develop. When they are ready to hatch, he places them in shallow water.

Size: 2 in (5 cm)
Range: Siberia, northeastern China, Korea
Habitat: farmland, high ground, fresh water

Size: up to 2 in (5 cm)
Range: western Europe
Habitat: inhabited areas, farmland, high ground, deciduous forest

# Oriental fire-bellied toad
### Bombina orientalis

The brilliantly colored rough skin of this toad gives off a milky substance that irritates the mouth and eyes of any attacker. The female fire-bellied toad lays her eggs on the underside of stones in water. The eggs are laid in small clumps of two to eight and are left to hatch by themselves.

Size: 4–9½ in (10–24 cm)
Range: South and Central America, introduced elsewhere
Habitat: inhabited areas, forest, farmland, fresh water

# Cane toad
### Rhinella marina

One of the largest toads in the world, the cane toad has been introduced to many areas outside its natural range. This is because it feeds on insects that destroy crops, such as sugar, and so helps to control them. In Australia, the cane toad has spread rapidly since being introduced and is now a pest, poisoning local species. Glands at the sides of its body make a poisonous liquid that causes irritation and even death in many of the reptiles and mammals that try to eat it. Eggs are laid in water, hatch into tadpoles up to a week later and grow rapidly.

## Pumpkin toadlet
*Brachycephalus ephippium*

This tiny frog often lives among dead leaves on the forest floor but may also hide in cracks in trees or rocks in dry weather. It has a bony shield on its back and may use this to block off the entrance of its hiding place to keep the atmosphere inside moist.

Size: up to ¾ in (2 cm)

Range: South America: southeastern Brazil

Habitat: tropical evergreen forest, high ground

Size: 1¼ in (3 cm)

Range: snowy mountains of southeastern Australia

Habitat: high ground, fresh water

## Corroboree frog
*Pseudophryne corroboree*

This critically endangered frog lives on land near water and shelters under logs or in a burrow that it digs itself. In summer, pairs dig a nesting burrow in a bog. The female lays up to 38 large eggs and one parent usually guards the eggs while they develop. The tadpoles normally stay in the eggs until there is enough rain to wash them into a creek, where they hatch at once.

Size: up to 1½ in (4 cm)

Range: South America

Habitat: tropical evergreen forest, high ground

## Marsupial frog
*Gastrotheca marsupiata*

The marsupial frog has an unusual way of caring for its eggs. As the female lays her eggs, the male helps her to pack them into a skin pouch on her back. A few weeks later, she finds some shallow water to release her brood. She uses the long toe on her back foot to open the pouch and free the tadpoles.

## Amazon horned frog
*Ceratophrys cornuta*

Size: 6 in (15 cm)

Range: northern and central South America

Habitat: forest, grassland, marsh

This horned frog is almost as broad as it is long and has a wide head and a large mouth. It has small eyes, with a lump on each upper eyelid. Even though it spends much of its life half-buried in the ground, its toes are partly webbed. It feeds on snails, small frogs and mice, and it probably eats tadpoles of its own species as well.

# Darwin's frog
*Rhinoderma darwinii*

This frog has unusual breeding habits. The female lays 20 to 45 eggs on land. Several males stand guard for up to 20 days until the young begin to move around inside the eggs. Each male then gathers up to 19 eggs in his mouth and lets them slide into the large sac under his chin. The tadpoles continue to develop inside the sac. When they have grown into tiny frogs the males let them go in water.

Size: 1¼ in (3 cm)
Range: southern Chile and southern Argentina
Habitat: temperate forest, rain forest

Size: up to 2 in (5 cm)
Range: most of Europe
Habitat: deciduous forest, conifer forest, fresh water

# Common tree frog
*Hyla arborea*

This smooth-skinned tree frog spends most of its life in trees. It can change color with amazing speed, turning from bright green in sunlight to dark gray in shade. The frogs breed in early summer and the female lays up to 2,000 eggs in water.

# Natterjack toad
*Epidalea calamita*

The male natterjack has the loudest call of any European toad. His croak carries 1¼ miles (2 km) or more. Natterjacks usually live on land but are often found near the sea and may even breed in salty water. Natterjacks mate at night and the female lays strings of up to 4,000 eggs in shallow water. The eggs hatch into tadpoles in about ten days.

Size: 2¾–4 in (7–10 cm)
Range: western and central Europe
Habitat: desert, coast, inhabited areas, farmland

# Spring peeper
*Pseudacris crucifer*

Size: ¾–1¼ in (2–3 cm)
Range: southeast Canada, U.S.A.
Habitat: deciduous forest, fresh water

Size: up to 1½ in (4 cm)
Range: South Africa
Habitat: fresh water

# Arum lily frog
*Hyperolius horstockii*

A good climber, this frog has large, sticky disks on each toe that help it grip. The undersides of its legs are orange but the rest of the body changes color according to conditions. In bright sun it is light cream and in shade it turns dark brown. Courting males often climb up on to arum lilies to call to females. They mate in water and eggs are laid on plants.

This agile frog can climb trees and leap to heights of more than 17 times its own body length. It feeds mainly on small spiders and insects — including flying insects, which it leaps into the air to catch. In the breeding season, males sit in trees courting females with their high-pitched whistle calls.

145

# Wallace's flying frog
*Rhacophorus nigropalmatus*

Size: 4 in (10 cm)

Range: Malaysia, Indonesia, Thailand

Habitat: tropical evergreen forest

This frog does not fly but glides from tree to tree in the forest. The large webbed feet and flaps of skin on its legs act like a parachute to help it float as far as 40 ft (12 m) through the air. It can even steer by changing the position of one or more of its feet. Little is known about this frog's breeding habits, but it is thought to lay its eggs in a mass of foam, which protects them while they incubate.

# South African rain frog
*Breviceps adspersus*

This plump frog has small legs and a sprinkling of warty lumps on its back. It spends much of its life in underground burrows, which it digs with its strong back feet. It comes above ground only during wet weather to hunt insects and other small creatures.

Size: 1¼ in (3 cm)

Range: southern Africa

Habitat: tropical grassland, deciduous forest, gardens

Size: 2 in (5 cm)

Range: Africa, south of the Sahara

Habitat: tropical grassland

# Termite frog
*Phrynomerus bifasciatus*

As its name suggests, termites and ants are the main food of this frog, which digs in burrows or climbs trees to find the insects. Its bright markings warn that its skin contains a nasty-tasting substance that irritates the mouths or skin of predators. Termite frogs breed in shallow pools. The jelly-coated eggs attach to plants or lie at the bottom of the water until they hatch.

# Eastern narrow-mouthed toad
*Gastrophryne carolinensis*

An excellent burrower, this small frog can disappear into the earth in a moment. It rests in a burrow during the day and comes out at night to hunt for ants and other insects. It breeds in summer when there is heavy rain.

Size: ¾–1½ in (2–4 cm)

Range: southeastern U.S.A.

Habitat: woodland, grassland, swamp

## Marsh frog
*Pelophylax ridibundus*

This noisy frog spends most of its life in water but comes out onto banks or to float on lily pads. It catches small invertebrates and also eats small birds and mammals. Males call night and day, particularly in the breeding season. The female lays thousands of eggs in several large clusters.

Size: up to 6 in (15 cm)

Range: Europe, western Asia

Habitat: fresh water

## Common frog
*Rana temporaria*

Size: up to 4 in (10 cm)

Range: Europe, east to Asia

Habitat: inhabited areas, farmland, deciduous forest, fresh water

Much of this frog's life is spent on land, feeding on insects, spiders and other small creatures. It breeds in spring, when males attract females with their deep croaking calls. They mate in water and the females lay clusters of 3,000 to 4,000 eggs.

Size: up to 1½ in (3.5 cm)

Range: Africa, south of Chad

Habitat: temperate grassland, farmland

## Mottled burrowing frog
*Hemisus marmoratus*

This frog has a small pointed head with a hard snout used for burrowing. It digs head first, pushing into the soil with its snout and clawing its way forward with its strong legs. The female lays her large eggs in a burrow. When the young hatch, she digs a tunnel for the tadpoles to swim to the nearest water.

## Northern leopard frog
*Rana pipiens*

This frog adapts to any watery home and eats almost any creatures it can find. If disturbed on land, it leaps away to water in a series of zigzagging jumps. In the breeding season, males attract females with low, grunting calls. Each female lays up to 7,600 eggs, which lie at the bottom of the water until they hatch about four weeks later.

Size: 2–4 in (5–11 cm)

Range: most of northern North America

Habitat: temperate grassland, high ground, fresh water

Size: 3½–8 in (9–20 cm)

Range: Canada, U.S.A., Mexico; introduced into South America, Europe, eastern Asia

Habitat: fresh water

## Bullfrog
*Rana catesbeiana*

The largest North American frog, the bullfrog lives in water but also spends time on land at the water's edge. It hunts at night, catching insects, fish, smaller frogs and even birds and snakes. It is a good jumper and can leap nine times its own length. In the breeding season the female lays up to 20,000 eggs in water.

# POISON-ARROW FROGS

These frogs live in the rain forests of Central and South America. Also known as poison-dart frogs, they are among the most colorful of all amphibians. For some species, their jewel-like appearance is a warning to predators to keep their distance because the skin contains extremely strong poisons. The frogs cannot inject their poison into enemies. It is produced in special glands and simply released into the skin, making a dangerous meal for a predator. But some poison-arrow frogs are not poisonous at all, but mimic the bright colors to scare off predators.

Among the most striking of all poison-arrow frogs is the dyeing poison frog (*Dendrobates tinctorius*) with its shiny blue markings. It is one of the poisonous species.

## STRAWBERRY POISON-ARROW FROG

The poison in the skin of the strawberry poison-arrow frog (*Oophaga pumilio*) may come partly from its food, such as small beetles and millipedes. Although deadly to its enemies, the frog's poison may have a value. Doctors are investigating its use as a medicine for heart-attack patients.

# CARING FOR YOUNG

The female flaming poison-arrow frog (*Oophaga pumilio*) looks after her tadpoles while they develop into frogs. She carries them up into a tree and places them in groups of about four in tiny pools of water contained in plants. She checks on them every few days and even gives them some unfertilized eggs to eat. The young are not poisonous at this stage, so they are very easy for other creatures to catch and eat.

1. The eggs are laid on a leaf.

2. Once hatched, the tadpoles wriggle on to the mother's back.

3. She carries them to a leaf-pool high in a tree.

## SMALL BUT LETHAL

The golden poison-arrow frog is one of the most deadly of this group. It is only 2 in (5 cm) long, but its poison is at least 20 times as strong as that of any other frog and can be lethal for humans even to touch. It is one of only three species traditionally used by local tribesmen for tipping hunting arrows. The arrow is simply rubbed over the frog's body and then it is ready to use. The poison remains strong for over a year.

# POISONS AND VENOMS

Many animals use poison for protection against enemies. By being unpleasant to eat, small creatures such as toads and caterpillars are able to defend themselves against larger creatures. Many have colorful markings that serve as a warning to others — predators learn to link these bright colors with the unpleasant taste and stay away. Venom is injected directly into the body, and makes a deadly weapon. Some snakes and spiders deliver a venomous bite to their prey with their fangs, while scorpions have venomous stings.

## SNAKE

The rattlesnake uses venom to kill its prey. As it bites the animal, venom passes from glands in the head, through special canals in the fangs at the front of the jaw into its prey. The snake warns potential predators of its threat by making a rattling sound with its tail.

Rattlesnake

## TOAD

The Oriental fire-bellied toad has small poison glands all over its body that produce an unpleasant-tasting substance. If threatened, the toad reveals the bright scarlet markings on the underside of its body to warn off its attacker.

Oriental fire-bellied toad

# SPIDER

The funnel-web spider delivers a venom so strong that that it can kill humans. The spider digs a burrow and lines the entrance with trip-wires made of silk. It hides in the burrow and feels for vibrations in the silk with its legs. When it senses an animal brushing the silk, the spider pounces, burying its fangs into its victim and injecting it with venom.

Funnel-web spider

# CATERPILLAR

The monarch butterfly caterpillar feeds on the poisonous milkweed plant. The poison in the plant does not affect the caterpillar but is stored in its body and makes the caterpillar taste extremely unpleasant. Its bold stripes warn predators to leave it alone. Even as a butterly, this insect is poisonous.

Monarch butterfly caterpillar

# FISH

THERE ARE ABOUT 32,500 SPECIES of fish, more than any other type of vertebrate. They range from tiny species such as the pygmy goby, which is only ¹/₃ in (1 cm) long, to giants such as the whale shark, which can measure as much as 40 ft (12 m). Most species of fish can live either in the sea or in fresh water, but not in both habitats. Some fish eat aquatic plants, others filter tiny animals from the water. Many are active, fast-moving hunters, while some lie hidden on the seabed and wait for prey to come close.

# WHAT IS A FISH?

Fish were the first vertebrates — animals with backbones — to live on Earth. The earliest fish lived about 440–500 million years ago. All fish, except for the group that includes lampreys, have a spine made of bones called vertebrae, although in sharks and rays this is made of cartilage.

Mackerel

Emperor angelfish

Coloration helps many fish hide from their enemies. The angelfish's markings and the mackerel's light belly and darker back break up their outlines and make them harder to see.

## STRUCTURE OF A FISH

There are three main groups of fish and their relatives. The most primitive group includes the lampreys. These fishlike animals have no jaws, only suckerlike mouths. The second group includes all the sharks and rays. These are known as cartilaginous fish because their skeletons are made of a gristly substance called cartilage, not bone. The third and largest group contains the bony fish. As their name suggests, these fish have skeletons made of bone.

### JAWLESS FISHLIKE ANIMALS

Tail fin

Fin rays

Tongue

Mouth

Teeth

River lamprey

Suckerlike mouth

### CARTILAGINOUS FISH

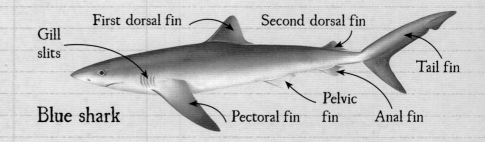

First dorsal fin

Second dorsal fin

Gill slits

Tail fin

Pelvic fin

Blue shark

Pectoral fin

Anal fin

## EGGS AND YOUNG

Adult

Laying eggs

Juvenile

Eggs

Larva

Most female fish lay large numbers of eggs into the water. Males then release sperm to fertilize the eggs, which float in surface waters or sink to the bottom. The eggs hatch into larvae, many of which are eaten by predators. Some survive to become juveniles, with a more adultlike body. The juveniles feed and grow into adult fish.

Brood pouch

There are many exceptions to the normal way of breeding in fish. A male seahorse develops eggs in a small pouch on its body until they hatch.

## Gills of bony fish

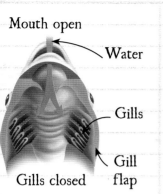

Mouth open

Water

Gills

Gill flap

Gills closed

Mouth closed

Gills open

## Gills of shark

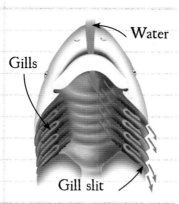

Water

Gills

Gill slit

# HOW FISH BREATHE

Fish breathe through special structures called gills at the sides of the head. These are made up of large numbers of delicate plates, packed with blood vessels. As water flows over the gills, molecules of oxygen pass into the blood, which is then carried around the body. The gills of a bony fish have one combined opening to the outside, which is covered by a protective flap. In sharks and rays, each gill has its own exit to the water.

## BONY FISH

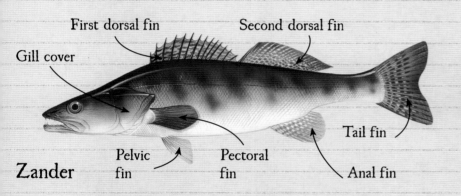

First dorsal fin

Second dorsal fin

Gill cover

Tail fin

Zander

Pelvic fin

Pectoral fin

Anal fin

Barracuda

Pufferfish

# FISH MOUTHS

The mouths of fish are adapted to suit the food that they eat. Hunting fish, such as the barracuda, have long snouts and sharp teeth for seizing prey. The angler uses its wide mouth for engulfing prey that it lures near with its fishing rod. Many, such as the parrotfish, have beaklike mouths for crushing hard-shelled creatures. The herring filters plankton through special structures called gill rakers.

## Bony fish skeleton

Dorsal fins

Skull

Tail fin

Pectoral fins

Jaw

Bones over gills

Vertebrae

Pelvic fins

Anal fin

Like all vertebrates, fish have a bony skull and a movable lower jaw. Special bones cover the gills on each side of a fish's head. In the fins there are small bones called fin rays. These bones keep the fins stiff and spread out.

Angler fish

Herring

# LAMPREYS, SHARKS AND RAYS

Lampreys are primitive fishlike animals that have no true jaws. They have sucking disks for feeding on the blood of other creatures. Sharks, sawfishes, rays and their relatives have skeletons made of cartilage, not bone. There are about 1,200 known species of cartilaginous fish and all live in the sea. Most are active hunters with sharp-edged teeth. A few of the largest, such as the whale shark, are not hunters — instead they filter small creatures from the water.

Size: up to 25 ft (7.6 m)

Range: temperate and tropical oceans

Habitat: coastal waters

## Common sawfish
*Pristis pectinata*

The sawfish has a long bladelike snout studded with at least 24 large teeth on each side. It lives on the seabed in shallow water and uses its saw to dig in the sand and mud for small invertebrates to eat. It also swims into schools of smaller fish and lashes its toothed saw from side to side to stun prey.

## Lesser spotted dogfish
*Scyliorhynus canicula*

Size: 15½–25½ in (40–65 cm)

Range: northeast Atlantic Ocean

Habitat: coastal waters

A small shark, the sandy dogfish lives on sandy and muddy seabeds, where it feeds on fish and bottom-living invertebrates. The female's eggs are laid in hard cases that lodge among weeds or other objects. The young dogfish hatch 5 to 11 months later and are about 4 in (10 cm) long.

Size: 9–13 ft (2.5–4 m)

Range: Atlantic, Pacific and Indian oceans

Habitat: all tropical and temperate seas

## Mako shark
*Isurus oxyrinchus*

A powerful fish with a slender body and pointed head, the mako is a fast aggressive hunter. It feeds on surface-living fish such as tuna and mackerel. The female gives birth to live young, which develop inside her body.

## Smooth hammerhead
*Sphyrna zygaena*

Size: 14 ft (4.3 m)

Range: all tropical and temperate seas

Habitat: oceanic

The hammerhead has a broad head that extends to each side. There is one eye and one nostril on either side of the elongated head. This spacing of eyes and nostrils may improve the shark's sight and sense of smell.

## Great white shark
### Carcharodon carcharias

A large aggressive hunter equipped with jagged triangular teeth, this shark kills seals, dolphins, and even other sharks. It also scavenges dead animals and waste. White sharks have been involved in a number of attacks on humans.

Size: 35½ in (90 cm)

Range: Atlantic coasts and Mediterranean Sea

Habitat: fresh water, coastal waters

## Sea lamprey
### Petromyzon marinus

The adult sea lamprey is a blood-feeding parasite. It has no true jaws and uses its sucking disklike mouth to attach itself to its victim so firmly that it is almost impossible to remove. A special substance in its mouth keeps the host's blood flowing so the lamprey can feed. Victims often die from blood loss.

Size: 19½ ft (6 m)

Range: Atlantic, Pacific and Indian oceans

Habitat: all tropical and temperate seas

Size: 39½ ft (12 m)

Range: all tropical and temperate seas

Habitat: oceanic, coral reefs

## Whale shark
### Rhincodon typus

The whale shark is the biggest of all fish. Despite its size, it is not a fierce hunter and eats animal plankton that it filters from the water. The shark opens its mouth and takes in a rush of water, which contains lots of small creatures. The water flows out through the gill slits, leaving the plankton in the mouth.

Size: 17 ft (5.2 m) long; 22 ft (6.7 m) wide

Range: all tropical and temperate seas

Habitat: coastal waters

## Giant manta
### Manta birostris

With its huge pointed pectoral fins, the manta is the biggest of the rays. Like the whale shark, this giant feeds mostly on tiny animal plankton, which it filters from the water. It also eats fish. The manta often basks near the surface with the tips of its pectoral fins out of the water.

157

# SKATES, RAYS AND SEABED SHARKS

There are more than 650 different species of skate and ray. Most have a very broad, flattened body and huge winglike fins, giving them a diamond shape. As they swim, the fish flap their fins and appear almost to fly through the water. Skates and rays spend much of their lives on or near the seafloor. Their flat bodies make them hard to see. Openings called spiracles on the upper surface of the head allow them to breathe. Sharks are thought of as fast swimmers that live near the surface, but some, such as horn sharks and carpet sharks, lurk on the bottom.

Camouflaged by its coloring and the many flaps of skin at the sides of its body, the carpet shark lies on the seabed waiting for prey to come near.

## SKATE

The skate's flattened body is covered with tiny spines and a line of larger spines runs down the middle of the tail. The spines help the skate defend itself against attackers. The female lays her eggs in a leathery case with long tips at each corner, which is left on the seabed. When the young hatch, they are about 7¾ in (20 cm) long.

Sting ray

Eagle ray

# STING RAY AND EAGLE RAY

Both of these fish have long whiplike tails that they use to lash out at enemies to defend themselves. The spines are linked to venom glands and can cause serious injury to humans. Rays have flattened teeth with which they crush the hard shells of crabs and mollusks.

# HORN SHARK

This shark has a long tapering body and a large blunt head. It gets its name from the sharp spines in front of the fins on its back. Active at night, it hunts for prey such as sea urchins, crabs and worms on the seabed. It crushes hard-shelled food with the large flat teeth at the back of its jaws.

# NURSE SHARK

A slow-moving bottom dweller, the nurse shark has lots of short sharp teeth, ideal for crushing shellfish. The sensitive fleshy whiskers on its flattened head help it find hidden prey on the seabed. This shark spends much of its time on the seabed and tends to crawl away if disturbed, rather than swim.

# STURGEONS, GARS AND RELATIVES

All of these fish live in fresh water, but most sturgeons spend part of their life in the sea. They travel into rivers to lay their eggs and the young remain there for several years, feeding and growing before making their first journey to the sea, where they spend their adult lives. Sturgeons are increasingly rare, partly because humans collect the female's unshed eggs to eat as a food called caviar. Gars, bichirs and bowfins are separate groups of fish. They generally occur in areas where there is a dense growth of water plants. Most goldeyes, pirarucus and elephant-snout fish live in the southern half of the world, but there are two species of goldeyes in North America. They all eat fish and insects.

## Bowfin
### Amia calva

This fish lives in slow-moving waters with dense plant life. In spring, the male clears a hollow in the riverbed, and makes a nest of plants roots and gravel. The female then lays her eggs and the male guards them for eight to ten days until they hatch out.

Size: up to 3¼ ft (1 m)
Range: northeastern U.S.A., southeastern Canada
Habitat: fresh water

## Mottled bichir
### Polypterus weeksii

A long-bodied fish covered with hard, diamond-shaped scales, the bichir lives among water plants at the edges of rivers and lakes. It has an unusual dorsal fin made up of small flaglike sections, each supported by a bony ray. The bichir feeds mainly on fish, frogs and newts.

Size: 15¾ in (40 cm)
Range: Africa: central basin of the Congo River
Habitat: fresh water

## Longnose gar
### Lepisosteus osseus

As its name suggests, this gar has extremely long jaws, which are studded with sharp teeth. It hides among water plants, waiting for fish and shellfish to come near. It then dashes forward and seizes its prey. It lays eggs in spring in shallow water. The eggs are sticky and attach themselves to water weed or stones so they are not carried away by the water current.

Size: up to 2 m (6½ f)
Range: North and Central America
Habitat: fresh water

Size: 31½ in (80 cm)

Range: Africa: Nile River and East African lakes

Habitat: fresh water

# Goldeye
*Hiodon alosoides*

The goldeye belongs to a small family of fish known as mooneyes. They have big golden eyes that provide good vision at night, when they are generally active. The goldeye has a large number of small fine teeth and it feeds mainly on insects and their larvae as well as on fish.

# Elephant-snout fish
*Mormyrus kannume*

This fish gets its name from its long trunklike snout. The muscles along its body are adapted to produce weak electric charges that set up an electric field in the water around the body. The fish can sense any disturbances in this field, which helps it find prey at night or in murky water.

Size: 11¾–15¾ in (30–40 cm)

Range: North America

Habitat: fresh water

Size: up to 13 ft (4 m)

Range: Amazon River basin

Habitat: fresh water

# Pirarucu
*Arapaima gigas*

One of the largest freshwater fish in the world, South America's pirarucu may weigh up to 440 lb (200 kg). It has large scales on its body but none on its head. Other fish and insect larvae are its main food. Pirarucus breed in sandy-bottomed water. The eggs are laid in a hollow in the riverbed and the parents guard them until they hatch.

# Common sturgeon
*Acipenser sturio*

Sturgeons spend most of their lives in the sea, feeding on worms and other invertebrates, but they lay their eggs in rivers. In spring, sturgeons migrate to rivers where each female lays thousands of sticky black eggs. The eggs hatch in about a week. The young fish remain in the river for about three years before traveling to the sea.

Size: up to 6½ ft (2 m)

Range: Mississippi River

Habitat: fresh water

# Paddlefish
*Polyodon spathula*

The paddlefish is a relative of the sturgeon. It swims with its large mouth open and uses the comblike structures in its mouth to catch small creatures in the water. Eggs are laid in spring. Newly hatched fish do not have long snouts, but these develop in two or three weeks.

Size: 10 ft (3 m)

Range: European coastline

Habitat: fresh water, coastal waters

161

# EELS, TARPONS AND HERRING

**M**ost of these fish live in the sea, but some eels and tarpons spend at least part of their lives in fresh water. There are more than 800 species of eel. They live in all oceans, except in polar areas, and there are also a few freshwater species. All have slender bodies and long fins on the back and belly. The herring group includes about 390 species, some of which are important food fish, such as herrings themselves, sardines and anchovies. Most are marine and live in schools in surface waters in the open sea or near coasts. The tarpons belong to a small family of marine fish, which are related to eels and herrings. They are slender-bodied fish with deeply forked tails.

## Sardine
### *Sardina pilchardus*

The sardine is similar to the herring but has a more rounded body and larger scales. Shoals of sardines swim in surface waters, feeding on animal plankton. Sardines are a valued food fish, and large numbers are caught every year.

Size: 9¾ in (25 cm)

Range: European and northwest African coasts

Habitat: coastal waters, oceanic

## Alewife
### *Alosa pseudoharengus*

A member of the herring group, the alewife feeds mostly on plankton and small fish. Although it lives in the sea, it swims into rivers to mate and lay its eggs, so it is often found in fresh water. Some alewife spend all their lives in lakes and these are only about half the size of sea-living alewives.

Size: 15 in (38 cm)

Range: Atlantic coast of North America

Habitat: fresh water, coastal waters

Size: 4–7¾ ft (1.2–2.4 m)

Range: Atlantic Ocean, Caribbean Sea, eastern Pacific Ocean via the Panama Canal

Habitat: coastal waters, fresh water

## Atlantic herring
### *Clupea harengus*

Herring has long been an important food for humans, and large numbers of these fish are caught every year. In the sea, herring are also preyed on by birds, other fish, dolphins and seals. Herring themselves feed on plankton, small crustaceans and fish.

## Tarpon
### *Megalops atlanticus*

A strong, fast-swimming fish, the tarpon is related to eels and herrings. It feeds on many types of fish and on crabs. The female lays millions of eggs in coastal waters, but many of the larvae drift into rivers where they remain until they grow larger.

Size: 15¾ in (40 cm)

Range: North Atlantic Ocean

Habitat: coastal waters, oceanic

Size: 4 ft (1.2 m)

Range: worldwide except tropical waters

Habitat: deep sea

## Spiny-eel
*Notacanthus chemnitzii*

The spiny-eel has a long slender body but it is not a true eel. It has short spines on its back and belly. Little is known about this deep-sea fish, but it is thought to feed head down on the seabed, eating bottom-living animals such as sea anemones.

Size: 3¼–4 ft (1–1.2 m)

Range: all tropical and temperate seas

Habitat: oceanic

## Slender snipe eel
*Nemichthys scolopaceus*

This deep-sea eel has an extremely long thin body with fins that run almost its whole length. It has narrow beaklike jaws and sharp backward-facing teeth that it uses to trap prey such as fish and crustaceans.

Size: 4½ ft (1.3 m)

Range: northeast Atlantic waters and Mediterranean Sea

Habitat: coastal waters, coral reefs

## Moray
*Muraena helena*

Like all of the 200 or so different species of moray eels found in warm seas, this moray has a scaleless, boldly patterned body, powerful jaws and strong sharp teeth. A fierce hunter, the moray usually hides among underwater rocks with only its head showing, watching out for prey such as fish, squid and cuttlefish.

Size: 8¾ ft (2.7 m)

Range: coastal waters of North Atlantic Ocean

Habitat: coastal waters

## Conger eel
*Conger conger*

This eel is common on rocky North Atlantic shores. It usually lives in shallow water, where it hides among rocks and comes out to find prey such as fish and octopus. It travels to deeper water to mate and lay its eggs. The eggs hatch out into small transparent larvae that drift in the sea for a year or two before they develop into small eels.

Size: 19¾–39½ in (50–100 cm)

Range: North Atlantic Ocean, Mediterranean Sea

Habitat: fresh water, coastal waters, oceanic

## European eel
*Anguilla anguilla*

Young eels live in fresh water where they feed in insects, crustaceans and fish. When they are ready to breed they swim to the sea where they mate, lay their eggs and then die. The eggs hatch and the larvae drift in surface waters for about three years. They then swim into rivers and the cycle starts again.

# CARP, BREAM AND PIRANHAS

Carp, bream, roach and their relatives, such as the bigmouth buffalo and the white sucker, belong to a group of about 3,250 freshwater fish. They dominate the streams, rivers and lakes of Europe, northern Asia and North America and are also found in Africa. Most have scales on the body, but not on the head, and a single fin on the back. Pacus and piranhas belong to a separate group of freshwater fish, most of which live in lakes and rivers in Central and South America. Some relatives of the piranhas also live in Africa. Meat-eating piranhas have sharp teeth for chopping flesh from their victims.

## Common carp
### Cyprinus carpio

The carp is a sturdy, deep-bodied fish. It usually lives in slow-moving water with plenty of plant life and feeds mostly on crustaceans, insect larvae and some plants. The eggs are laid in shallow water and stick to plants until they hatch.

Size: 20-3¼ in (50-100 cm)

Range: parts of Europe and Asia; introduced worldwide

Habitat: fresh water

Size: up to 27½ in (70 cm)

Range: Europe and western to central Asia

Habitat: fresh water

## Tench
### Tinca tinca

A relative of the carp, the tench has a thickset body and rounded fins. The scales on the body are extremely small and covered with mucus. It usually feeds on the river or lake bed on insect larvae, crustaceans and mollusks. Tench breed in shallow water, shedding their eggs onto plants.

## Goldfish
### Carassius auratus

The colorful goldfish belongs to the carp family. In the wild, it lives in ponds and lakes where there are plenty of water plants, but it is also bred for keeping in aquariums and ornamental pools.

Size: up to 12 in (30 cm)

Range: Europe and Asia; introduced worldwide

Habitat: fresh water

## White sucker
### Catostomus commersonii

This bottom-living fish has thick, suckerlike lips and feeds on insect larvae, crustaceans, mollusks and some plants. The eggs are laid at night in gravel-bottomed streams. They sink to the bottom and stay among the gravel until they hatch.

Size: 12-20 in (30-52 cm)

Range: North America

Habitat: fresh water

Size: 27½ in (70 cm)
Range: South America
Habitat: fresh water

# Red piranha
## *Pygocentrus nattereri*

The piranha is not a large fish but swims in such large shoals that together they can catch and kill animals much larger than themselves. Usually, however, they feed on fish, seeds and fruit. Piranhas have strong jaws and razor-sharp teeth.

Size: up to 11¾ in (30 cm)
Range: northern South America
Habitat: fresh water

# Pacu
## *Colossoma macropomum*

Not all piranhas are fierce hunters. Some are plant-eaters, such as the pacu. This fish feeds on the many fruits and seeds that fall from the forest trees bordering the rivers where it lives. It uses its strong teeth to crush them to a pulp. Plant-eating piranhas are slower swimmers than the hunting species and do not have such powerful jaws.

Size: up to 3¼ ft (1 m)
Range: North America
Habitat: fresh water

# Bigmouth buffalo
## *Ictiobus cyprinellus*

This powerful fish feeds on crustaceans and insect larvae and on some plant material. In spring, adults gather in shallow water where females lay as many as 500,000 eggs. The young fish stay in the shallow breeding area for some months, feeding on plankton.

Size: 10 in (25 cm)
Range: Europe and western Asia
Habitat: fresh water

# Bream
## *Abramis brama*

This fish uses its a tubelike mouth to gather insect larvae, snails and worms from the river bottom. It lives in shoals and usually feeds at night. Bream breed in late spring of summer in shallow water. The eggs stick to water plants and hatch in about 12 days.

Size: 10 in (25 cm)
Range: Europe, northern Asia
Habitat: fresh water

# Roach
## *Rutilus rutilus*

This common river fish eats insects and their larvae as well as mollusks, crustaceans and plants. It, in turn, is food for many fish-eating birds and mammals. Roach breed in shallow water, where the eggs stick to plants. The young hatch in about two weeks.

# CATFISH AND RELATIVES

There are more than 2,400 species in the catfish group, ranging from tiny fish a few centimetres long to giant forms measuring 5 ft (1.5 m) or more and weighing as much as 100 lb (45 kg). Most live in rivers and freshwater lakes in the warmer parts of the world, but there are some sea-living species. Most catfish live in South America.

These fish do not have ordinary scales, but some have bony plates which cover their bodies like armor. They are bottom-dwellers and find their food by touch and taste, digging in the mud of a river or lake bed until the sensitive whiskers, or barbels, around their mouth find prey.

## Cascarudo
### *Callichthys callichthys*

The body of this little catfish is covered with overlapping bony plates, which help protect it from enemies. The male fish makes a nest for the eggs among floating plants by blowing bubbles of air and mucus to form a foamy mass.

Size: up to 6½ in (17 cm)
Range: South America
Habitat: fresh water

Size: 18 in (45 cm)
Range: southern and eastern Australia
Habitat: fresh water

## Tandan catfish
### *Tandanus tandanus*

The fins of this catfish run right around its body from its back to its belly. The spines on its back and on its pectoral fins can cause painful wounds if touched. Sensory whiskers, or barbels, around the mouth help it find food, mainly mussels, prawns and worms.

## Candirú
### *Vandellia cirrhosa*

A tiny, delicate catfish, the candirú is a parasite — it lives on the blood of other fish. With small fish, it simply bites the skin and then feeds, but it may get inside the gill system of larger fish and stay there sucking blood. It is usually active at night and buries itself in the riverbed when not feeding.

Size: 1 in (2.5 cm)
Range: South America: Amazon River basin
Habitat: fresh water

Size: up to 3¼ ft (1 m)
Range: South America
Habitat: fresh water

## Barred sorubim
### *Pseudoplatystoma fasciatum*

This South American catfish has a long snout and a slender body, marked with dark stripes and blotches. It spends most of its life on the river bed where it feeds on invertebrate animals. The sensitive whiskers, or barbels, around its mouth help it find food.

Size: 5 ft (1.5 m)
Range: U.S.A., Mexico
Habitat: fresh water

## Blue catfish
### *Ictalurus furcatus*

This catfish, one of the largest in North America, can grow to more than 100 lb (45 kg) and is a valuable food fish. It often lives in fast-moving water, even waterfalls and rapids, and feeds on fish and crayfish. Its eggs are laid on the bottom and both parents guard the nest and then the young.

Size: 11¾ in (30 cm)
Range: Indonesia; introduced to neighboring areas
Habitat: fresh water

## Walking catfish
### *Clarias batrachus*

This catfish lives in ponds or temporary pools that may disappear in long dry periods. When this happens, the fish can move over land to another pool, making snakelike movements of its body and using its pectoral fins as "legs." It feeds on fish and invertebrate animals.

## Glass catfish
### *Kryptopterus bicirrhis*

As its name suggests, this fish is transparent and many of the internal organs can be seen through the body. Unlike most catfish, it moves in small schools in surface waters during the day.

Size: 4 in (10 cm)
Range: Cambodia, Indonesia, Laos, Malaysia, Thailand, Vietnam
Habitat: fresh water

## Wels
### *Silurus glanis*

A large catfish, the wels has a broad head and long anal fin. It lives in slow-moving or still waters and is usually active at night, hiding in plants near the bottom during the day. Fish are its main food, but it also eats frogs, birds and even small mammals such as water voles.

Size: 11¾ in (30 cm)
Range: western Atlantic Ocean
Habitat: coastal waters

## Sea catfish
### *Ariopsis felis*

This sea-living catfish is most active at night when it feeds on crabs, shrimp and fish. It breeds in summer and as the eggs are laid, the male takes them in his mouth, where they incubate. He cannot eat during this time. The young fish may also swim into the male's mouth for safety after hatching.

Size: up to 10 ft (3 m)
Range: Europe and western Asia
Habitat: fresh water

# ELECTRIC EEL, SALMON, HATCHETFISH AND PIKE

The electric eel is one of about 39 species in its family. It is not a true eel but has a similar long body and is able to produce electric charges. In a separate group of about 73 species is the hatchetfish, a deep-sea fish which has light-producing organs on its body. These help the hatchetfish recognise its own kind in the darkness of the deep sea. The salmon family contains about 222 species which live in fresh water and the sea. Some migrate from the sea into rivers to lay eggs. The smelts belong to a different group of sea fish but they, too, travel up rivers to breed. Pike are a small group of freshwater fish.

Size: 2¾ in (7 cm)

Range: warm and tropical areas of all oceans

Habitat: oceanic, deep sea

Size: 5 ft (1.5 m)

Range: central Asia, Europe, Russia, Alaska, Canada, northern U.S.A.

Habitat: fresh water

## Northern pike
### *Esox lucius*

A fierce predator, the pike lurks among plants, keeping watch for any prey. Young pike feed mainly on invertebrates, but adults catch other fish and even birds and mammals. Female pike are larger than males and may weigh 50 lb (23 kg) or more.

## Lovely hatchetfish
### *Argyropelecus aculeatus*

This fish lives in water 330–2,000 ft (100–600 m) deep, but at night it comes up near the surface to feed on plankton. On its belly, rows of light-producing organs give out a pale blue light. This confuses predators about its size and shape, making it harder to catch.

## Electric eel
### *Electrophorus electricus*

Special muscles in the electric eel's body release high-voltage electric charges into the water. The eel uses these shocks to kill prey, usually other fish, or to defend itself from enemies. The charge can even give a human a severe shock.

Size: 7 in (17 cm)

Range: North Atlantic Ocean

Habitat: fresh water, coastal waters

## Smelt
### *Osmerus eperlanus*

Smelts are sea-living fish, but in winter adult fish leave the sea to travel up rivers to breed. In spring the females shed their eggs on to gravel on the riverbed or onto plants. When the young fish are large enough, they swim to the sea where they grow and mature.

Size: up to 7¾ ft (2.4 m)

Range: South America: Orinoco and Amazon river basins

Habitat: fresh water

Size: 18 in (46 cm)
Range: northern Europe
Habitat: fresh water

Size: up to 33 in (84 cm)
Range: North Pacific Ocean
Habitat: fresh water, coastal
waters, oceanic

# Grayling
*Thymallus thymallus*

A member of the salmon family, the grayling has a high, saillike fin on its back and a forked tail. It eats insects and their larvae as well as crustaceans and mollusks. In spring, the female grayling makes a hollow in shallow water for her eggs. The eggs hatch three to four weeks after laying.

# Sockeye salmon
*Oncorhynchus nerka*

Sockeye salmon live in the ocean until they are two to four years old. They then enter rivers and swim to the breeding grounds where they were hatched, sometimes as far as 1,000 miles (1,600 km) inland. After laying their eggs, the adult salmon die. The young spend up to three years in fresh water before migrating to the sea.

Size: up to 3¼ ft (1 m)
Range: western North America;
introduced worldwide
Habitat: fresh water, coastal
waters

# Rainbow trout
*Oncorhynchus mykiss*

Another member of the salmon family and now farmed in large quantities, this trout is an important food fish. In the wild, rainbow trout live in rivers and feed on insect larvae, mollusks and crustaceans. In spring, the female makes a shallow nest and lays her eggs, which are then fertilized and covered over by the male.

Size: up to 5 ft (1.5 m)
Range: North Atlantic Ocean
Habitat: fresh water, coastal
waters, oceanic

# Arctic char
*Salvelinus alpinus alpinus*

This member of the salmon family spends most of its life in polar seas, feeding on fish and mollusks. When ready to breed, it swims into rivers, and lays its eggs among gravel on the riverbed. The young eventually make their way back to the sea. Some Arctic char live in lakes.

# Atlantic salmon
*Salmo salar*

Like the sockeye salmon, most Atlantic salmon swim into rivers to breed. The female makes a shallow nest on the riverbed in winter and lays her eggs, which are fertilized by the male. The eggs hatch the following spring and the young spend two to six years in the river before going to sea.

Size: 16 in (40 cm)
Range: Arctic and North
Atlantic oceans
Habitat: fresh water, coastal
waters, oceanic

# COD, ANGLERS AND CUSK-EELS

There are about 610 species of fish in the cod group. All but five live in the sea, mostly in the northern hemisphere. They include popular food fish such as cod, haddock, hake and ling. Many have a sensory whisker, or barbel, on the chin, which helps them find prey on the seabed. The anglers include about 320 species, all with a large head, a wide mouth and rows of sharp teeth. Most have a spine on the head, which they use as a lure to attract prey. Cusk-eels are a group of small, eel-like fish.

## New Providence cusk-eel
*Lucifuga spelaeotes*

This little eel-like fish is mostly known from a few fresh water pools in the Bahamas. It has a broad flattened head and a tapering body with a continuous back, tail and anal fin. Most of its head is bare, but small scales cover its body.

Size: up to 4¼ in (11 cm)

Range: Bahamas and western Atlantic Ocean

Habitat: fresh water, coastal waters

Size: 5–6½ ft (1.5–2 m)

Range: northeastern Atlantic Ocean, Arctic Ocean

Habitat: oceanic, deep sea

## Ling
*Molva molva*

The ling is most common in rocky-bottomed waters where it eats fish and large crustaceans. Although usually a deepwater fish, it may live in shallower areas where there are rocks. It breeds in spring and summer and one female may lay as many as 60 million eggs.

Size: 35½–39½ in (90–100 cm)

Range: North Atlantic Ocean

Habitat: deep sea

## Roughhead grenadier
*Macrourus berglax*

A relative of the cod, this deep-sea fish has a large head and a tapering tail. Its body scales are rough and toothed. Males make loud sounds by vibrating the swim bladder (a gas-filled sac inside the body) with special muscles.

Size: 16 in (40 cm)

Range: Canada, northern U.S.A., northern Europe, Asia

Habitat: fresh water

## Burbot
*Lota lota*

One of the few freshwater fish in the cod group, the burbot hides among water plants by day and comes out at dawn and dusk to feed. Adults eat fish, crustaceans and insects; young feed on insect larvae and small shrimps. Eggs are laid at night in winter — up to three million eggs per female.

Size: 14 in (35 cm)

Range: North Atlantic Ocean

Habitat: coastal waters

# Haddock
## *Melanogrammus aeglefinus*

The haddock is a member of the cod family and feeds on bottom-living worms, mollusks and brittlestars as well as fish. It gathers in shoals to spawn and the eggs are left to float in the surface waters until they hatch. Young haddock often shelter among the tentacles of large jellyfish.

# Atlantic footballfish
## *Himantolophus groenlandicus*

This deep-sea angler has a round body studded with bony plates, each with a central spine. On its head is a lure, which carries a light-producing organ. It uses this lure to attract prey in the darkness of the deep sea.

Size: up to 60 cm (23½ in)

Range: all temperate and tropical oceans

Habitat: deep sea

Size: 4 ft (1.2 m)

Range: North Atlantic Ocean

Habitat: coastal waters

# Atlantic cod
## *Gadus morhua*

The cod has three fins on its back, a long whisker, or barbel, on its chin and a mouth lined with sharp teeth. It usually swims in schools in surface waters but will search for food such as fish and worms on the seabed. It is an extremely valuable food fish.

Size: 3¼–6½ ft (1–2 m)

Range: European and North African coasts

Habitat: coastal waters, deep sea

# Angler
## *Lophius piscatorius*

The angler, or monkfish, has a special spine on its head, tipped with a flap of skin which it uses as a fishing lure. The fish lies on the seabed and moves its lure to attract other fish. When prey comes within reach, the angler opens its huge mouth and water flows in, with the prey.

Size: up to 35½ in (90 cm)

Range: North Pacific and Arctic oceans

Habitat: coastal waters, oceanic, deep sea

# Alaska pollock
## *Theragra chalcogramma*

The pollock has a long tapering body, with three fins on its back and two on its underside. Its head and mouth are large and it has bigger eyes than most other cod. Unlike most cod, it feeds in midwaters, catching crustaceans and small fish.

# PERCHLIKE FISH

This is the largest and most varied of all groups of fish and species live in almost every watery habitat. It includes more than 10,000 types of fish such as the sea bass, cichlids, gobies and wrasses. They have a wide range of body forms and include fish as different as the barracuda, angelfish, swordfish and Siamese fightingfish. Despite their differences, all perchlike fish have one or two fins on the back and most have pelvic fins close to the head. The pelvic fins usually have a spine and five rays.

## Perch
### Perca fluviatilis

Barred markings camouflage this fish among water plants. Perch live in slow-moving water, feed on fish and breed in shallow water in spring. Long strings of eggs hatch in about eight days and the young fish feed on plankton.

Size: 10 in (25 cm)

Range: Europe and parts of Asia

Habitat: fresh water

Size: up to 3¼ in (8 cm)

Range: central U.S.A.

Habitat: fresh water

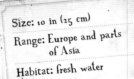

## Orangethroat darter
### Etheostoma spectabile

This little member of the perch family feeds on insects and animal plankton. A breeding male has an orange throat and breast, while females have pale throats. The male chooses a nest site and guards the eggs once they are laid.

## Greater amberjack
### Seriola dumerili

A relative of the pompano, the greater amberjack is a large fish with a sleek body and a deeply forked tail. It feeds on many species of fish and is itself caught as a food fish.

Size: up to 6 ft (1.8 m)

Range: all temperate and tropical seas

Habitat: coastal waters, coral reefs

Size: 17¾–25½ in (45–65 cm)

Range: western Atlantic Ocean

Habitat: coastal waters

## Florida pompano
### Trachinotus carolinus

The pompano has a rounded snout and a fairly deep body, which tapers sharply to a forked tail. It feeds mainly on mollusks and crustaceans, which it finds in the mud and sand of the seabed. It is an excellent and valuable food fish.

Size: 6½ ft (2 m)

Range: eastern and northwestern Pacific Ocean

Habitat: coastal waters

## Red mullet
*Mullus surmuletus*

This fish uses the sensory whiskers, or barbels, on its chin to help it find bottom-living invertebrates, which it then digs it out of the sand or mud. Red mullet are able to change color to blend in to their surroundings, varying between day and night.

## Giant sea bass
*Stereolepis gigas*

Some of these fish weigh more than 550 lb (250 kg) and live for more than 70 years. They eat fish and crustaceans and are popular food fish. The young are reddish in color but slowly develop the adult appearance by about 12 or 13 years of age.

Size: 15¾ in (40 cm)

Range: eastern Atlantic Ocean and Mediterranean Sea

Habitat: coastal waters

Size: up to 6½ ft (2 m)

Range: warm and tropical waters of all oceans

Habitat: coastal

## Dolphinfish
*Coryphaena hippurus*

The brightly colored dolphinfish is easily identified by the large fin along its back. The forehead of the male becomes steeper with age; otherwise male and female look alike. Dolphinfish move in small shoals and eat fish, squid and crustaceans. They are often seen around patches of floating seaweed where their prey may hide.

Size: 15¾ in (40 cm)

Range: western Atlantic Ocean

Habitat: coastal waters, coral reefs

Size: 13¾–19¾ in (35–50 cm)

Range: Atlantic Ocean and Mediterranean Sea

Habitat: coastal waters, oceanic

## Blackspot seabream
*Pagellus bogaraveo*

This fish has a reddish flush and a dark spot above its pectoral fin. The young are paler in color and may not have a dark spot. They swim in large shoals in shallow waters, feeding on crustaceans. Adults live in smaller groups in deeper waters and eat fish as well as crustaceans.

## Yellowtail snapper
*Ocyurus chrysurus*

Snappers are common around coral reefs and are a popular fish for humans to eat. This species is easily recognized by its bright yellow tail and the yellow stripe along each side. It feeds mostly on other fish and small crustaceans.

Size: up to 17¾ in (45 cm)

Range: western Atlantic
Ocean and
Caribbean Sea

Habitat: coral reefs

# Queen angelfish
## Holacanthus ciliaris

This colorful angelfish has long fins on its back and belly that extend past the tail fin. It feeds on sponges and other invertebrate animals. Young queen angelfish may act as cleaners — they pick and eat parasites off other fish.

Size: up to 35½ in (90 cm)

Range: northern and western
Australia and islands

Habitat: coastal waters,
coral reefs

# Dragonet
## Callionymus lyra

The male dragonet has long, blue and yellow fins. Females are smaller and do not have extended fins. Dragonets lie half-buried in the sand on the seabed, watching for bottom-dwelling crustaceans and worms — their main food. They breed in spring or summer and males perform displays with their decorative fins to win females.

Size: up to 11¾ in (30 cm)

Range: eastern Atlantic Ocean
and Mediterranean Sea

Habitat: coastal waters, oceanic

# Rock goby
## Gobius paganellus

There are more than 1,800 kinds of goby, mostly in the sea. The rock goby is one of the larger gobies but typical of the group with its big blunt head and rounded tail. It uses its pelvic fins to cling to rocks. It feeds on small invertebrates and fish.

Size: up to 4¾ in (12 cm)

Range: North Atlantic Ocean
and Mediterranean Sea

Habitat: coastal waters

# Sweetlip emperor
## Lethrinus miniatus

This heavy-bodied fish is one of the many that hunt for their food around coral reefs. It has a rather large head for its body, a long snout and no scales on its cheeks. It has deep red fins, dark barring on its sides and red patches around the eyes. It can grow to more than 20 lb (9 kg) and is an extremely popular food fish.

Size: up to 7¾ in (20 cm)

Range: Indian and
Pacific oceans

Habitat: coral reefs,
coastal waters

# Copperband butterflyfish
## Chelmon rostratus

This fish uses its long beaklike snout to reach into crevices in the coral and find small creatures to eat. The large "eyespot" near its tail fin may confuse predators into thinking the copperband is larger than it really is.

# Black drum
## *Pogonias cromis*

This large fish can weigh as much as 112 lb (51 kg). A bottom-feeder, it eats mollusks and crustaceans, which it crushes with the special flat teeth in its throat. Oysters are a favorite food and black drums can cause a great deal of damage to commercial oyster beds.

Size: 4–6 ft (1.2–1.8 m)
Range: western Atlantic Ocean
Habitat: coastal waters

# Atlantic spadefish
## *Chaetodipterus faber*

This fish has a deep flattened body and long dorsal and anal fins. The young are black, becoming silvery gray as they grow, with dark vertical bars that become less clear in large adults. Spadefish feed mostly on small invertebrates.

Size: 10 in (25 cm)
Range: western Atlantic Ocean and Caribbean Sea
Habitat: coastal waters, coral reefs

Size: 18–35½ in (46–90 cm)
Range: western Atlantic Ocean
Habitat: coastal waters

# Blue tang
## *Acanthurus coeruleus*

This fish has extremely sharp spines on each side of its tail, which it can raise to wound an enemy. The young are bright yellow with blue markings, as shown above. This color changes as the fish matures, becoming blue all over by the time it is an adult.

Size: 8 in (21 cm)
Range: Indian and Pacific oceans
Habitat: coastal waters, coral reefs

# Northern clingfish
## *Gobiesox maeandricus*

This common fish has a smooth body and a broad head. Its dorsal and anal fins are set back near its tail. Like all clingfish, its pelvic fins form part of a sucking disk on its belly. It uses this to cling to rocks to avoid being washed away by strong tides in the coastal waters where it lives. Mollusks and crustaceans are its main foods.

# Moorish idol
## *Zanclus cornutus*

This relative of the blue tang has bold stripes, a protruding snout and long swept-back fins. It lacks tail spines, but the young have a sharp spine at each corner of the mouth, which drop off as the fish grow bigger.

Size: up to 6½ in (16 cm)
Range: eastern Pacific Ocean
Habitat: coastal waters

## Great barracuda
*Sphyraena barracuda*

Size: up to 6½ ft (2 m)

Range: worldwide, tropical and subtropical seas

Habitat: coastal waters, coral reefs, oceanic

There are about 27 types of barracuda living in warm and tropical seas. The great barracuda is typical, with its long slender body and large jaws and teeth. A fierce predator, it can be dangerous to humans if disturbed. Young barracudas may swim in schools, but larger fish hunt alone.

## Northern stargazer
*Astroscopus guttatus*

The northern stargazer has a large head with its mouth pointing upward and eyes on top of its head, also facing upward. This allows the stargazer to lie partly buried on the seabed, with only its eyes and mouth uncovered, watching for prey such as fish and crustaceans.

Size: up to 23½ in (59 cm)

Range: Atlantic coast of North America

Habitat: coastal waters

Size: up to 2¼ in (6 cm)

Range: Cambodia, Laos, Thailand, Vietnam

Habitat: fresh water

## Siamese fightingfish
*Betta splendens*

Male Siamese fightingfish are bred in captivity to take part in staged fights, but wild males battle with rivals over territory. In the breeding season, the male blows a bubble nest from air and mucus. When the female lays her eggs, the male fertilizes them and spits them into the nest to keep them safe.

## Striped snakehead
*Channa striata*

This long-bodied fish belongs to a small group of freshwater fish that live in tropical Africa and Asia. Usually found in oxygen-poor waters, it has special structures in its gills that help it take oxygen from the air. It can even survive out of water if it burrows into mud to keep its skin moist.

Size: up to 3¼ ft (1 m)

Range: India, China, and Southeast Asia

Habitat: fresh water

Size: 8¾ in (22 cm)

Range: tropical and temperate waters

Habitat: oceanic, coastal waters

## Man-of-war fish
*Nomeus gronovii*

Named for its habit of living among the trailing tentacles of the Portuguese man-of-war jellyfish, this little fish does not seem to be affected by the jellyfish's stinging cells. It may even prevent them working and remove parasites and other debris from its host's body.

# Redlip blenny
*Ophioblennius macclurei*

This fish is identified by the bristles on its rounded snout as well as its red lips and red-tipped fin. It lives on rocky- or coral-bottomed seabeds, where it searches for small invertebrates to eat. The female lays her eggs among coral or under rocks and the male guards them until they hatch.

Size: up to 4¾ in (12 cm).
Range: western Atlantic Ocean, Gulf of Mexico and Caribbean Sea
Habitat: coastal waters, coral reefs

# Atlantic mackerel
*Scomber scombrus*

In spring and summer, large schools of mackerel go north to breed; in winter they return south. A female may produce as many as 450,000 eggs, which float until they hatch about four days later. Adult mackerel eat small fish and crustaceans, while young fish feed mainly on plankton and fish larvae.

Size: 16–26 in (41–66 cm)
Range: Atlantic Ocean and Mediterranean Sea
Habitat: coastal waters, oceanic

Size: up to 14 ft (5 m).
Range: Atlantic Ocean, tropical and temperate waters
Habitat: oceanic

# Blue marlin
*Makaira nigricans*

One of the fastest of all fish, the blue marlin has the streamlined body and crescent-shaped tail typical of high-speed swimmers. It weighs at least 400 lb (180 kg) and has a long beaklike nose, which it may use to stun its prey such as smaller schooling fish and squid.

Size: 6½–16 ft (2–4.9m)
Range: worldwide, warm and tropical seas
Habitat: oceanic, coastal waters

# Indo-pacific sailfish
*Istiophorus platypterus*

This fast-swimming fish has a tall, saillike fin on its back and long pointed jaws. It is a fierce predator and eats almost any fish it can find, as well as squid. Sailfish breed in open sea. The female sheds several million eggs, which float in surface waters until they hatch.

Size: up to 12 ft (3.6 m)
Range: worldwide, warm and tropical waters
Habitat: oceanic, coastal waters

# Swordfish
*Xiphias gladius*

The huge spectacular swordfish is a fast active hunter with a streamlined body and a sickle-shaped fin on its back. It feeds on small fish as well as squid, and it may use its extremely long snout to strike at schooling fish. Young swordfish do not have a long snout; it develops as they grow.

# TUNA

Among the fastest of all fish, tuna are shaped for speed and can swim at 70 km/h (44 mph). They are among the most streamlined fish, with a pointed head and a torpedo-shaped body tapering to a narrow tail stalk and a crescent tail. The 14 species of tuna usually live near the surface waters of warm and tropical oceans. All are hunters, feeding mainly on fish and squid. Many swim in large schools, but the biggest fish swim in smaller groups or alone. Fish obtain oxygen from water, not air; the oxygen is taken out of the water flowing past the gills. Most fish pump water over the gills by muscle action — but not tuna. Instead, tuna must keep swimming at all times, with their mouths open, to create a constant flow of water over the gills. The faster they swim, the more water passes over the gills and the more oxygen can be absorbed.

Albacore
*Thunnus alalunga*

Skipjack
*Katsuwonus pelamis*

Bluefin
*Thunnus thynnus*

Bigeye
*Thunnus obesus*

## TYPES OF TUNA

The bluefin is the biggest tuna. It can grow up to 4.5 m (14¾ ft) long and weigh more than 685 kg (1,500 lb) — as much as nine people. A fast swimmer, it has been known to cross the Atlantic in 60 days. The bigeye grows to nearly 7¾ ft (2.4 m) long and can weigh more than 400 lb (180 kg). The albacore and skipjack are smaller — up to 5 ft (1.5 m) and 3½ ft (1.1 m) respectively. The skipjack "skips" over the surface of the water as it chases its prey.

# YELLOWFIN

This tuna swims in schools that often attack mackerel. It has long pectoral fins and yellow finlets as well as yellow markings on its sides. The yellowfin lives in the Atlantic, Indian and Pacific oceans. It grows to about 5 ft (1.5 m) long and weighs up to 440 lb (200 kg).

Yellowfin tuna (*Thunnus albacares*) are the most valuable of all the tuna as food fish. All over the world fishermen pursue schools of these tuna and catch large numbers.

# FLYINGFISH, LANTERNFISH AND LIZARDFISH

The flyingfish belongs to a large group of mostly sea-living fish, which also includes halfbeaks, needlefish, sauries and garfish. Most are active near or at the surface of the water, and flyingfish can actually lift themselves into the air with their pectoral fins and use their rapidly beating tails to help them glide short distances. Lanternfish are deep-sea fish and are found in all oceans. They have light-producing organs on the body. The lizardfish and its relative the bummalow both live in shallow coastal waters, where they prey on small fish.

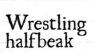

## Wrestling halfbeak
*Dermogenys pusilla*

Size: up to 2¾ in (7 cm)

Range: Southeast Asia: from India to Malaysia and the Philippines

Habitat: fresh water

This small slender fish feeds on mosquito larvae and so helps to control these pests. Male fish are aggressive and fight one another by wrestling with their long jaws.

## Tropical two-wing flyingfish
*Exocoetus volitans*

Size: up to 11¾ in (30 cm)

Range: worldwide, tropical and subtropical seas

Habitat: coastal waters, oceanic

The flyingfish escapes enemies by leaping up and gliding over the surface of the water with the aid of its winglike fins. It can glide for 300 ft (90 m), up to 5 ft (1.5 m) above the surface.

## Garfish
*Belone belone*

The slender garfish has long jaws, studded with many needlelike teeth. An active hunter, the garfish eats small fish and crustaceans. It breeds in coastal waters and its small round eggs attach themselves to floating debris or seaweed.

Size: up to 37 in (94 cm)

Range: North Atlantic Ocean: Mediterranean and Black seas

Habitat: coastal waters, oceanic

Size: 13 in (32 cm)

Range: Arctic and Atlantic oceans, Mediterranean Sea

Habitat: oceanic

## Atlantic saury
*Scomberesox saurus saurus*

The saury swims in shoals in surface waters, feeding on small fish and crustaceans. It has beaklike jaws, the lower longer than the upper. Young fishes hatch with short jaws of equal length; the long lower jaw develops as they grow.

## Spotted lanternfish
*Myctophum punctatum*

This fish has groups of light-producing organs on its body. The light organs may help the fish to light up the dark depths of the sea to find prey or they may be used to confuse its own enemies. Lanternfish feed on animal plankton.

Size: up to 4 in (10 cm)

Range: North Atlantic Ocean, Mediterranean Sea

Habitat: deep sea, oceanic

Size: up to 12½ in (32 cm)

Range: warm waters of the Atlantic Ocean

Habitat: coastal waters, coral reefs

## Diamond lizardfish
*Synodus synodus*

The lizardfish has unusually long pelvic fins and often lies on the seabed, supporting its body on these fins. A fierce hunter, it lies in wait for prey, then suddenly darts up from the seabed and catches the victim in its long sharp teeth.

## Bummalow
*Harpadon nehereus*

The bummalow has a long body and huge jaws, armed with sharp curving teeth. It is often found near the mouths of large rivers, where it eats small fish and crustaceans. This fish is split and dried in the sun for eating. In this form it is known as Bombay duck.

Size: up to 16¼ in (41 cm)

Range: Indian and western Pacific oceans

Habitat: coastal waters, deep sea

## Needlefish
*Belonian apodion*

A long slender body and the position of its fins near its tail give this tiny freshwater fish its dartlike appearance. It uses its long lower jaw to scoop up animal plankton.

Size: 14 in (35 cm)

Range: warm waters of the Atlantic Ocean

Habitat: coastal waters

Size: up to 2 in (5 cm)

Range: South America

Habitat: fresh water

## Ballyhoo
*Hemiramphus brasiliensis*

This fish cannot leap above the water like its relative the flying fish, but it can skim over the surface. It moves in schools, feeding on sea grass and small fish, and it may use its long lower jaw to scoop up food from the water surface.

# GUPPIES, GRUNIONS AND RELATIVES

Guppies belong to a group of freshwater fish that contains more than 1,250 species, including lyretails, mummichogs, sheepshead minnows and the four-eyed fish. Most are surface swimmers, feeding on insects and plant matter that has fallen on to the water, and are able to survive in slow-moving or even stagnant water. Grunions belong to a group of about 340 species that includes silversides, sand smelts and rainbow fish. Most feed on animal plankton and live in large shoals in lakes, estuaries and shallow coastal waters.

Size: 7 in (18 cm)
Range: eastern Pacific Ocean
Habitat: coastal waters

## California grunion
*Leuresthes tenuis*

Grunions time their breeding with the tides. On a night of an extreme high, or spring, tide, they swim ashore, lay their eggs in the sand and swim back out to sea on next wave. Two weeks later, at the next spring tide, the eggs hatch and the young are carried out to sea.

Size: 3½ in (9 cm)
Range: Australia
Habitat: fresh water

Size: 3 in (7.5 cm)
Range: western Atlantic Ocean
Habitat: coastal waters

## Hardhead silverside
*Atherinomorus stipes*

During the day the slender body of this little fish looks almost transparent, with a narrow silvery stripe running down each side. When night falls, the color darkens. Silversides are common fish and they swim in large schools. Their eggs have tiny threads which attach them to water plants while they develop.

## Murray River rainbowfish
*Melanotaenia fluviatilis*

This colorful fish is one of about 59 types of rainbow fish found in Australia and New Guinea. In early summer it lays eggs, which become anchored to water plants by fine threads.

## Sand smelt
*Atherina presbyter*

This small fish has a long slender body and two widely spaced fins on its back. It swims in schools and eats mainly animal plankton, but also tiny fish. Sand smelts are themselves eaten by larger fishes and by seabirds such as terns.

Size: 6–7¾ in (15–20 cm)
Range: eastern Atlantic Ocean. Mediteranean
Habitat: coastal waters

Size: 2¼ in (6 cm)

Range: Angola, Cameroon, Congo, Gabon

Habitat: fresh waters

# Guppy
## *Poecilia reticulata*

The guppy is an extremely common fish. It is popular with humans because it feeds on mosquito larvae and so helps to control this pest. It also eats other insect larvae, small crustaceans and the eggs and young of other fish. Many colorful forms of the guppy are bred as aquarium fish.

# Lyretail panchax
## *Aphyosemion australe*

The male lyretail is a brightly colored fish with large pointed fins. The female is plainer and has smaller fins. She lays her eggs in mud. If there is a long dry season, the eggs stop developing until the rains return. The embryos then start to grow again and hatch shortly afterward.

Size: 2¼ in (6 cm)

Range: northern South America

Habitat: fresh water

Size: up to 3½ in (9 cm)

Range: east coast of North and South America

Habitat: coastal waters

# Sheepshead minnow
## *Cyprinodon variegatus variegatus*

Outside the breeding season, male and female sheepshead minnows look similar, but breeding males develop brighter coloration. The female lays her eggs a few at a time and the male fertilizes them as they are shed. The eggs have sticky threads on the surface, which attach them to each other and to plants.

# Mummichog
## *Fundulus heteroclitus heteroclitus*

The mummichog is a hardy little stout-bodied fish that can survive in salt or fresh water and eats almost any plants and animals it can find. It breeds in spring, in shallow water. The male clasps the female with his fins so he can fertilize the eggs as they are laid. The eggs stick together and sink to the bottom in a cluster.

Size: 4–6 in (10–15 cm)

Range: east coast of North America

Habitat: fresh water, coastal waters

# Four-eyed fish
## *Anableps anableps*

This unusual fish has, in fact, only two eyes that are divided into two parts. The top part of each eye is for seeing in the air and the lower part is for seeing in water. The two parts are separated by a dark band. The fish swims at the surface, the water reaching the dividing bands on the eyes. It is able to watch for insect prey in the air or other prey in the water at the same time.

Size: 11¾ in (30 cm)

Range: northern South America

Habitat: fresh water, coastal waters

183

# OARFISH, SQUIRRELFISH AND RELATIVES

All of these fish live in the sea. The pinecone fish, squirrelfish, roughie and beardfish all belong to a group of about 163 species of deep-bodied fishes with spiny fins. The John Dory belongs to a separate group of deep-bodied fish, many of which live in deep sea. The whalefish is also a deep-sea species. Although their body shapes appear to be very different, the oarfish and the opah both belong to a rare group of fish, about which little is known.

Size: 5 in (12.5 cm)
Range: Indian and Pacific oceans
Habitat: oceanic, coastal waters

## Pinecone fish
*Monocentris japonica*

The body of the pinecone fish is protected by an armor of heavy platelike scutes, or scales. It has a dorsal fin made up of thick spines, more spines on in its belly and two light-producing organs under the lower jaw. Pinecone fish swim in schools near the bottom of the sea.

Size: up to 36 ft (11 m)
Range: worldwide, especially in cool waters
Habitat: oceanic

## Oarfish
*Regalecus glesne*

This unusual fish has a long ribbonlike body, with a dorsal fin running along most of its length. It swims with rippling snakelike movements and is thought to have been the cause of many tales about giant sea serpents. The oarfish has no teeth in its small mouth and feeds mainly on small shrimplike crustaceans.

Size: 11¾ in (30 cm)
Range: Atlantic Ocean
Habitat: deep sea

## Stout beardfish
*Polymixia nobilis*

This fish gets its name from the pair of whiskers, or barbels, that hang from its lower jaw. These may help it find food on the seabed. It usually lives at depths of about 330 to 2,500 ft (100 to 770 m).

Size: 5 ft (1.2 m)
Range: worldwide, except the Southern Ocean
Habitat: oceanic

## Opah
*Lampris guttatus*

Despite its almost comical appearance, this fish is a successful hunter, feeding on squid and fish such as hake and whiting. It has a large rounded body, dotted with white spots, and bright red fins. It may weigh as much as 161 lb (73 kg).

## John Dory
*Zeus faber*

The John Dory has 9 or 11 thick spines in the front part of its dorsal fin and four on the belly in front of its anal fin. Not a fast swimmer, it slowly approaches its prey — mostly crustaceans and small fish — until near enough to snatch them up in its huge mouth.

Size: 11¾ in (30 cm)
Range: Atlantic, Indian and Pacific oceans
Habitat: deep sea

## Orange roughy
*Hoplostethus atlanticus*

The brightly colored roughy has a large head and a deep body. It has sharp spines on its back in front of its dorsal fin and on its belly. Its mouth is large and upturned, its jaws are lined with lots of tiny teeth and it is thought to feed on small crustaceans.

Size: up to 35½ in (90 cm)
Range: worldwide
Habitat: coastal waters

## Whalefish
*Cetichthys indagator*

The whalefish belongs to a small group of deep-sea fish. It has a big head for its size and no scales on its body. The area at the base of the dorsal and anal fins is thought to glow in the dark. It hunts for its food and seizes prey in its large jaws lined with many tiny teeth.

Size: up to 4¾ in (12 cm)
Range: Atlantic, Pacific and Indian oceans
Habitat: deep sea

Size: 24 in (61 cm)
Range: Atlantic Ocean
Habitat: coastal waters, coral reefs

## Squirrelfish
*Holocentrus adscensionis*

This brightly colored fish is common on coral reefs. Hiding in crevices by day, it comes out at night to hunt for small crustaceans and other prey. Its large eyes help it to see well in the dark, and it can make a range of sounds by vibrating its swim bladder (a gas-filled sac inside the body) with special muscles.

# SEAHORSES, STONEFISH AND RELATIVES

Seahorses and sticklebacks belong to a group of about 320 fish, which also includes tubesnouts and pipefish. Sticklebacks have between 3 and 16 spines on their backs and are found in the sea and in fresh water. Seahorses, with their horselike heads, all live in the sea. The stonefish, lionfish, northern searobin and sculpin belong to the scorpionfish group. This includes more than 1,300 species, most of which live in the sea. Many of these fish are chunky and spiny. The flying gurnard belongs to a small group of only seven species of marine fish. Despite their name, these fish have never been seen flying above the surface of the water.

Size: 15 in (38 cm)

Range: Indian and Pacific oceans

Habitat: coastal waters, coral reefs

Size: 10½ in (27 cm)

Range: Indian and Pacific oceans

Habitat: coastal waters, coral reefs

## Stonefish
*Synanceia verrucosa*

The stonefish's mottled coloration and irregular shape keep it well hidden as it lies half-buried among stones on the seabed. The sharp spines on its back are linked to glands containing a deadly poison that can even kill any human unlucky enough to tread on a stonefish's spines.

## Lionfish
*Pterois volitans*

With its brightly striped body and large fanlike fins, this fish is one of the most extraordinary in the sea. The spines on its back are poisonous and can be dangerous even for humans. The fish uses its spines to defend itself against its enemies, not to attack prey.

Size: 9¾–23½ in (25–60 cm)

Range: Arctic and North Atlantic oceans

Habitat: coastal waters

## Shorthorn sculpin
*Myoxocephalus scorpius*

This fish has spines on its head, near its gills and along each side. Females are usually larger than males. A bottom-dweller, the shorthorn sculpin has mottled coloring that blends well with the seabed. It eats seabed crustaceans, worms and small fish.

# Flying gurnard
*Dactylopterus volitans*

A bottom-dwelling fish, the flying gurnard uses its long winglike pelvic fins to "walk" over the seabed as it searches for crustaceans to eat. When alarmed, the gurnard spreads its fins wide to show off their blue spots.

# Weedy seadragon
*Phyllopteryx taeniolatus*

The many leaflike flaps of skin on the body of this strange little seahorse are thought to help it hide from its enemies among fronds of seaweed. The male incubates his mate's eggs on a flap of skin beneath his tail.

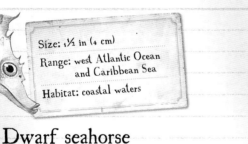

# Dwarf seahorse
*Hippocampus zosterae*

This unusual fish moves slowly, gently pushing itself along with movements of its tiny dorsal fin. It can also attach itself to seaweed with its curling tail. In the breeding season the female lays 50 or more eggs, which she places in a pouch on the male's body where they incubate.

# Three-spined stickleback
*Gasterosteus aculeatus*

In the breeding season, the male stickleback develops a bright red belly. He make a nest from tiny bits of plants, glued together with mucus. He then displays to attract females to his nest, where they lay their eggs. He fertilizes the eggs and guards them carefully until they hatch about three weeks later.

# Northern searobin
*Prionotus carolinus*

A relative of the lionfish, the northern sea robin spends much of its life on the seabed, often supporting itself on its pectoral fins. It uses the first three rays of its pectoral fins to feel for prey on the seabed. If in danger, the sea robin buries itself in sand, leaving only the top of its head and eyes showing.

# FLATFISH

The flatfish belong to a group of about 777 species. All but three of these live in the sea. Young flatfish have normal bodies at first, but as they grow, their bodies flatten and the eye on one side moves so that both eyes are on the upper surface. A typical flatfish spends much of its life on the seabed, lying with the eyed side facing up. Some flatfish have both eyes on the right side and lie on the left; others have both eyes on the left side and lie on the right.

### Adalah
*Psettodes erumei*

The adalah is less dramatically flattened than most other flatfish. Some have both eyes on the left side, others on the right, but one eye is on the edge of the head. Like other flatfish, the adalah spends much of its life on the seabed, but it also swims in midwaters looking for fish and other creatures to eat.

Size: up to 25 in (64 cm)
Range: Red Sea, Indian Ocean, western Pacific Ocean
Habitat: coastal waters

Size: 3¼ ft (1 m)
Range: eastern Atlantic Ocean and Mediterranean and Baltic seas
Habitat: coastal waters

### Turbot
*Scophthalmus maximus*

This extremely broad-bodied flatfish varies in color, but usually has speckled markings that help to camouflage it on the seabed. A food fish, the adult turbot preys mostly on fish, but young turbots eat small crustaceans. Turbot breed in spring or summer and females produce as many as 10 million eggs.

### Summer flounder
*Paralichthys dentatus*

A slender active fish, the summer flounder feeds on crustaceans, mollusks and fish and will chase prey up into surface waters if necessary. But this fast swimmer spends much of its time lying half-buried on the seabed. Its color varies according to the type of seabed it is on, but is usually grayish brown, with dark spots.

Size: up to 3¼ ft (1 m)
Range: western Atlantic Ocean
Habitat: coastal waters

Size: 5 ft (1.5 m)
Range: eastern Pacific Ocean
Habitat: coastal waters

# European plaice
## *Pleuronectes platessa*

The topside of this important food fish is brown, dotted with orange spots. Both eyes are usually on the top, right side of the body. Plaice breed in early spring and the larvae live in surface waters for up to six weeks before settling on the seabed.

Size: 40 cm (15¾ in)
Range: North Atlantic Ocean
Habitat: coastal waters

# California flounder
## *Paralichthys californicus*

This flounder has a large mouth and strong sharp teeth. It feeds on fish, particularly anchovies, and is itself eaten by creatures such as rays, sea lions and porpoises. It is also an important food fish for humans. A large individual can weigh up to 70 lb (32 kg).

Size: 11¾–27½ in (30–70 cm)
Range: eastern Atlantic Ocean and Mediterranean Sea
Habitat: coastal waters

# Sole
## *Solea solea*

A food fish, the common or Dover sole usually feeds at night and spends the day buried in sand or mud. It breeds in shallow water and its eggs float at the surface. The larvae move to the seabed when they are about ½ in (1.25 cm) long.

# North American naked sole
## *Gymnachirus melas*

With no scales on its skin, the naked sole has dark stripes on its uppermost side and a whitish underside. Mostly both eyes are on the right side and the small mouth is also twisted to the right. This flatfish spends most of its life on the seabed, but it is an active hunter and can swim well when necessary.

Size: 7¾ in (20 cm)
Range: west Atlantic Ocean
Habitat: coastal waters

Size: up to 9 in (23 cm)
Range: western Atlantic Ocean
Habitat: coastal waters

# Blackcheek tonguefish
## *Symphurus plagusia*

This flatfish's body tapers to a pointed tail, and its dorsal and anal fins join with the tail fin. Both its eyes are on the left side and its small mouth is twisted to the left. Like other flatfish, it lives on the seabed and feeds on small invertebrate animals such as worms and crustaceans.

189

# COELACANTH, LUNGFISH, TRIGGERFISH AND RELATIVES

The coelacanth is thought to resemble some of the earliest fish and is more closely related to amphibians than any other living fish. Common millions of years ago, only two species now survive. Lungfish are related to early air-breathing fish. They have lunglike breathing organs, which they use to take breaths of air at the surface of the water. Triggerfish, pufferfish, boxfish and relatives belong to a group of about 340 species. Many of these have round or boxlike bodies, and most live in the sea.

Size: 22 in (56 cm)

Range: western Atlantic Ocean and Caribbean Sea

Habitat: coastal waters, coral reefs

## Queen triggerfish
*Balistes vetula*

On the triggerfish's back are three spines. When the first spine is upright, it is locked into place by the second. If in danger, the triggerfish can wedge itself into a crevice with this "locking" spine and is extremely hard to move. It feeds on small invertebrate creatures, particularly sea urchins.

Size: 6½ ft (2 m)

Range: African coast of Indian Ocean

Habitat: coastal waters

## Coelacanth
*Latimeria chalumnae*

Coelacanths were thought to have been extinct for millions of years until one was caught off South Africa in 1938. This living species is very like its fossil relatives. It has a heavy body and fleshy sections at the base of all its fins except the first dorsal fin. It may hunt other fish to eat.

## South American lungfish
*Lepidosiren paradoxa*

This lungfish lives in swamps that dry out for part of the year. During this time, it lives in a burrow that it digs in the mud and breathes air with the help of lunglike organs in its body. When the rains return, the fish comes out of its burrow.

Size: 4½ ft (1.25 m)

Range: central South America

Habitat: fresh water

# Ocean sunfish
## *Mola mola*

A relative of the triggerfish, the ocean sunfish
is unlike any other fish. Its body is almost
round and ends in a frill-like tail. Despite its
huge size, it has a small beaklike mouth and
feeds on small creatures such as
animal plankton and
tiny jellyfish.

Size: up to 11 ft (3.3 m)
Range: Atlantic, Pacific and
Indian oceans
Habitat: oceanic

Size: 36 in (91 cm)
Range: tropical waters of Pacific,
Indian and Atlantic oceans
Habitat: coastal waters

# Porcupinefish
## *Diodon hystrix*

This fish is covered with long, sharp
spines. These normally lie flat, but if the
fish is in danger, it puffs up its body so
the spines stand out, making it hard to
attack. Its teeth are joined together into
a sharp beak for crushing hard-shelled
prey such as mollusks and crabs.

Size: 18 in (46 cm)
Range: Indian and Pacific oceans
Habitat: coastal waters, coral reefs

Size: 6 in (15 cm)
Range: Bangladesh, Burma
(Myanmar), India,
Malaysia, Sri Lanka
Habitat: fresh water

# Ocellate puffer
## *Tetraodon cutcutia*

If threatened, this fish can blow its body up until it is almost completely
round and difficult for any predator to swallow. Many kinds of pufferfish
are popular food fish, even though some parts of their bodies are very
poisonous. In Japan, chefs are trained in the preparation of pufferfish.

# Yellow boxfish
## *Ostracion cubicus*

Like all boxfish, this one has a hard
shell around its body, made up of
joined plates. Its mouth, eyes, fins
and gill openings are the only breaks
in the armor, which protects the fish
from its enemies. It feeds mostly on
bottom-living invertebrates.

Size: 21½ in (55 cm)
Range: tropical waters of
Atlantic, Pacific and
Indian oceans
Habitat: coastal waters

# Scrawled filefish
## *Aluterus scriptus*

A relative of the triggerfish, this filefish has a long
spine on its head and small prickly spines on the scales
of its body. It feeds nose-down on bottom-living
invertebrates and seaweeds. It often lurks in eel grass,
where its greenish coloration keeps it well hidden.

191

# WHY DO SOME ANIMALS WORK TOGETHER?

When animals develop close links with creatures of another species both partners can benefit. The cleaner fish, for example, feeds on parasites and tiny scraps of food it finds on the bodies of larger fish. The cleaner fish gains a good meal and the host has its body cleared of debris and harmful parasites. Sometimes only one partner benefits. Cattle egrets follow large mammals such as elephants to feed on the insects disturbed as they pass. The egrets get plenty of food but there is no clear advantage to the elephant.

The honeyguide feeds on wax and bee larvae, while honey-eating mammals such as the honey badger, or ratel, raid the bees' nests for honey. Humans gathering honey in the wild use both the bird and the badger as guides to finding the nests.

Ant

Aphids

## PROTECTION

Black ants protect groups of the tiny bugs called aphids from other insects. When an ant strokes an aphid's body with its antennae, the aphid produces a drop of a sugary substance called honeydew — delicious food for the ant.

The oxpecker provides a very useful service for this buffalo while getting a good meal for itself. The bird eats the ticks and other parasites that live on the buffalo's skin.

# SAFETY

The clownfish finds safety from enemies among a sea anemone's stinging tentacles. Its own skin is immune to the sting. The clownfish may attract other fish near enough for the anemone to catch.

# INSECTS, SPIDERS AND OTHER INVERTEBRATES

Insects outnumber every other creature on Earth. There are almost two million known animal species in the world, and about half of those species are insects. Arachnids, like insects, are found all over the world in every kind of habitat. There are at least 103,000 species of arachnid, of which spiders are the biggest group. Other invertebrates include worms, snails, centipedes and millipedes on land and an amazing range of species at sea, including sponges, clams, mussels, jellyfish and crabs.

# WHAT IS AN INVERTEBRATE?

An invertebrate is an animal with no backbone — creatures such as crabs, worms, insects and spiders are all invertebrates. There are invertebrates on land, in the sea and in fresh water, and many insects fly in the air. These animals have an extraordinary range of lifestyles and feeding habits.

## ARTHROPODS

Arthropods are the largest group of invertebrates and some of the most successful creatures of all time. They include such creatures as insects, spiders and crabs. One of the reasons for their success is that they have a hard external skeleton, called an exoskeleton, which protects the soft body within.

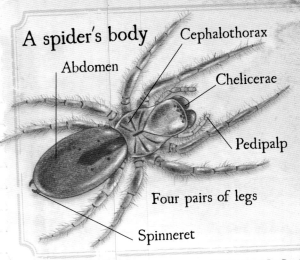

### A spider's body

Abdomen

Cephalothorax

Chelicerae

Pedipalp

Four pairs of legs

Spinneret

The typical spider's body is divided into two parts. The head and thorax are joined to make one structure called the cephalothorax. This is linked to the abdomen by a narrow waist. At the front of the head are the spider's jaws, called chelicerae, and behind these is the mouth. Spiders have four pairs of segmented legs, and each leg is tipped with claws.

Spider

Centipede

Crustacean

Millipede

Insect

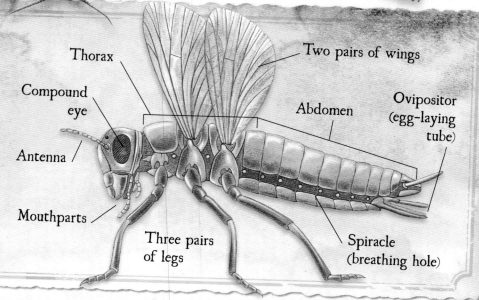

### An insect's body

An insect is divided into three parts — head, thorax and abdomen. The head carries the eyes, a pair of sensory antennae, which the insect uses to find out about its surroundings, and the mouthparts. These vary in shape according to the insect's diet. On the thorax are three pairs of legs and usually two pairs of wings.

Thorax

Compound eye

Antenna

Mouthparts

Two pairs of wings

Abdomen

Ovipositor (egg-laying tube)

Three pairs of legs

Spiracle (breathing hole)

# OTHER INVERTEBRATE GROUPS

## COMB JELLIES

Comb jellies have a simple baglike body, with eight lines of tiny hairs that beat to move the comb jelly through the water.

Beroe comb jelly

## ANNELID WORMS

There are about 21,000 species of these worms, in water and on land. Their bodies are divided into segments.

Medical leech

## LAMP SHELLS

There are about 400 species in this group, also known as brachiopods. All lampshells have an upper and a lower shell.

Lamp shell

## MOLLUSKS

The three main groups of mollusks are the gastropods (creatures such as limpets); bivalves (clams, scallops and mussels); and cephalopods (squid, octopus and the nautilus).

Nautilus

## ECHINODERMS

There are four main groups of echinoderms — brittle stars, starfish, sea cucumbers, and sea urchins and sand dollars. Most move around using tiny stilts called tube feet.

Flower urchin

## CNIDARIANS

This group includes creatures such as sea anemones and corals. Most have tubelike bodies with a central mouth surrounded by tentacles.

Purple jellyfish

## SPONGES

Sponges are the simplest many-celled animals. Their shapes vary from tiny cups, tubelike pipes and tall vases to rounded masses. Special filtering cells in their bodies trap food particles in the water.

Glass sponge

# COCKROACHES, EARWIGS, CRICKETS, GRASSHOPPERS AND RELATIVES

**W**hile these insects are not closely related, they share certain features. They all have strong jaws for chewing, mobile heads, and most have large back wings. They also include some of the most ancient of all insect groups — cockroaches have been around for about 350 million years. Most of these creatures are familiar to humans, and some are even unwelcome guests in our homes.

## COCKROACHES, EARWIGS AND BRISTLETAILS

**A**lthough most cockroaches live outdoors, in every kind of habitat from mountains to rain forests, they are best known as indoor pests. Earwigs, found in every garden, are also considered pests, since many feed on plants and flowers. Also common in houses, but less often seen, are the wingless insects known as silverfish or bristletails.

Family: Blattidae
Size: ¾–2 in (1.9–5 cm) long
Number of species: about 650
Habitat: worldwide

Family: Forficulidae
Size: ⅜–1 in (0.9–2.5 cm) long
Number of species: about 450
Habitat: worldwide

### American cockroach

Common in buildings, these cockroaches hide by day and feed on anything they can find by night. The female lays her eggs in a case attached to her body, which she leaves in a dark safe place before the eggs hatch.

### Common earwig

The female earwig lays her eggs in a burrow and stays close to look after them. Unusually for an insect, she tends her young until they are able to manage by themselves. The abdomen ends in a pair of pincers that is used to capture prey and defend against attack.

Family: Lepismatidae

Size: ⅓–¾ in
(0.8–1.9 cm) long

Number of species: about 295

Habitat: worldwide

Family: Labiduridae

Size: ⅜–1 in (0.9–2.5 cm) long

Number of species: 75

Habitat: worldwide

## Firebrat

The firebrat is a bristletail.
It usually lives indoors
near warm places such
as ovens or boilers.
A fast runner, it scurries
around finding crumbs and
scraps of food to eat.

## Long-horned earwig

These insects are also known as striped
earwigs because of the dark markings on
the thorax and short front wings. Like all
earwigs, the long-horned hides by day and
comes out at night to hunt other insects. If
attacked, it can squirt a bad-smelling liquid
from special glands on the abdomen.

## Silverfish

Fast-moving, silverfish usually shy away from
the light and live in dark corners indoors, where
they eat paper, glue and spilled foods. The long
tapering body is covered with tiny scales.

Family: Lepismatidae

Size: ⅓–¾ in (0.8–1.9 cm) long

Number of species: about 295

Habitat: worldwide

## Madagascan hissing cockroach

Large and wingless, these cockroaches make a
hissing sound through breathing holes in their
abdomen to warn off any enemies. Males also make
a softer hissing noise when courting females.

Family: Blattellidae

Size: ¾–1 in (0.6–2.5 cm) long

Number of species: about 2,240

Habitat: worldwide

Family: Blaberidae

Size: 2–3 in (5–7.5 cm) long

Number of species: about 1,200

Habitat: tropical

## German cockroach

These cockroaches are found all over the world,
usually indoors. They are fast runners and their
flattened bodies are ideally shaped for squeezing
into cracks and under floorboards.

# CRICKETS, GRASSHOPPERS AND RELATIVES

More often heard than seen, grasshoppers are best known for their calls, usually made by the male rubbing together its wings or legs when courting females. There are two main families of grasshoppers: short-horned, such as locusts, and long-horned, such as katydids. Crickets are relatives of grasshoppers and also make chirping sounds. Stick and leaf insects are famous for their ability to hide themselves by looking like twigs or leaves.

Family: Acrididae
Size: ½–3 in (1.2–7.5 cm) long
Number of species: about 10,500
Habitat: worldwide

## Locust

Locusts are a type of grasshopper and are among the most damaging of all insects. Swarms of locusts swoop down on to crops and feed until there are scarcely any leaves left. A swarm may contain as many as 50 billion insects.

Family: Acrididae
Size: ½–3 in (1.2–7.5 cm) long
Number of species: about 10,500
Habitat: worldwide

## Long-horned grasshopper

As their name suggests, long-horned grasshoppers have long antennae. They feed on plants but also catch and eat small insects. Many are green or brown in color and can be hard to spot in the trees and bushes where they live.

Family: Tettigoniidae
Size: ½–3 in (1.2–7.5 cm) long
Number of species: about 6,750
Habitat: worldwide

## Short-horned grasshopper

Short-horned grasshoppers have short antennae. Like all grasshoppers, they have powerful back legs and can leap more than 200 times their own length.

# Leaf insect

These extraordinary insects are shaped just like the leaves they live on, complete with veins. Even their eggs look like the plant's seeds. Leaf insects live in tropical parts of Asia and Australia.

Family: Phylliidae
Size: 2–4 in (5–10 cm) long
Number of species: about 30
Habitat: tropical

Family: Gryllidae
Size: up to 2 in (5 cm) long
Number of species: about 4,700
Habitat: tropical

# True cricket

True crickets "sing" by rubbing together specially ridged and thickened areas of their front wings to make a high-pitched sound. They are usually colored green, black or brown and have broad bodies and well-developed feelers at the end of the abdomen.

# Mole cricket

Like tiny moles, these crickets live under the ground, where they burrow with their large spadelike front legs. Fine hairs protects the body from soil. Plant roots are their main food and they often damage crops and trees. They also catch and eat worms and larvae.

Family: Gryllotalpidae
Size: ¾–2 in (2–5 cm) long
Number of species: about 105
Habitat: worldwide

Family: Phasmatidae
Size: up to 11¾ in (30 cm) long
Number of species: about 2,450
Habitat: worldwide

# Stick insect

With its slender green or brown body, the stick insect looks so like a leafless twig that it is hard for hungry birds to see. During the day it clings to a plant, with only its long thin legs swaying gently, as though blown by a breeze. At night the stick insect moves around, feeding on leaves.

# Katydid

This insect has wings that look like leaves to help it hide among plants. The female katydid has a knifelike ovipositor, which is an egg-laying tube. She uses this to insert her eggs into slots that she cuts in the stems of plants.

Family: Tettigoniidae
Size: ½–3 in (1.2–7.5 cm) long
Number of species: about 6,750
Habitat: worldwide

Ovipositor

# MANTIDS, DRAGONFLIES AND RELATIVES

These insects are some of the fiercest hunters in the insect world. Mantids are equipped with long front legs, which they extend at lightning speeds to grasp their prey. More energetic hunters are the dragonflies, among the fastest-flying of all insects. They seize their prey in the air or pluck tiny creatures from leaves. Lacewings, antlions, snakeflies and mantidflies are known as nerve-winged insects. They have two pairs of delicate veined wings that can be folded like an arch over the body. Their larvae feed on other small creatures, which they catch in their powerful jaws.

## Flower mantis

Some mantids are colored to match the flowers that they perch on. This helps them to stay hidden from both their victims and their enemies. Mantids usually prey on other insects but they can also catch frogs and small lizards.

Family: Mantidae
Size: ½–6 in (1.2–15 cm) long
Number of species: about 1,100
Habitat: worldwide

Family: Hymenopodidae
Size: up to 5 in (13 cm) long
Number of species: 290
Habitat: tropical

## Angola mantis

This mantis is hard to see when it lies on a lichen-covered branch. It remains very still as it watches for food but can reach out to grab its prey in a fraction of a second. Mantid larvae hatch as tiny versions of their parents and start hunting for themselves right away.

Family: Mantidae
Size: ½–6 in (1.2–15 cm) long
Number of species: about 1,100
Habitat: worldwide

## Praying mantis

When a mantid holds its front legs up together, it may look like it is at prayer, but these two powerful limbs are its hunting tools. They are lined with sharp spines, which help the insect hold on to its struggling prey as it feeds. Females are usually larger than males and sometimes attack or even eat males after mating.

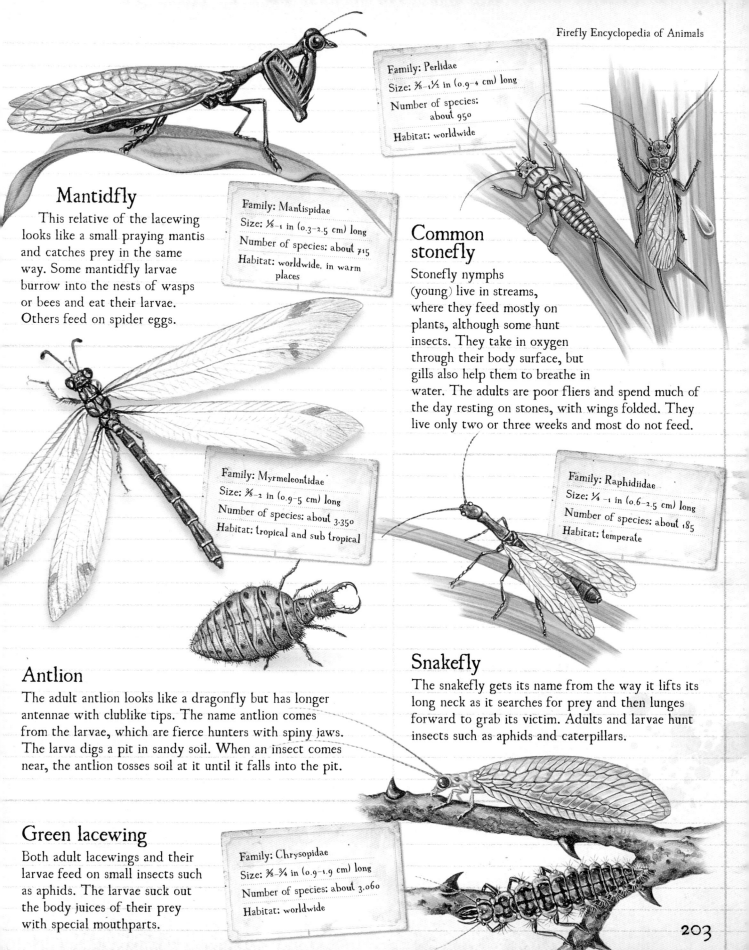

Family: Perlidae

Size: ⅜–1½ in (0.9–4 cm) long

Number of species: about 950

Habitat: worldwide

## Mantidfly

This relative of the lacewing looks like a small praying mantis and catches prey in the same way. Some mantidfly larvae burrow into the nests of wasps or bees and eat their larvae. Others feed on spider eggs.

Family: Mantispidae

Size: ⅛–1 in (0.3–2.5 cm) long

Number of species: about 715

Habitat: worldwide, in warm places

## Common stonefly

Stonefly nymphs (young) live in streams, where they feed mostly on plants, although some hunt insects. They take in oxygen through their body surface, but gills also help them to breathe in water. The adults are poor fliers and spend much of the day resting on stones, with wings folded. They live only two or three weeks and most do not feed.

Family: Myrmeleontidae

Size: ⅜–2 in (0.9–5 cm) long

Number of species: about 3,350

Habitat: tropical and sub tropical

Family: Raphidiidae

Size: ¼–1 in (0.6–2.5 cm) long

Number of species: about 185

Habitat: temperate

## Antlion

The adult antlion looks like a dragonfly but has longer antennae with clublike tips. The name antlion comes from the larvae, which are fierce hunters with spiny jaws. The larva digs a pit in sandy soil. When an insect comes near, the antlion tosses soil at it until it falls into the pit.

## Snakefly

The snakefly gets its name from the way it lifts its long neck as it searches for prey and then lunges forward to grab its victim. Adults and larvae hunt insects such as aphids and caterpillars.

## Green lacewing

Both adult lacewings and their larvae feed on small insects such as aphids. The larvae suck out the body juices of their prey with special mouthparts.

Family: Chrysopidae

Size: ⅜–¾ in (0.9–1.9 cm) long

Number of species: about 3,060

Habitat: worldwide

# Darner dragonfly

Darners are some of the largest and fastest of all dragonflies. When hunting, they zoom back and forth with legs held ready to seize prey. The male is very territorial — he has a particular area that he patrols and defends. Females are allowed to enter the territory, but other male darners are chased away.

Family: Aeshnidae
Size: 2¼–4¾ in (6–12 cm) long
Number of species: about 450
Habitat: worldwide

Family: Libellulidae
Size: ¾–2½ in (2–6 cm) long
Number of species: about 1,000
Habitat: worldwide

## Darter

This type of dragonfly gets its name from its fast darting flight. Like all dragonflies, darters lay their eggs in or close to water. The young are called nymphs or naiads. They look quite different from adults and live in water, catching prey such as tadpoles.

## Skimmer

A skimmer is a kind of dragonfly with a wide flattened body that is shorter than its wings. Some have a wingspan of up to 10 cm (4 in). Skimmers are usually seen flying near still or slow-moving water, such as ponds and swamps.

Family: Libellulidae
Size: ¾–2½ in (2–6 cm) long
Number of species: about 1,000
Habitat: worldwide

Family: Lestidae
Size: 1¼–2 in (3–5 cm) long
Number of species: about 150
Habitat: worldwide

## Damselfly

These insects are sometimes known as spread-winged damselflies because they hold their wings partly spread out when at rest. They live around ponds and marshes, where they catch insects such as small flies.

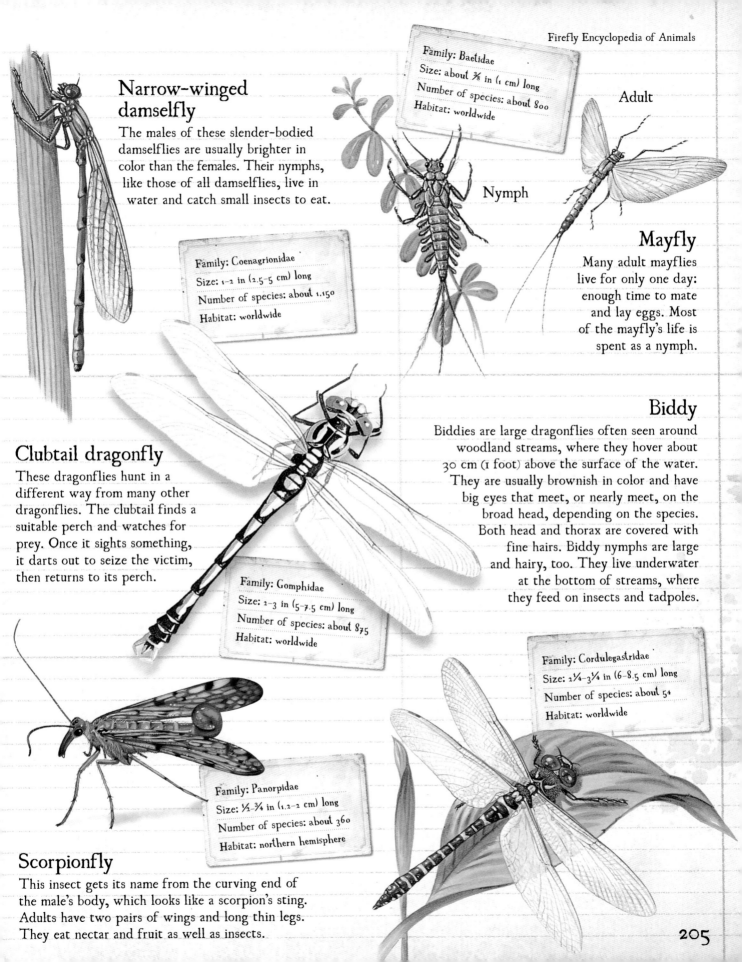

## Narrow-winged damselfly

The males of these slender-bodied damselflies are usually brighter in color than the females. Their nymphs, like those of all damselflies, live in water and catch small insects to eat.

Family: Coenagrionidae
Size: 1–2 in (2.5–5 cm) long
Number of species: about 1,150
Habitat: worldwide

Family: Baetidae
Size: about ⅜ in (1 cm) long
Number of species: about 800
Habitat: worldwide

Nymph

Adult

## Mayfly

Many adult mayflies live for only one day: enough time to mate and lay eggs. Most of the mayfly's life is spent as a nymph.

## Biddy

Biddies are large dragonflies often seen around woodland streams, where they hover about 30 cm (1 foot) above the surface of the water. They are usually brownish in color and have big eyes that meet, or nearly meet, on the broad head, depending on the species. Both head and thorax are covered with fine hairs. Biddy nymphs are large and hairy, too. They live underwater at the bottom of streams, where they feed on insects and tadpoles.

## Clubtail dragonfly

These dragonflies hunt in a different way from many other dragonflies. The clubtail finds a suitable perch and watches for prey. Once it sights something, it darts out to seize the victim, then returns to its perch.

Family: Gomphidae
Size: 2–3 in (5–7.5 cm) long
Number of species: about 875
Habitat: worldwide

Family: Cordulegastridae
Size: 2¼–3¼ in (6–8.5 cm) long
Number of species: about 54
Habitat: worldwide

Family: Panorpidae
Size: ½–¾ in (1.2–2 cm) long
Number of species: about 360
Habitat: northern hemisphere

## Scorpionfly

This insect gets its name from the curving end of the male's body, which looks like a scorpion's sting. Adults have two pairs of wings and long thin legs. They eat nectar and fruit as well as insects.

# BUGS, LICE, FLEAS AND BEETLES

These are some of the most numerous of all insects. Beetles form the largest group of insects and account for 40 percent of known insect species. One of the reasons for their success is that they can adapt to almost any type of food. Bugs, too, eat a wide range of foods from plant juices to human blood. Lice and fleas live as parasites, feeding on the blood, skin, feathers or hair of other animals.

Family: Cicadidae
Size: up to 2 in (5 cm) long
Number of species: about 2,500
Habitat: worldwide

Adult

## Cicada

This insect is best known for the shrill, almost constant call from the males. The sound is made by tymbals, a pair of structures located on the abdomen, which are vibrated by special muscles. Female cicadas usually lay their eggs in slits they make in tree branches. The nymphs live under the ground and feed on plant roots. As they grow, they molt — shedding their exoskeleton — until they finally make their way to the surface and emerge as adults.

## BUGS, LICE AND FLEAS

The name bug is used for insects generally, but it also describes a particular group of insects. These include a wide variety of aphids, cicadas and stinkbugs. All have special needlelike mouthparts for piercing food and sucking out the juices. Lice are small wingless insects which live on birds and mammals. There are two types: sucking lice and chewing lice. Fleas, too, are wingless. They have powerful legs to help them leap on to other animals to feed.

Family: Membracidae
Size: ¼–½ in (0.6–1.2 cm) long
Number of species: about 2,500
Habitat: worldwide

Family: Pentatomidae
Size: ¼–¾ in (0.6–2 cm) long
Number of species: about 5,500
Habitat: worldwide

## Stinkbug

Stinkbugs squirt a foul-smelling liquid at any creature that tries to attack them. The liquid comes from glands on the underside of the stinkbug's body. The bug uses its beaklike snout for piercing the surface of a plant or animal to get at the sap or body juices.

## Treehopper

Many of these little bugs have strangely shaped extensions on the thorax, which makes them look like the sharp thorns of plants. They feed mostly on sap from trees and other plants.

Family: Aphididae
Size: up to ⅜ in (0.9 cm) long
Number of species: about 2,250
Habitat: worldwide

## Plant bug

The biggest group of true bugs, plant bugs live in every kind of habitat. Most feed on leaves, seeds and fruit and some are serious pests of food crops such as alfalfa. Other plant bugs are more welcome to farmers since they feed on insects such as aphids, which are also pests. Plant bugs have delicate, often brightly colored bodies.

Family: Miridae
Size: ⅛–¾ in (0.3–1.9 cm) long
Number of species: about 8,000
Habitat: worldwide

## Aphid

These small, soft-bodied insects are familiar to gardeners because they feed on sap from the leaves and stems of plants and can damage them. They reproduce extremely quickly, but many are destroyed by insects such as ladybugs and parasitic wasps.

Family: Cercopidae
Size: up to ¾ in (2 cm) long
Number of species: about 2,400
Habitat: worldwide

## Bedbug

Bedbugs usually stay hidden during the day, then come out at night to feed on the blood of birds and mammals. They do not live on their host but in its home or nest, and their flattened bodies make it easy for them to hide in crevices. Adults can survive for weeks without food.

Family: Cimicidae
Size: up to ½ in (1.2 cm) long
Number of species: 90
Habitat: worldwide

Family: Pediculidae
Size: ⅟₁₆–¼ in (0.15–0.6 cm) long
Number of species: 7
Habitat: worldwide

## Froghopper

Like tiny frogs, froghoppers hop about on plants as they feed. They lay their eggs on plant stems and when the nymphs hatch they cover themselves with a substance much like spit, or saliva. This comes from glands on the abdomen and mixes with air to form a frothy mass. The froth helps to protect the nymphs and hides them from enemies.

## Head louse

The head louse is a sucking louse that lives on human heads, feeding on blood. It stays on the head by holding on to hairs with its strong legs and claws, and also glues its small eggs to the hairs of its host.

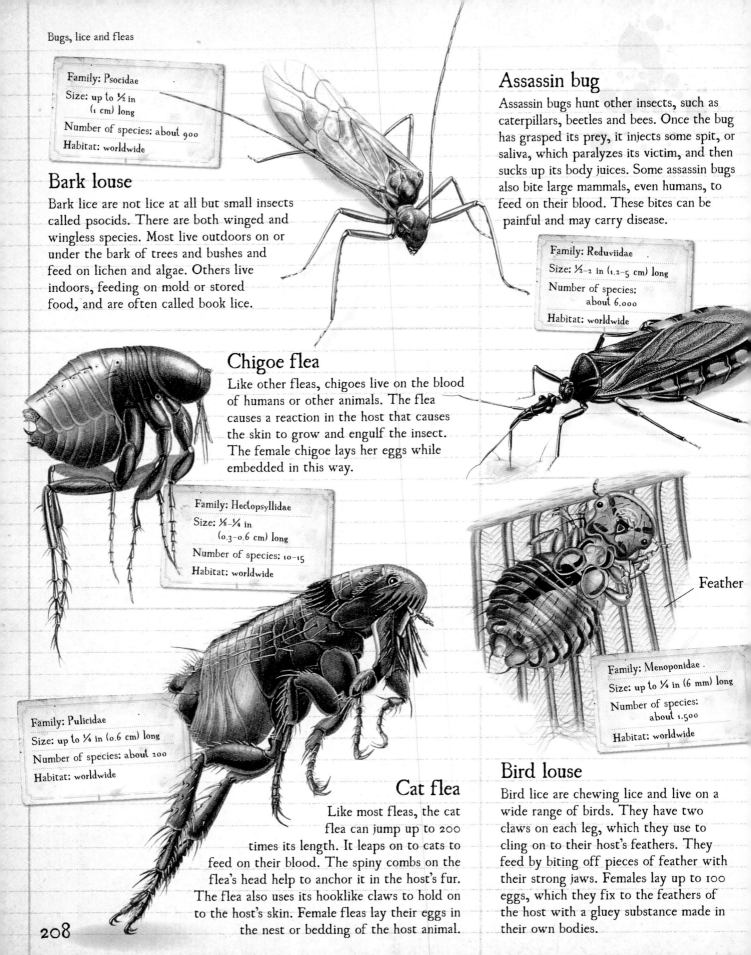

Family: Psocidae
Size: up to ½ in
(1 cm) long
Number of species: about 900
Habitat: worldwide

## Bark louse

Bark lice are not lice at all but small insects called psocids. There are both winged and wingless species. Most live outdoors on or under the bark of trees and bushes and feed on lichen and algae. Others live indoors, feeding on mold or stored food, and are often called book lice.

## Assassin bug

Assassin bugs hunt other insects, such as caterpillars, beetles and bees. Once the bug has grasped its prey, it injects some spit, or saliva, which paralyzes its victim, and then sucks up its body juices. Some assassin bugs also bite large mammals, even humans, to feed on their blood. These bites can be painful and may carry disease.

Family: Reduviidae
Size: ½–2 in (1.2–5 cm) long
Number of species:
about 6,000
Habitat: worldwide

## Chigoe flea

Like other fleas, chigoes live on the blood of humans or other animals. The flea causes a reaction in the host that causes the skin to grow and engulf the insect. The female chigoe lays her eggs while embedded in this way.

Family: Hectopsyllidae
Size: ⅛–¼ in
(0.3–0.6 cm) long
Number of species: 10–15
Habitat: worldwide

Feather

Family: Menoponidae
Size: up to ¼ in (6 mm) long
Number of species:
about 1,500
Habitat: worldwide

Family: Pulicidae
Size: up to ¼ in (0.6 cm) long
Number of species: about 200
Habitat: worldwide

## Cat flea

Like most fleas, the cat flea can jump up to 200 times its length. It leaps on to cats to feed on their blood. The spiny combs on the flea's head help to anchor it in the host's fur. The flea also uses its hooklike claws to hold on to the host's skin. Female fleas lay their eggs in the nest or bedding of the host animal.

## Bird louse

Bird lice are chewing lice and live on a wide range of birds. They have two claws on each leg, which they use to cling on to their host's feathers. They feed by biting off pieces of feather with their strong jaws. Females lay up to 100 eggs, which they fix to the feathers of the host with a gluey substance made in their own bodies.

# BEETLES

About 370,000 species of beetle are known and there are certainly many more yet to be discovered. They live in almost every type of habitat, from polar lands to rain forests, and feed on almost every type of food with their strong, chewing mouthparts. Typically, beetles have two pairs of wings — the front pair, called elytra, are thick and hard and act as covers for the more delicate back wings. When the beetle is at rest, its back wings are folded safely away under the front wings.

Family: Staphylinidae .
Size: up to 1½ in (4 cm) long
Number of species:
about 29,000
Habitat: worldwide

## Rove beetle

This beetle has a long body and short wing cases that cover only a little of the abdomen. When it is disturbed, it holds the back end of its body up, like a scorpion does. Both adult rove beetles and their larvae prey on insects and other small creatures such as worms.

## Tiger beetle

The colorful tiger beetle has long legs and is a fast runner. A fierce active hunter, it catches smaller insects in its strong jaws. The female beetle lays its eggs in the sand. When the larvae hatch, they dig burrows where they hide, waiting to grab passing prey.

Family: Carabidae
Size: ¹/₁₆–3 in
    (0.2–8 cm) long
Number of species:
about 29,000
Habitat: worldwide

Family: Scarabaeidae .
Size: ¹/₁₆–6¾ in
    (0.2–17 cm) long
Number of species:
about 16,500
Habitat: worldwide

## Whirligig beetle

Glossy whirligig beetles swim on the surface of ponds and streams, feeding on insects that fall into the water. Their eyes are divided into two parts so that they can see above and below the water surface at the same time. Larval whirligigs eat water insects, but they also hunt other small creatures such as snails.

## Goliath beetle

One of the largest and heaviest of all insects is the goliath beetle, found in Africa. Males are the giants; females are smaller and less brightly patterned. These beetles have strong front legs and are excellent climbers. They clamber up into trees in search of sap and soft fruit to eat.

Family: Gyrinidae
Size: ⅛–⅝ in
    (0.3–1.5 cm) long
Number of species: 750
Habitat: worldwide

# Diving beetle

Diving beetles live in ponds and lakes. They swim by moving their paddlelike back legs together as oars. When they dive, these beetles can stay under for some time, using air trapped under the wing cases. Both adults and larvae hunt prey.

Family: Dytiscidae
Size: ¹⁄₁₆–1⅝ in (0.15–4 cm) long
Number of species: about 3,500
Habitat: worldwide

# Jewel beetle

With their gleaming metallic colors, jewel beetles deserve their name. They live in woodland, usually in tropical areas, where the adults feed on flower nectar and leaves. The larvae bore into dead or living wood as they eat, and can cause a great deal of damage.

Family: Buprestidae
Size: ¾–2½ in (2–6 cm) long
Number of species: about 15,000
Habitat: worldwide

Family: Curculionidae
Size: ¹⁄₁₆–3½ in (0.15–9 cm) long
Number of species: about 48,000
Habitat: worldwide

# Boll weevil

This insect belongs to the weevil family, all of which eat plants and can cause serious damage. The boll weevil uses its long snout to bore into the seedpods — called bolls — and buds of cotton plants. Females also lay their eggs in holes made in seedpods.

# Carrion beetle

These brightly colored beetles and their larvae feed on dead animals, such as mice and birds. Some carrion beetles dig under the corpse so that it sinks into the ground. They then lay their eggs on the buried, decaying creature so that their young have a ready supply of food to eat when they hatch.

Family: Elateridae
Size: up to 2¼ in (6 cm) long
Number of species: about 9,000
Habitat: worldwide

Family: Silphidae
Size: up to 1½ in (4 cm) long
Number of species: about 250
Habitat: worldwide

# Click beetle

The clicking sound made as they leap in the air to escape predators and to right themselves gives these beetles their name. They can jump as high as 30 cm (12 in). Adult beetles feed on plants and live on the ground or in rotting wood.

## Longhorn beetle

This beetle has extremely long antennae — up to three times the length of its body. Adults feed on mainly on leaves, roots and pollen and do not usually catch prey. While her mate stands guard, the female lays her eggs in crevices in living trees or logs. When the larvae hatch, they tunnel into the wood as they feed and may cause considerable damage to timber and trees.

Family: Cerambycidae
Size: up to 7 in (18 cm) long, including antennae
Number of species: about 30,000
Habitat: worldwide

Family: Tenebrionidae
Size: ¾–1¾ in (2–4.5 cm) long
Number of species: about 17,000
Habitat: worldwide

## Darkling beetle

Common in dry areas, where they lurk under stones, darkling beetles scurry out at night to feed. They are scavengers and eat many kinds of foods, including rotting wood, insect larvae and stored grain. Some desert-living darklings have long legs and can move quickly as they run from one patch of shade to another.

## Ladybug

The ladybug's round, spotted body makes it one of the most easily identifiable of all insects. Its bright colors warn the ladybug's enemies that it tastes unpleasant and may be poisonous. Adults and larvae feed mainly on aphids, which suck the juices of plants and can be serious pests. Without ladybugs, these insects would be a far greater problem for farmers and gardeners.

Family: Coccinellidae
Size: up to ½ in (1.5 cm) long
Number of species: 5,000
Habitat: worldwide

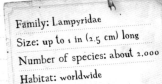

## Firefly

Fireflies can produce a yellowish-green light in a special area at the end of the abdomen. Each species of firefly flashes its light in a particular pattern to attract mates of its own kind. Male fireflies have wings, but females are often wingless and look like larvae.

Family: Lampyridae
Size: up to 1 in (2.5 cm) long
Number of species: about 2,000
Habitat: worldwide

# STAG BEETLES

With their large heads and massive jaws, male stag beetles look fierce, but these insects are harmless and feed mostly on tree sap and other liquids. There are about 1,300 species of stag beetle, some as long as 10 cm (4 in). Mostly black or brownish in color, they usually live in woodland and are particularly common in tropical areas. The jaws of the males are branched like the antlers of a stag and, like stags, these beetles take part in fierce battles with one another to win females. They rarely bite, but they do sometimes damage each other's wing cases. The beetle with the biggest jaws usually wins the contest. Female stag beetles lay their eggs in cracks in logs or dead tree stumps. When the larvae hatch, they feed on the juices of the rotting wood.

Its wing cases raised, this magnificent stag beetle is about to take to the air. When the beetle is not in flight, the tough front wings, which act as the wing cases, protect the more delicate back wings, which are folded underneath.

Larva

Pupa

## FEMALE STAG BEETLE

The female stag beetle is smaller than the battling male and does not have such large jaws. However, she can give a much more powerful nip if under threat. The male's mighty jaws are so specialized for fighting that they are almost useless for feeding or biting.

## LARVA AND PUPA

Stag beetle eggs hatch into wormlike C-shaped larvae called grubs. They spend most of their time feeding and grow quickly. As a larva grows, it molts several times – it sheds its skin to allow for the increase in body size. When the larva is full grown, it becomes a pupa – the stage during which the larva changes into an adult beetle. Finally, a winged, adult beetle comes out of the pupa.

# THE HELPLESS LOSER

If a stag beetle lands on its back after a battle, it is very hard for it to right itself again. In this position, it is extremely easy for other enemies, such as birds, to snatch the beetle up.

# BATTLING RIVALS

The beetles usually meet on the branch of a tree. As they struggle, each male tries to lock the other in its jaws — the jaws are just the right shape to fit around the top part of the stag beetle's body. Once one competitor succeeds in grabbing the other, he lifts the loser up and tries to throw him off the branch.

# FLIES, MOTHS AND BUTTERFLIES

Flies are sometimes thought of as dirty and disease-carrying but, like bees, they pollinate plants as they feed and they are an important source of food for many other creatures, such as birds. Also, their scavenging habits help to get rid of decaying waste, such as dung and dead bodies. With large, often beautifully patterned wings, butterflies and moths pollinate plants too, as they flit from flower to flower sipping nectar.

Family: Chironomidae
Size: 1/16–3/8 in (0.15–0.9 cm) long
Number of species: about 5,0
Habitat: worldwide

## Midge

Tiny, delicate insects, these midges do not bite. They fly in huge swarms, usually in the evening, and are often seen near ponds and streams. Their larvae live in damp places or in water. Most feed on rotting plants and algae but some are predators.

## FLIES

Among the larger groups of insects, with more than 150,000 known species, flies are common almost everywhere — one of the few land-based creatures in Antarctica is a midge, a type of fly. Flies have only one pair of wings. The hind wings are reduced to small knobbed structures called halteres, which help the fly to balance in flight. Flies usually take liquid food. Many sip nectar and sap from plants or lap up juices from rotting plants. Some, such as mosquitoes, suck blood from humans and other animals.

Family: Asilidae
Size: 1/4–1 3/4 in (0.6–4.5 cm) long
Number of species: about 5,000
Habitat: worldwide

Family: Tabanidae
Size: 1/4–1 in (0.6–2.5 cm) long
Number of species: about 4,100
Habitat: worldwide

## Horse fly

These flies have particularly large, iridescent (shimmering) eyes. Males feed on pollen and nectar, but female horse flies take blood from mammals, including humans. Their bites can be painful and the flies may carry diseases such as anthrax.

## Robber fly

A fast-moving hunter, the robber fly chases and catches other insects in the air or pounces on them on the ground. It has strong, bristly legs for seizing its prey. Once it has caught its victim, the robber fly sucks out its body fluids with its sharp mouthparts. Larvae live in soil or rotting wood, where they feed on the larvae of other insects.

# Hover fly

Also known as flower flies, adult hover flies feed on pollen and nectar and are often seen around flowers. They are expert fliers and can hover with ease and even fly backward. Many species are brightly colored and look much like bees or wasps but do not sting. Some hover fly larvae hunt insects such as aphids. Others feed on plants or live in the nests of bees or wasps, where they feed on the larvae.

Family: Syrphidae
Size: ¼–1¼ in (0.6–3 cm) long
Number of species: about 6,000
Habitat: worldwide

Family: Tipulidae
Size: ¼–2½ in (0.6–6 cm) long
Number of species: about 15,000
Habitat: worldwide

# Crane fly

With their long thin legs, crane flies look like large mosquitoes, but they do not bite or suck blood. The largest have a wingspan of as much as 2¾ in (7 cm). Most adults live only a few days and probably do not eat at all. The larvae feed mainly on plant roots and rotting plants, although some do hunt for their food.

# Blow fly

Many blow flies are colored metallic blue or green. Adults feed on pollen and nectar as well as fluids from rotting matter. Many lay their eggs in carrion — the bodies of dead animals — or in dung, so that the larvae, called maggots, have plenty of food to eat when they hatch.

Family: Calliphoridae
Size: ¾–⅝ in (0.6–1.5 cm) long
Number of species: about 1,200
Habitat: worldwide

Family: Muscidae
Size: ⅛–½ in (0.3–1.2 cm) long
Number of species: about 4,000
Habitat: worldwide

# Fruit fly

These little flies are common around flowers and overripe fruit. Their larvae feed on plant matter and some are serious pests, causing great damage to fruit trees and other crops.

# Housefly

Found almost everywhere in the world, houseflies suck liquids from manure and other decaying matter and from fresh fruit and plants. These insects can be dangerous as they may carry diseases.

Family: Tephritidae
Size: ⅛–⅜ in (0.3–0.9 cm) long
Number of species: about 4,500
Habitat: worldwide

215

# BUTTERFLIES AND MOTHS

Wherever plants grow, there are butterflies and moths. Known as the Lepidoptera, this is the second largest group of insects, containing about 165,000 species. Caddisflies look similar to butterflies and moths but are in fact a separate group called the Trichoptera. The young butterfly or moth is called a caterpillar. It spends most of its life feeding on plants and growing fast. When it has reached its full size, a caterpillar becomes a pupa. During this stage, it makes its transformation from wingless larva to winged adult.

Family: Tineidae
Size: wingspan ¼–¾ in (0.6–2 cm) long
Number of species: about 2,500
Habitat: worldwide

## Clothes moth

The caterpillars of the clothes moth feed on hair and feathers in animal nests and on the dried corpses of small mammals and birds. Few creatures, other than some beetle larvae, can digest these tough foods. Because our clothes are often made of animal wool, the caterpillars often come into our homes to feed on cloth. The adult moths are small and brownish in color, with narrow front wings that are folded neatly over the body when at rest. They do not usually eat anything.

Family: Geometridae
Size: wingspan ¾–3 in (1.7–7.4 cm) long
Number of species: about 20,000
Habitat: worldwide

## Geometrid moth

Geometrids have slender bodies and fragile wings. When they are at rest, they spread their wings out flat. Their caterpillars are known as inchworms because they seem to be measuring, inch by inch, as they move. They eat leaves and may cause serious damage to trees.

Family: Sphingidae
Size: wingspan 1¼–6 in (3–15 cm) long
Number of species: about 1,100
Habitat: worldwide

## Hummingbird hawkmoth

Many of the scales on the wings of this hawkmoth drop off after its first flight, leaving large, clear areas. It feeds on flower nectar, using its long proboscis, or feeding tube, to reach deep into the flowers. It hovers as it feeds, making a noise like the sound of a hummingbird's wings.

## Large caddisfly

Caddisflies look like moths but have hairs not scales on the body and wings, and short mouthparts for lapping up food instead of a proboscis. The caterpillarlike larvae are usually aquatic and live and pupate in water, in cases made of leaves, stones or twigs.

Family: Phryganeidae
Size: wingspan ½ –1 in (1.2–2.5 cm) long
Number of species: about 450
Habitat: worldwide

Larva

Large Caddis fly

## Cotton boll moth

This moth belongs to one of the biggest families of moths. Most moths in this family are night-flying and dull in color. The cotton boll caterpillar feeds on cotton seedpods and can damage the plants.

Family: Noctuidae
Size: wingspan ½ –3 in (1.2–7.5 cm) long
Number of species: about 22,000
Habitat: worldwide

## Atlas moth

These brightly patterned moths are some of the largest in the world. Most have transparent scaleless patches on their broad wings and feathery antennae. The antennae help male moths pick up the scent signals given off by females when looking for mates. Adults have very small mouthparts and do not generally feed during their short lives.

Family: Saturniidae
Size: wingspan 1–10 in (2.5–25 cm) long
Number of species: about 1,200
Habitat: worldwide

## Luna moth

This beautiful moth has wings that can measure up to 4 in (11 cm) across with long tails trailing from them. It lives in forests and its caterpillars feed on the leaves of trees such as hickory, walnut and birch. The caterpillars pupate in a cocoon on the ground.

Family: Saturniidae
Size: wingspan 1–10 in (2.5–25 cm) long
Number of species: about 1,200
Habitat: worldwide

Family: Arctiidae
Size: wingspan ¾ –2¾ in (2–7 cm) long
Number of species: 2,500
Habitat: worldwide

## Tiger moth

Tiger moths have broad hairy bodies and boldly patterned wings. The bright markings of these moths, and of their hairy caterpillars, warn birds and mammals that they are unpleasant to eat. The caterpillars feed on plants that are poisonous to vertebrate animals, and store the poison for their own protection.

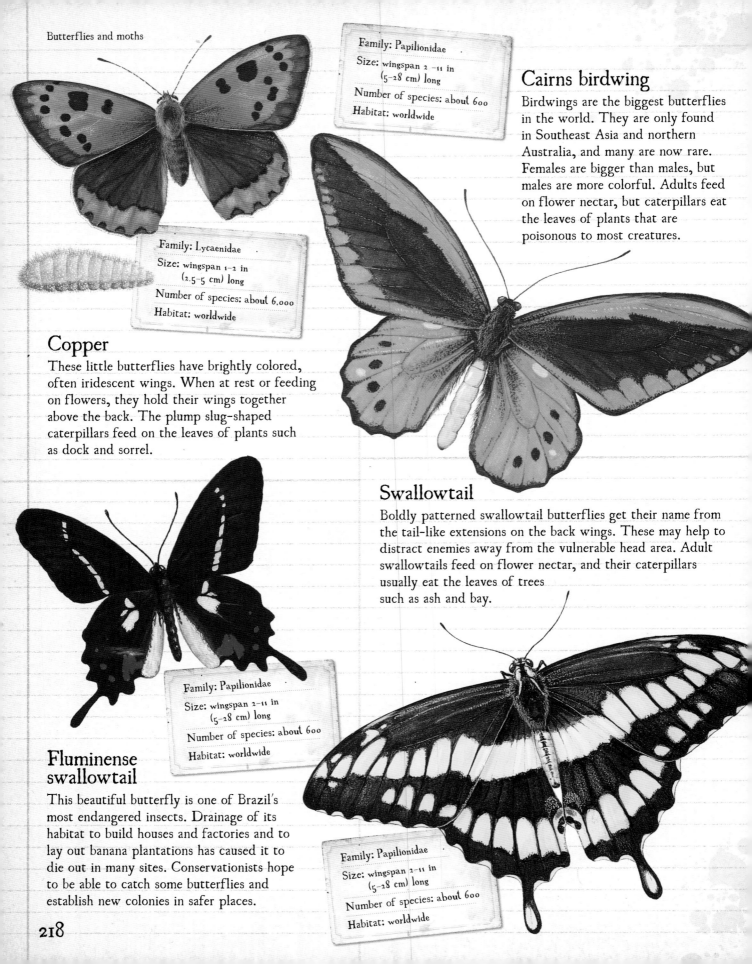

Family: Papilionidae

Size: wingspan 2 –11 in
(5–28 cm) long

Number of species: about 600

Habitat: worldwide

## Cairns birdwing

Birdwings are the biggest butterflies
in the world. They are only found
in Southeast Asia and northern
Australia, and many are now rare.
Females are bigger than males, but
males are more colorful. Adults feed
on flower nectar, but caterpillars eat
the leaves of plants that are
poisonous to most creatures.

Family: Lycaenidae

Size: wingspan 1–2 in
(2.5–5 cm) long

Number of species: about 6,000

Habitat: worldwide

## Copper

These little butterflies have brightly colored,
often iridescent wings. When at rest or feeding
on flowers, they hold their wings together
above the back. The plump slug-shaped
caterpillars feed on the leaves of plants such
as dock and sorrel.

## Swallowtail

Boldly patterned swallowtail butterflies get their name from
the tail-like extensions on the back wings. These may help to
distract enemies away from the vulnerable head area. Adult
swallowtails feed on flower nectar, and their caterpillars
usually eat the leaves of trees
such as ash and bay.

Family: Papilionidae

Size: wingspan 2–11 in
(5–28 cm) long

Number of species: about 600

Habitat: worldwide

## Fluminense
## swallowtail

This beautiful butterfly is one of Brazil's
most endangered insects. Drainage of its
habitat to build houses and factories and to
lay out banana plantations has caused it to
die out in many sites. Conservationists hope
to be able to catch some butterflies and
establish new colonies in safer places.

Family: Papilionidae

Size: wingspan 2–11 in
(5–28 cm) long

Number of species: about 600

Habitat: worldwide

# Cabbage white

The cabbage white, like others in its family, is a very common butterfly. Unlike many butterflies, it has well-developed front legs, which are used for walking. Adults feed on nectar. Their caterpillars eat cabbage and other leafy crops, and can do great damage.

Family: Pieridae

Size: wingspan ¾–2¾ in (0.9–7 cm) long

Number of species: about 1,200

Habitat: worldwide

Family: Nymphalidae

Size: wingspan 1¼–6 in (3–15 cm) long

Number of species: about 5,000

Habitat: tropical

# Morpho

Morpho butterflies live in the rain forests of Central and South America. The males are brilliantly colored – the beautiful iridescence of their wings is caused by the arrangement of the rows of scales, which reflect the light. Females are much plainer.

# Monarch

Every fall, millions of monarch butterflies fly south from Canada to Mexico — a distance of about 3,200 km (2,000 miles). The following spring, the females lay their eggs as they return north. Then the new monarch butterflies fly north to Canada before fall returns.

Family: Papilionidae

Size: wingspan 2–11 in (5–28 cm) long

Number of species: about 600

Habitat: worldwide

Family: Nymphalidae

Size: wingspan 1¼–6 in (3–15 cm) long

Number of species: about 5,000

Habitat: worldwide

# Queen Alexandra's birdwing

The female of this giant butterfly is the biggest in the world, with a wingspan of up to 28 cm (11 in). It is highly prized by collectors, so local people catch it to sell to traders. It is hoped that if some of the forest in which the butterflies live can be saved in reserves, local people might be able to earn a living from tourism instead.

# SPHINX MOTHS

Of all butterflies and moths, the sphinx moths — also called hawkmoths — are some of the most powerful fliers. Their wings beat so fast that they make a whirring noise. Some sphinx moths can even hover like hummingbirds in front of flowers as they feed. Like all moths, the adults eat liquid food such as nectar. They suck up the food with a strawlike tongue called a proboscis, which is coiled under the head when not in use. They have the longest tongues of any moths and can feed on nectar at the bottom of long tubelike flowers. There are about 1,100 species of hawkmoth, some with wingspans of up to 6 in (15 cm). Most have large heavy bodies and long narrow front wings.

A privet hawkmoth lands on a flower to feed on nectar with the help of its long proboscis. The moth's caterpillar feeds on the leaves of privet, lilac and ash.

## OLEANDER SPHINX MOTH

This is one of the most beautifully patterned of all moths. Its caterpillar feeds on the leaves of plants such as oleander and grows up to 15 cm (6 in) long. It has bold eyespots on its body, which can fool a predator into thinking it a much larger creature than it really is.

## BEE SPHINX MOTH

A bee sphinx moth plunges its long tongue deep into a flower. With its broad striped body and the large clear areas without scales on its wings, this moth looks amazingly like a bee as it hovers over plants — the resemblance to a stinging insect may help to scare away potential predators. Many moths are nocturnal, but the bee sphinx flies during the day, not at night.

# WHITE-LINED SPHINX MOTH

The white-lined sphinx moth visits flowers at night to feed. Like most moths, it has antennae that are extremely sensitive to smell as well as touch. It can pick up the faintest scents, which helps it to find flowers in the darkness.

# POPLAR SPHINX MOTH

The color and irregular shape of the poplar sphinx moth's wings help it to hide on bark as it rests during the day. Its caterpillars feed on the leaves of trees such as poplar and willow.

# EGG TO PUPA

As soon as a caterpillar hatches from its egg it starts to feed, devouring plants with its strong chewing mouthparts. It grows fast and sheds its skin several times as it gets bigger. When fully grown, the caterpillar becomes a pupa. The bee sphinx moth pupates on the ground in a cocoon made of silk.

Egg

Caterpillar

Pupa in cocoon

# BEES, WASPS, ANTS AND TERMITES

Bees, wasps and ants belong to a large group of about 198,000 insects. Although they vary greatly, most have a definite "waist" at the front of the abdomen. They have mouthparts for chewing and tonguelike structures for sipping liquids such as flower nectar. Species that have wings have two pairs, but many worker ants are wingless. Ants and some bees and wasps live in social colonies in elaborate nests. Termites are not related to ants, bees and wasps, but they too live in huge colonies. They make nests in soil or trees, or in specially built mounds.

Family: Megachilidae

Size: ⅜–¾ in (0.9–2 cm) long

Number of species: about 3,000

Habitat: worldwide

## Leafcutter bee

This bee gets its name from its habit of cutting circular pieces of leaves and flowers with its jaws. It uses these pieces to line larval cells in its tunnel nest, made in soil or rotting wood. Stores of nectar and pollen are put into the cells and an egg is then laid in each one.

## BEES

These flying insects have two pairs of wings and their bodies are covered with tiny hairs. Some, such as leafcutter bees, live alone and make their own nests for their young. Others, such as honeybees and bumblebees, live in huge colonies that may contain thousands of bees. Only bee colonies produce honey.

Family: Apidae

Size: ⅛–1 in (0.3–2.5 cm) long

Number of species: about 1,000

Habitat: worldwide

## Bumblebee

Bumblebees are large hairy insects, usually black in color with some yellow markings. In spring, queens look for underground nest sites. Each queen collects pollen and nectar and makes food called beebread. Later she lays eggs, and when the larvae hatch they feed on the beebread. These larvae become adult worker bees and they take over the work of the colony while the queen continues to lay eggs.

Family: Colletidae

Size: ⅛–¾ in (0.3–2 cm) long

Number of species: over 2,000

Habitat: worldwide

## Plasterer bee

Plasterer bees nest in the ground in burrows with branching tunnels. They line the tunnels with a secretion from glands in the abdomen, which dries to a clear waterproof substance. Cells for larvae are made in the tunnels.

Family: Apidae
Size: ⅛–1 in (0.3–2.5 cm) long
Number of species: about 1,000
Habitat: worldwide

# Orchid bee

Most orchid bees live in tropical areas and are brightly colored. Males are attracted to orchid flowers for their nectar. They pollinate the flowers and collect scent, which may play a part in their mating rituals.

Family: Apidae
Size: ⅛–1 in (0.3–2.5 cm) long
Number of species: about 1,000
Habitat: worldwide

# Carpenter bee

The female carpenter bee chews a tunnel-like nest in wood. She makes a line of separate cells inside the tunnel, fills them with pollen and nectar food stores and lays one egg in each cell. She stays nearby and guards the nest against any enemies.

# Cuckoo bee

Like its namesake the cuckoo bird, this wasplike bee lays its eggs in the nests of other bees, which have prepared food stores for their eggs. The cuckoo bee's eggs hatch first and the larvae eat up all the food intended for the host's larvae.

Family: Anthophoridae
Size: ⅜–½ in (0.9–1.2 cm) long
Number of species: about 4,200
Habitat: worldwide

Family: Apidae
Size: ⅛–1 in (0.3–2.5 cm) long
Number of species: about 1,000
Habitat: worldwide

Family: Andrenidae
Size: ⅛–¾ in (0.3–2 cm) long
Number of species: about 4,000
Habitat: worldwide

# Stingless bee

As their name suggests, these bees cannot sting, but they have strong jaws that they use to bite any intruders. They live in colonies and make nests under the ground in a tree trunk or even in part of a nest of a termite colony.

# Mining bee

Mining bees nest in long branching tunnels that they dig in the ground. Cells in the tunnels are stocked with nectar and pollen, and an egg is laid in each one. Each bee digs its own nest but large numbers may live close together.

# WASPS

Wasps feed their young on other insects, such as caterpillars and aphids that harm garden and food plants. Without wasps there would be many more of these pests. Adult wasps feed mainly on nectar and the juice of ripe fruit. Many wasps, including mud daubers and spider wasps, live alone and make their own nests for their eggs. Others, such as common wasps and hornets, live in large colonies and make group nests. Wasp colonies do not store food like honeybees. Only the new queens survive the winter, in other shelters.

Family: Vespidae
Size: ⅜–1¼ in (1–3 cm) long
Number of species: about 4,000
Habitat: worldwide

Family: Pompilidae
Size: ¼–3 in (0.5–8 cm) long
Number of species: about 4,000
Habitat: worldwide

## Blue-black spider wasp

Adult spider wasps feed on nectar but the female catches spiders to feed her young. She paralyzes the spider with her sting, then places it in a nest cell with an egg and seals the top with mud. When the wasp larva hatches, it eats the spider.

Family: Vespidae
Size: ⅜–1¼ in (1–3 cm) long
Number of species: about 4,000
Habitat: worldwide

## Giant hornet

Adult hornets feed on insects and nectar and grow to up to 1¼ in (3 cm) long. They live in colonies in nests built of a papery material they make by mixing saliva with chewed up plant material. The nest is usually in a tree or an old building. Larvae feed on insects caught by the adults.

## Paper wasp

The paper wasp builds her nest with a papery material that she makes from chewed wood mixed with her spit. She lays her eggs in the cells, and more females join her to help feed the young with other insects. About 20 wasps usually live in a nest.

## Velvet ant

Velvet ants are not ants but hairy wasps. Only the males have wings. The females search for the nests of bees and other kinds of wasp and lay their eggs on their larvae. When each velvet ant hatches, it eats its host.

Family: Mutillidae
Size: ¼–1 in (0.6–2.5 cm) long
Number of species: about 5,000
Habitat: worldwide

Family: Cynipidae
Size: 1/16–3/8 in
(0.15–0.9 cm) long
Number of species: about 1,250
Habitat: worldwide

# Gall wasp

These tiny wasps lay their eggs on particular species of plants. For reasons that are not fully understood, the host plant forms a growth, called a gall, around the egg. When the larva hatches it feeds on the gall tissue.

# Common wasp

Common wasps, or yellow jackets, feed on nectar and other sweet things such as ripe fruit. They also catch other insects to feed their young. Like other vespid wasps, the females are well known for their sting. The pointed sting is at the end of the body and is linked to a bag of poison. The wasp uses its sting to kill prey and to defend itself against enemies — including humans.

Family: Ichneumonidae
Size: 1/8–2 in (0.3–5 cm) long
Number of species: about 60,000
Habitat: worldwide

Family: Vespidae
Size: 3/8–1 1/4 in
(1–3 cm) long
Number of species: about 4,000
Habitat: worldwide

# Ichneumon wasp

The female ichneumon wasp can bore through wood to lay her eggs near the larvae of other insects such as wood wasps. She has a special long egg-laying tube, called an ovipositor. When the egg hatches, the ichneumon larva feeds on the host larva.

# Mud dauber

Mud daubers are solitary wasps, which feed on other insects and nectar. The female mud dauber wasp makes a nest of damp mud. Into each cell she puts an egg and some paralyzed insects for her young to eat when it hatches.

Family: Tenthredinidae
Size: up to 1 1/4 in
(3.2 cm) long
Number of species: about 6,000
Habitat: worldwide

Family: Sphecidae
Size: 3/8–2 in
(0.9–5 cm) long
Number of species: 8,000
Habitat: worldwide

# Sawfly

The sawfly is related to wasps but lacks the "waist" between the abdomen and thorax. The female sawfly uses her ovipositor (egg-laying tube) to cut slits in the stems and leaves of plants where she then lays her eggs. The caterpillarlike larvae feed on leaves when they hatch.

# HONEYBEES

Honeybees are probably the best known bees of all. They pollinate countless food crops and produce billions of dollars' worth of honey and wax every year. They live in huge colonies of thousands of bees, with a complex social organization. Each colony has a queen. She is larger than the other bees and lays all the eggs of the colony. Most of the members of the colony are female workers. They care for the young, build and repair the nest and gather food, but they do not lay eggs. At certain times of year the colony includes male bees, called drones, whose only role is to mate with new queens. The nest is made in a hollow tree or in a beekeeper's hive and consists of sheets of hexagonal (six-sided) cells that make up the honeycomb. These cells contain eggs and young as well as food stores of pollen and honey.

## BUSY BEES

When a worker bee returns from a foraging trip laden with pollen and nectar, the other bees gather around to collect the food stores. Workers also make the nest cells, building them from wax produced in glands on the underside of the bee's abdomen. The bee pulls out thin flakes of wax and kneads it with her mouthparts until it is soft enough to use for building the honeycomb.

## WORKERS

A worker honeybee lives only about six weeks. For the first week of her adult life she cares for the eggs and larvae of the colony. Then she helps build cells and maintain the nest. Finally she becomes a food gatherer, bringing nectar and pollen back to the nest.

A worker honeybee has just returned to the nest, with her pollen baskets full of golden-yellow pollen. Other workers gather round to help her unload the pollen and pack it into cells.

# ROYAL CELLS

Special cells for future queens hang from the edge of the comb. The larvae in these queen cells are fed on royal jelly — a protein-rich substance from glands on the workers' heads. Worker larvae are fed royal jelly for a few days and then pollen and nectar.

# EQUIPPED FOR WORK

All the tools needed by a worker bee are on her own body. On each front leg there are long hairs used for removing pollen from the body and a special notch for cleaning the antennae. On the middle legs there are fringes of hair for removing pollen from the forelegs and a spike for taking wax from glands in the abdomen. On each hind leg there is a pollen basket — a special area lined with hairs for carrying pollen.

227

# ANTS AND TERMITES

Ants live in huge well-organized groups, or colonies, of thousands of individuals Most colonies make a nest of interconnecting tunnels in rotting wood or under the ground. Each colony includes at least one queen that lays all the eggs. The workers are also female but cannot lay eggs. They do all the work, gathering food and looking after eggs and young. Termites are more closely related to cockroaches than to ants, but they too build large nests.

Family: Formicidae
Size: ⅟₁₆–1 in (0.15–2.5 cm) long
Number of species: about 9,000
Habitat: worldwide

## Fire ant

This ant gets its name from its powerful bite and sting, which is extremely painful even to humans. It hunts other insects, which it stings to death, but also eats seeds, fruit and flowers. Fire ants make nests in the ground or under logs or stones.

Family: Formicidae
Size: ⅟₁₆–1 in (0.15–2.5 cm) long
Number of species: about 9,000
Habitat: worldwide

## Harvester ant

These ants get their name from their habit of feeding on seeds and grain crops. When the ants find a plentiful supply of seeds near their nest, they leave scent trails to lead others in their colony to the food. In times of plenty, the ants collect more seeds than they can eat and store them in special granary areas in the nest.

## Red ant

The main food of red ants is aphid honeydew, a sweet liquid that is a by-product of the digestive system of these tiny bugs. The ant "milks" the aphid by stroking it to encourage it to release the sugary liquid. In return for this food, the ants protect the aphids from predators. Some even store the aphids in their nest over winter.

Family: Formicidae
Size: ⅟₁₆–1 in (0.15–2.5 cm) long
Number of species: about 9,000
Habitat: worldwide

Family: Formicidae
Size: ⅟₁₆–1 in (0.15–2.5 cm) long
Number of species: about 9,000
Habitat: worldwide

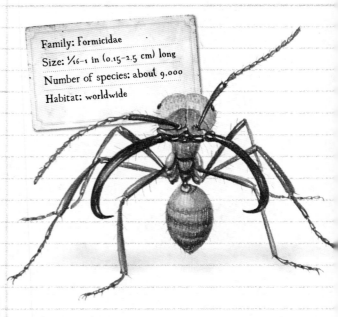

## Army ant

Unlike other ants, army ants do not build permanent nests. They march in search of prey, and only periodically stop to produce eggs. The worker ants link their bodies together, making a temporary nest called a bivouac to protect the queen and young. When the young have developed, they move on.

Family: Rhinotermitidae
Size: ¼–⅜ in
(0.6–0.9 cm) long
Number of species: about 360
Habitat: worldwide

Family: Formicidae
Size: ⅟₁₆–1 in (0.15–2.5 cm) long
Number of species:
about 9,000
Habitat: worldwide

## Subterranean termite

As their name suggests, these termites live in underground nests. They live in warm wooded areas and eat the wood of rotting trees and roots.

## Snouted termite

Most termite colonies have special soldier termites to defend them against enemies such as ants, which may attack their nests. The soldiers of this type of termite have long snouts, which they use to spray sticky bad-smelling fluids at ants and other enemies.

Family: Termitidae
Size: up to 2¼ in (6 cm) long
Number of species:
about 2,000
Habitat: worldwide

## Leafcutter ant

These ants grow their own food. They cut bits of leaves with their strong scissorlike jaws and carry them back to their underground nest. Here, the leaves are chewed up and mixed with droppings to make compost heaps. The ants eat the special fungus that grows on the compost.

## Drywood termite

These termites attack the wood of buildings, furniture and even stored timber. Special microscopic organisms in their gut help them digest their tough food. The special soldier termites have larger heads and jaws than the others and it is their job to defend the colony against enemies.

Family: Formicidae
Size: ⅟₁₆–1 in (0.15–2.5 cm) long
Number of species: about 9,000
Habitat: worldwide

Soldier

Drywood
termite

Family: Kalotermitidae
Size: up to 1 in (2.5 cm) long
Number of species: about 450
Habitat: worldwide

## Carpenter ant

Colonies of carpenter ants make their nests in wooden buildings or poles or in rotting tree trunks and often cause a great deal of damage. As with all ants, the queen lays all the eggs for the colony. As she lays, worker ants remove the eggs and take them to special brood chambers where they are cared for.

# SPIDERS AND SCORPIONS

Often confused with insects, the arachnids — which include spiders, scorpions, ticks and mites — are a separate group of invertebrates. They first lived on land at least 400 million years ago. Today, arachnids include a wide range of body forms, but they have four pairs of legs and do not have wings or antennae. Most live on land and hunt other creatures to eat.

## SPIDERS

Most spiders are harmless. Only a few have a venomous bite that is dangerous to people. In fact, spiders help us by keeping insect numbers under control. All are hunters and feed mostly on small insects. Some of the larger species catch birds and other small animals. All spiders can make silk with the special glands at the end of the body, but not all build webs. Spiders use silk to line their burrows and some make silken traps that they hold between their legs to snare prey. Young spiders use long strands of silk as parachutes to drift away and find new territories.

Family: Salticidae

Size: ⅛–⅝ in (0.3–1.5 cm) long

Number of species: about 5,700

Habitat: worldwide

### Jumping spider

Unlike most spiders, the jumping spider has good eyesight, which helps it find prey. Once it has spotted something, the spider leaps on to its victim. Before jumping, it attaches a silk thread to the ground as a safety line along which it can return to its hideout.

Family: Theridiidae

Size: up to ½ in (1.2 cm) long

Number of species: about 2,400

Habitat: worldwide

### Black widow spider

The female black widow has comblike bristles on her back legs, which she uses to throw strands of silk over prey that gets caught in her web. She has a venomous bite. One drop is more deadly than the same amount of rattlesnake venom. Male black widows do not bite.

Family: Lycosidae

Size: ⅛–1½ in (0.3–4 cm) long

Number of species: about 2,400

Habitat: worldwide

### Wolf spider

Fast-moving hunters, wolf spiders creep up on prey and seize it after a final speedy dash. Most do not make webs. Wolf spiders have excellent eyesight, which helps them find prey at night.

Family: Theraphosidae

Size: up to 11 in (28 cm) long

Number of species: about 1,000

Habitat: worldwide

## Crab spider

This spider scuttles sideways like a crab. Some crab spiders are dark brown or black, but those that usually sit on certain flowers to wait for prey are brightly colored to match the petals.

Family: Thomisidae

Size: 1⁄16 –3⁄8 in (0.15–0.9 cm) long

Number of species: about 2,200

Habitat: worldwide

## Lichen spider

Mottled colors help keep this spider well hidden on lichen-covered tree bark. Tufts of tiny hairs on its legs break up any shadows which might otherwise reveal its presence. If the spider suspects an enemy is near, it flattens itself against the bark and is even more difficult to see.

## Red-kneed tarantula

Tarantulas are some of the largest of all spiders, with legs spanning more than 8 in (20 cm). Most hide by day and come out at night to hunt insects and other small creatures, which they kill with a venomous bite. Harmless to people, they are becoming popular pets. So many are collected for sale that they may soon become scarce in the wild.

Family: Ctenizidae

Size: 3⁄8–2 in (0.9–5 cm) long

Number of species: about 130

Habitat: worldwide

Family: Sparassidae

Size: 3⁄8–1 1⁄4 in (0.9–3 cm) long

Number of species: about 1,150

Habitat: tropical

Family: Scytodidae

Size: 3⁄8 in (0.9 cm) long

Number of species: about 230

Habitat: worldwide

## Spitting spider

This unusual hunter approaches its victim and spits out two lines of a sticky substance from glands near its mouth. These fall in zigzags over the prey, pinning it down. The spider then kills it with a bite.

## Trapdoor spider

The burrow of the trapdoor spider has a hinged lid at the top. The spider waits in its burrow until it senses the movement of prey overhead. It then pops out of the door, grabs the prey and takes it back into its burrow.

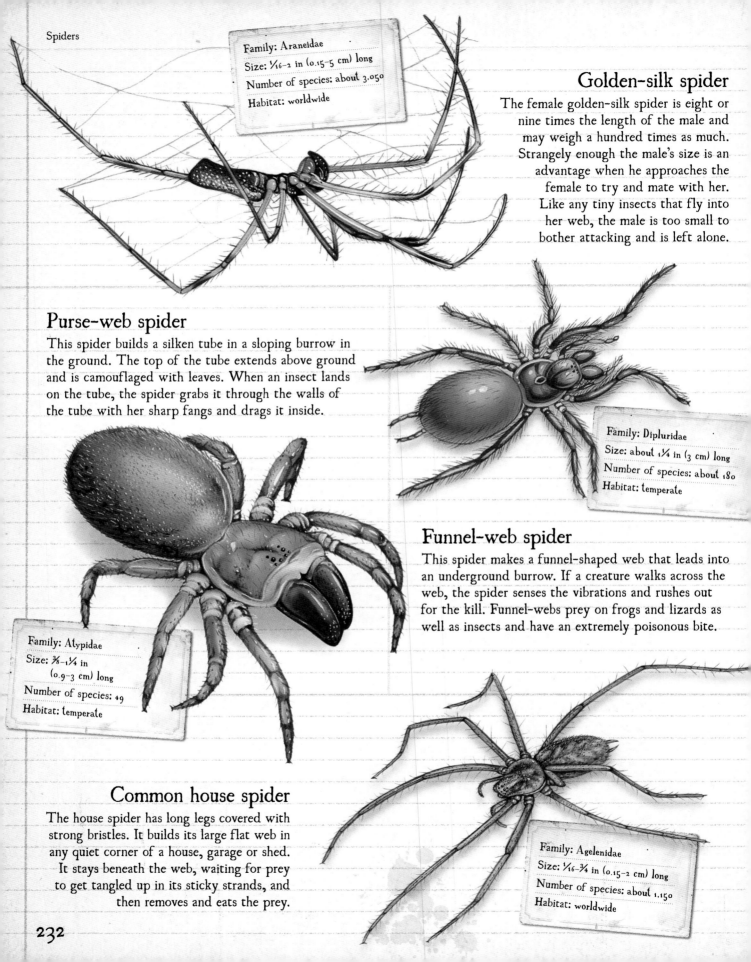

Family: Araneidae
Size: 1/16–2 in (0.15–5 cm) long
Number of species: about 3,050
Habitat: worldwide

## Golden-silk spider

The female golden-silk spider is eight or nine times the length of the male and may weigh a hundred times as much. Strangely enough the male's size is an advantage when he approaches the female to try and mate with her. Like any tiny insects that fly into her web, the male is too small to bother attacking and is left alone.

## Purse-web spider

This spider builds a silken tube in a sloping burrow in the ground. The top of the tube extends above ground and is camouflaged with leaves. When an insect lands on the tube, the spider grabs it through the walls of the tube with her sharp fangs and drags it inside.

Family: Dipluridae
Size: about 1¼ in (3 cm) long
Number of species: about 180
Habitat: temperate

## Funnel-web spider

This spider makes a funnel-shaped web that leads into an underground burrow. If a creature walks across the web, the spider senses the vibrations and rushes out for the kill. Funnel-webs prey on frogs and lizards as well as insects and have an extremely poisonous bite.

Family: Atypidae
Size: 3/8–1¼ in
(0.9–3 cm) long
Number of species: 49
Habitat: temperate

## Common house spider

The house spider has long legs covered with strong bristles. It builds its large flat web in any quiet corner of a house, garage or shed. It stays beneath the web, waiting for prey to get tangled up in its sticky strands, and then removes and eats the prey.

Family: Agelenidae
Size: 1/16–¾ in (0.15–2 cm) long
Number of species: about 1,150
Habitat: worldwide

Family: Dysderidae
Size: ¾ in (2 cm) long
Number of species: about 530
Habitat: temperate

# Cell spider

These spiders have only six eyes — most spiders have eight. They spend the day hiding under stones and come out at night to hunt woodlice. Woodlice have strong external skeletons but this spider can pierce the body armor with its huge sharp fangs.

# Green lynx spider

This fast-moving active hunter does not build webs but chases its prey over plants, jumping from leaf to leaf. It has good eyesight, which helps it spot its prey, and its green color helps keep it hidden when it rests on leaves. The female spins a silken egg sac that she attaches to plants.

Family: Araneidae
Size: ⅟₁₆–1¼ in (0.15–3 cm) long
Number of species: about 3,050
Habitat: worldwide

Family: Oxyopidae
Size: ⅛–⅝ in (0.3–1.5 cm) long
Number of species: about 500
Habitat: worldwide

# Orchard spider

Although a member of the orb weaver family, the orchard spider does not make a web. She simply sits on the branch of a tree and grabs any moth that comes near with her strong front legs. She may release a scent that attracts the moths to her.

# Water spider

This is the only spider that lives its whole life in water. So that it can breathe underwater, it spins a bell-shaped home of silk, attached to water plants, and supplies it with bubbles of air collected at the surface. Then it sits inside its bell, waiting for prey to come near. It pounces on the prey and takes it back to the bell to eat.

Family: Pisauridae
Size: ¼–1 in (0.6–2.5 cm) long
Number of species: about 340
Habitat: worldwide

Family: Agelenidae
Size: ⅟₁₆–¾ in (0.15–2 cm) long
Number of species: about 1,150
Habitat: worldwide

# Nursery-web spider

These spiders build a web not to catch prey but to protect their young. The female carries her egg sac with her until the eggs are almost ready to hatch. Then she spins a web over the eggs to protect them while they hatch.
She stands guard nearby.

# ORB WEAVERS

Very few creatures build traps to catch their prey. Among the best-known are the orb weaver spiders that build the webs most often seen in our houses and gardens. There are about 3,050 species of these spiders living all over the world. Spiders build their webs with two types of silk that comes from glands at the end of the body. The silk is liquid when it comes out of the nozzlelike openings of small structures at the end of the abdomen, called spinnerets. One type of silk hardens into extremely tough nonsticky thread; the other type is sticky and used for the center of the web. Once the web is built, the spider waits near the center or hides nearby, linked to the web by a signal thread. Through this, the spider can sense any movement or disturbance in the web. Once prey is caught in the sticky part of the web, the spider rushes over, bites it and wraps it in strands of silk to prevent it from escaping.

## OGRE-FACED SPIDER

This spider takes its web to the prey. It makes a small but strong net of very sticky threads in a framework of dry silk. Once the trap is made, the spider hangs from a twig on silken lines, holding the net in its four front legs. When an insect comes near, the spider stretches the net wide so the prey flies into it and becomes entangled. The catch is then bundled up in the net and taken away to eat.

## BUILDING A WEB

First, the orb weaver spider makes a framework of strong nonsticky thread that are firmly attached to surrounding plants or other supports. Spokes are added and the spider spins a widely spaced temporary spiral. With everything locked in place, the spider then moves inward, spinning the sticky spiral that will trap the prey and removing the temporary spiral. The whole process takes less than an hour and the spider may build a new web every night.

# SHEET-WEB SPIDER

Yet another kind of trap is woven by this spider. It makes a flat sheetlike web, which may measure as much as 12 in (30 cm) across, and lies in wait beneath it. Above the web there are many threads holding it in place. When a prey hits these threads it falls down on to the sheet web, where it is grabbed from below by the spider.

This orb weaver spider has caught a butterfly in her web and is wrapping the prey in threads of silk so that it cannot escape. She will then carry it off to eat in her hiding place near the web.

# A WIDE WEB

The European garden spider, also known as the cross or diadem spider, builds a large orbital web that measures as much as 15¾ in (40 cm) across and catches butterflies, wasps and flies. The spider has extra clawlike structures on each foot , which help it grip on to the dry lines of the web while avoiding the sticky threads. If the spider touches the sticky part, a special oily covering on its legs prevents it getting trapped.

# SCORPIONS AND OTHER ARACHNIDS

There are about 1,500 kinds of scorpions living everywhere from deserts to rain forests in warm parts of the world. They use the venomous sting at the end of the body to kill prey and to defend themselves. A few kinds of scorpions have venom so strong that it can kill a human, but the sting of most is no worse than that of a bee or wasp. Also in the arachnid group are tiny mites and ticks. Mites eat aphid eggs and prey on other small insects. Some also live as parasites on other animals. Ticks feed on the blood of birds, mammals and reptiles.

> Family: Cheliferidae
> Size: up to ¼ in (0.6 cm) long
> Number of species: about 300
> Habitat: worldwide

## Pseudoscorpion

These tiny soil-dwelling relatives of the scorpion have venom glands in their pedipalps, which they use when attacking prey. They do not have a sting. Pseudoscorpions have silk glands and they spin cocoons in which to spend the winter.

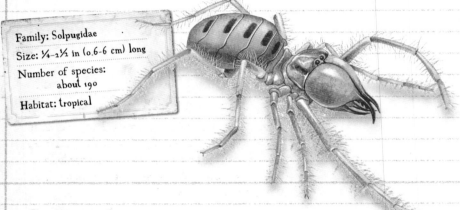

> Family: Solpugidae
> Size: ¼–2½ in (0.6–6 cm) long
> Number of species: about 190
> Habitat: tropical

## Wind scorpion

A group related to true scorpions, wind scorpions, also known as sunspiders, are fast-running hunters. Common in desert areas, they come out at night to hunt insects and even small lizards. They use their pedipalps and front legs as feelers.

> Family: Thelyphonidae
> Size: 5¾ in (14.5 cm) long including tail
> Number of species: about 110
> Habitat: tropical North and South America

## Centruroides scorpion

This scorpion hides under stones on the ground during the day and comes out at night to seize insects and spiders in its powerful pincers. The female carries her newborn young around on her back for a few weeks until they are big enough to fend for themselves.

> Family: Buthidae
> Size: up to 4¾ in (12 cm) long
> Number of species: about 650
> Habitat: worldwide

## Whip scorpion

Not a true scorpion, the whip scorpion has a long thin whiplike tail and no stinger. It has four pairs of legs but uses the first pair as feelers. The whip scorpion's other common name is vinegaroon because it can spray an acidic vinegary liquid from glands near the base of its tail when threatened.

## Velvet mite

This mite gets its common name from the thick, soft hair that covers its rounded body. Adult velvet mites are not parasites and feed mostly on insect eggs. They lay their own eggs on the ground and when the larvae hatch they live as parasites on insects and spiders, feeding on their body fluids.

Family: Trombidiidae
Size: up to 3⁄16 in (0.5 cm) long
Number of species: about 280
Habitat: worldwide

## House dust mite

These mites are common in houses throughout the world. They feed on scales of skin found in house dust. Their droppings contain materials that can cause an allergic reaction or asthma (difficulty breathing) in some sensitive people.

Family: Pyroglyphidae
Size: (1⁄100–2⁄100 in (0.25–0.5 mm) long
Number of species: 20
Habitat: worldwide

Family: Scorpionidae
Size: up to 8½ in (21 cm) long
Number of species: about 200
Habitat: tropical

## Harvestman

Also known as the daddy-long-legs, this relative of spiders has a rounded body without the narrow waist typical of spiders. All its legs are very long and thin but the second pair are the longest. Usually active at night, the harvestman hunts insects. The female lays her eggs in the ground where they stay through the winter and hatch out in the spring.

## Scorpion

The scorpion finds prey mostly by its sense of touch, using fine hairs attached to nerves on the body, legs and claws to sense movements. It grabs the prey in its huge claws and then swings its sting forward over its body to inject poison into its victim to paralyze or kill it before eating.

Family: Phalangiidae
Size: up to 1⅜ in (4 cm) long
Number of species: about 380
Habitat: worldwide

Family: Ixodidae
Size: ⅛–⅜ in (0.3–1 cm) long
Number of species: about 690
Habitat: worldwide

## Tick

Ticks are parasites — they live by feeding on the blood of birds, mammals and reptiles. They stay on the host for several days while feeding, attached by their strong mouthparts. Some species may pass along diseases as they feed.

# SNAILS, SLUGS AND OTHER LAND INVERTEBRATES

As well as insects and spiders, many other kinds of invertebrates spend their lives on land. Most mollusks live in the sea, but there are land species of slugs and snails. Woodlice are related to crustaceans, such as the sea-living crabs and shrimps. Earthworms are relatives of the segmented worms in the sea, but they spend their lives burrowing through the soil. All of these animals are common worldwide. Like insects and spiders, millipedes and centipedes are arthropods. They live everywhere from tropical rain forests to tundra. They may be mistaken for insects, but they have many more legs and do not have wings. Their bodies are sensitive to drying out in the sun and so they usually come out only at night.

## Woodlouse
### Armadillidium vulgare

A woodlouse is related to the crustaceans, like a crab or shrimp, but it has become adapted to live on land. Its body is made up of 13 segments and it has 7 pairs of legs. It hides in moist, dark places during the day and comes out at night to feed on decaying plants and tiny dead creatures.

Size: ⅜ in (1 cm) long

Range: worldwide

Habitat: inhabited areas and farmland, deciduous and tropical grassland and forest, northern forest

## Earthworm
### Lumbricus terrestris

Earthworms are common in soil all over the world. They spend most of their lives underground and only come to the surface at night or in wet weather. Dead leaves and other plant material are their main food, but they also eat soil, digesting what they can and excreting the rest.

Size: up to 11¾ in (30 cm) long

Range: worldwide

Habitat: inhabited areas and farmland, deciduous forest, temperate grassland

## Great black slug
### Arion ater

The slug is a mollusk, like a snail, but has no external shell. All land mollusks make mucus. This slime helps stop the slug's body drying out and allows the creature to move more easily. The slug leaves trails of slime wherever it goes and these help it find its way. It feeds mostly on rotting plant and animal material, which it finds by smell.

Size: 6 in (15 cm) long

Range: Europe and North America

Habitat: inhabited areas and farmland, deciduous forest, temperate grassland

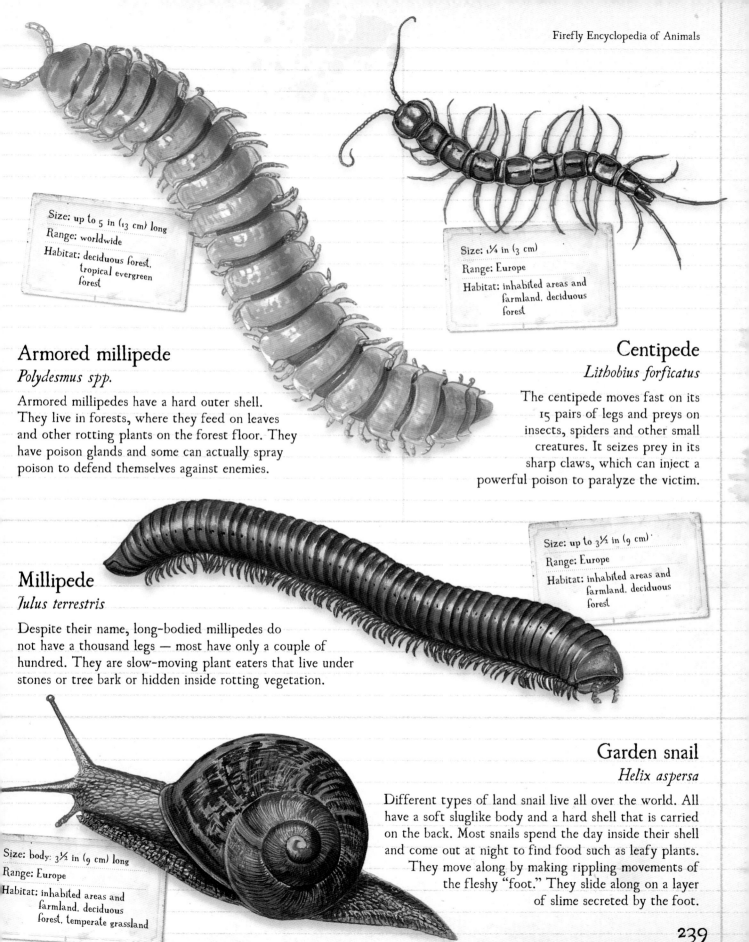

Size: up to 5 in (13 cm) long

Range: worldwide

Habitat: deciduous forest, tropical evergreen forest

Size: 1¼ in (3 cm)

Range: Europe

Habitat: inhabited areas and farmland, deciduous forest

## Armored millipede
### *Polydesmus spp.*

Armored millipedes have a hard outer shell. They live in forests, where they feed on leaves and other rotting plants on the forest floor. They have poison glands and some can actually spray poison to defend themselves against enemies.

## Centipede
### *Lithobius forficatus*

The centipede moves fast on its 15 pairs of legs and preys on insects, spiders and other small creatures. It seizes prey in its sharp claws, which can inject a powerful poison to paralyze the victim.

## Millipede
### *Julus terrestris*

Despite their name, long-bodied millipedes do not have a thousand legs — most have only a couple of hundred. They are slow-moving plant eaters that live under stones or tree bark or hidden inside rotting vegetation.

Size: up to 3½ in (9 cm)

Range: Europe

Habitat: inhabited areas and farmland, deciduous forest

## Garden snail
### *Helix aspersa*

Different types of land snail live all over the world. All have a soft sluglike body and a hard shell that is carried on the back. Most snails spend the day inside their shell and come out at night to find food such as leafy plants. They move along by making rippling movements of the fleshy "foot." They slide along on a layer of slime secreted by the foot.

Size: body: 3½ in (9 cm) long

Range: Europe

Habitat: inhabited areas and farmland, deciduous forest, temperate grassland

# SEA CREATURES

As well as the thousands of kinds of fish that live in the oceans there is also a huge range of invertebrates. Marine invertebrates, including clams, crabs and jellyfish, live in every part of the ocean from the surface waters to the deepest sea. The most highly populated waters are those near the surface. Here, plenty of light penetrates to about 330 ft (100 m) and plant plankton thrive. These microscopic plants are eaten by animal plankton — tiny animals that drift in surface waters and are themselves eaten by larger sea creatures.

> Size: 6 in (15 cm) long
> Range: Arctic, Atlantic and North Pacific oceans
> Habitat: oceanic

## SPONGES, JELLYFISH AND RELATIVES

Sponges have such simple bodies that they look more like plants than animals. Their larvae are free-swimming, but adult sponges remain in one place on a rock or on the seabed. Sea anemones belong to a large group of creatures called cnidarians, as do coral and jellyfish. Most have a simple tubelike body and tentacles armed with stinging cells. Comb jellies are a separate group. They are small, translucent animals that float in surface waters. Lamp shells are shelled creatures that can anchor themselves to rocks or the seabed by a fleshy stalk.

### Common comb jelly
*Bolinopsis infundibulum*

The comb jelly moves with the help of tiny hairs arranged in lines down its baglike body. These hairs are called comb plates and they beat together to push the comb jelly through the water. It catches prey such as shrimp and other small creatures.

> Size: bell: 4 in (10 cm) wide; tentacles: 10 ft (3 m) long
> Range: Atlantic, Indian and Pacific oceans
> Habitat: oceanic

> Size: up to 19¾ in (50 cm) long
> Range: tropical waters worldwide
> Habitat: coastal waters

### Vase sponge
*Callyspongia spp.*

Sponges are among the simplest of animals. To feed, they draw water into the chambers of the body, where tiny particles of food are trapped and digested. The water also brings oxygen to the creatures and removes carbon dioxide.

### Mauve stinger
*Pelagia noctiluca*

Like most jellyfish, this creature has many stinging cells on its long tentacles. These cells protect it from enemies and help it to catch plankton to eat. Although known as the mauve stinger, it may be yellow, red or even brown in color.

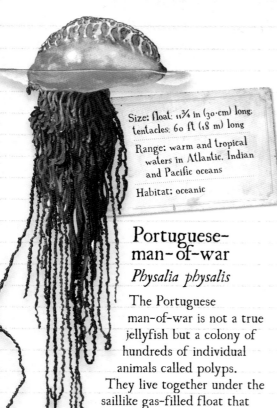

Size: float: 11¾ in (30 cm) long;
tentacles: 60 ft (18 m) long

Range: warm and tropical
waters in Atlantic, Indian
and Pacific oceans

Habitat: oceanic

## Portuguese-man-of-war
### *Physalia physalis*

The Portuguese man-of-war is not a true jellyfish but a colony of hundreds of individual animals called polyps. They live together under the saillike gas-filled float that lies on the water's surface. Each type of polyp performs different tasks for the colony, such as capturing food or producing eggs.

## Phosphorescent sea pen
### *Pennatula phosphorea*

The featherlike sea pen is not one animal but a group of many individuals called polyps. One large stemlike polyp stands in the seabed and supports the whole group. On the side branches there are many small feeding polyps. If touched, the sea pen glows with phosphorescence.

## Brain coral
### *Meandrina spp.*

Brain coral is most common in water 19½–39½ ft (6–12 m) deep. It lives in dome-shaped colonies of tiny anemonelike creatures called polyps. Each of the polyps has a hard skeleton. The skeletons make up the rocky base of the colony.

Size: Colony up to 3¼ ft (1 m) wide

Range: tropical Indian and Pacific oceans and Caribbean Sea

Habitat: coral reefs

Size: 1¼ in (3 cm) long

Range: Atlantic Ocean

Habitat: deep sea, coastal waters

## Lamp shell
### *Terebratulina septentrionalis*

The lamp shell belongs to a group of animals called brachiopods, members of which have lived on Earth for about 550 million years. It has two shells and a short stalk on which it can move around. When the shells open they expose folded tentacles lined with tiny hairs. These hairs drive water over the tentacles, which trap tiny particles of food.

## Sea anemone
### *Urticina spp.*

The sea anemone may look like a flower, but it is actually an animal that catches other creatures to eat. At one end of its body is a sucking disk that keeps it attached to a rock. At the other end is the mouth, surrounded by tentacles.

Size: up to 9¾ in (25 cm) tall

Range: Atlantic and Pacific coasts

Habitat: coast

# CRUSTACEANS

There are about 70,000 species of crustaceans, including such creatures as barnacles, crabs, lobsters and shrimps. Woodlice live on land and there are some shrimps and other species in fresh water, but most crustaceans live in the sea. Typically, they have a tough outer skeleton, which protects the soft body within. The head is made up of six segments, on which there are two pairs of antennae and several different sets of mouthparts. The rest of the body may be divided into a thorax and abdomen, and carries the walking legs.

Size: 4 in (10 cm) long

Range: worldwide

Habitat: deep sea

## Deep-sea shrimp
### *Pasiphaea spp.*

The deep-sea shrimp's antennae are longer than its body. It spreads its antennae out in the water to help it find food in the darkness of the deep sea. It eats any dead and decaying matter that it comes across.

Size: up to 31½ in (80 cm).
including stalk

Range: Atlantic and
Pacific oceans

Habitat: oceanic

## Common goose barnacle
### *Lepas anatifera*

Goose barnacles live fixed by their stalks to any object floating in the open sea, including logs and buoys as well as boats. The barnacle's body is enclosed by a shell made of five plates. These open at the top so that the barnacle can extend its six pairs of feathery arms and collect tiny particles of food from the water.

Size: up to 3½ in (9 cm) long

Range: Antarctic Ocean

Habitat: ocean seabed

Size: up to 3⅝ ft (1.1 m)

Range: North Atlantic coasts

Habitat: coast, coastal waters

## American lobster
### *Homarus americanus*

During the day this large crustacean hides in rock crevices, but at night it comes out to hunt. It uses its huge pincers to crack and tear apart prey such as mollusks and crabs. In the summer, the female lobster lays thousands of eggs, which she carries around with her on the underside of her body. The eggs hatch into shrimplike larvae, which float in surface waters for a few weeks. They then settle on the seabed and start to develop into adults.

## Giant isopod
### *Glyptonotus antarcticus*

A sea-living relative of the wood louse, the giant isopod lives in the Antarctic, where it catches any food it can find. It also scavenges on the seabed for dead and dying creatures. Antarctic isopods are much bigger than those elsewhere in the world.

# Antarctic krill
## *Euphausia superba*

Shrimplike krill feed on plant plankton and tiny creatures that they sieve from the water. In turn, krill are the main food of many fish, penguins and even whales. A blue whale can eat as many as four million krill in a day. Krill are extremely common and sometimes occur in such large numbers that the sea looks red.

Size: up to 2 in (5 cm) long
Range: southern oceans
Habitat: oceanic

Size: up to 4 in (10 cm) long
Range: North Atlantic coasts
Habitat: coast, coastal waters

Size: up to 1 in (2.5 cm) long
Range: Atlantic coasts
Habitat: coast, coastal waters

# Hermit crab
## *Pagurus bernhardus*

Unlike other crabs, the hermit crab has no hard shell of its own. It protects its soft body by living in the discarded shell of another creature, such as a snail. The crab has large pincers on its first pair of legs, which it uses to grab its prey.

# Amphipod
## *Gammarus locusta*

This small crustacean lives on the lower shore under rocks or among seaweed, and feeds on tiny pieces of plant and animal matter. On its abdomen are three pairs of jumping legs. The female amphipod holds her developing young in a pouch on the underside of her body.

# Pink shrimp
## *Pandalus montagui*

Shrimps have much lighter shells than crabs or lobsters. The limbs on the abdomen are used for swimming, while some of those on the thorax are for walking and others are used as mouthparts.

Size: up to 5 in (12.5 cm)
Range: Arctic Ocean, North Atlantic coasts
Habitat: coast, coastal waters

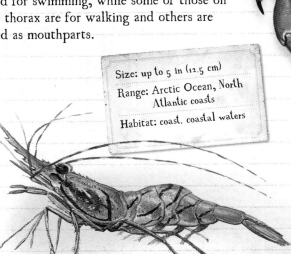

Size: up to 12 in (30 cm) wide
Range: North Atlantic coasts
Habitat: coast

# Edible crab
## *Cancer spp.*

Most crabs have a strong shell, which protects the body, and five pairs of legs. On the first pair are powerful pincers used to break open the shells of prey, such as mollusks. The other legs are smaller. Crabs live among rocks on the lower shore.

243

# MOLLUSKS

There are at least 110,000 living species of mollusks. They are divided into three main groups: gastropods, such as limpets and snails; bivalves, which include clams, mussels and scallops; and cephalopods, such as squid, cuttlefish and octopus. Slugs and some kinds of snails live on land and there are freshwater snails and clams, but the greatest range of mollusks is found in the sea. In most mollusks, the body is divided into three parts: the head, which contains the mouth and sense organs; the body and the foot, a fleshy part of the body on which the animal moves along. Most, but not all, mollusks have a tough shell that protects the soft body.

Size: up to 5 in (12.5 cm) long
Range: Atlantic Ocean and Caribbean Sea
Habitat: coral reefs

## Atlantic deer cowrie
*Macrocypraea cervus*

This type of sea snail has a beautiful shiny shell. Unlike most snails, the cowrie's mantle can be extended to cover the outside of the shell and camouflage the animal. (The mantle is a thin fold of tissue, part of which makes the shell.) The opening of the shell is edged with 35 teeth.

## Clam
*Saxidomus nuttalli*

The usual home of the clam is a burrow deep in a sandy or muddy seabed. It digs the burrow with its foot, a fleshy part of its body. Two long tubes extend from the shell. Water and food (tiny living particles) go in through one tube. The water then goes out the other tube.

Size: 4 in (10 cm) long
Range: Atlantic coasts
Habitat: coastal waters

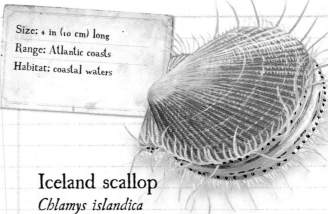

## Iceland scallop
*Chlamys islandica*

The scallop has a soft body protected by two shells. A row of well-developed eyes can be seen when the shells are slightly parted. The scallop moves by flapping its shells together, forcing out jets of water that push it forward.

Size: 6 in (15 cm) long
Range: North Pacific Ocean
Habitat: coastal waters

Size: up to 4 in (10 cm) long
Range: Atlantic and Pacific coasts
Habitat: coast, coastal waters

## Oyster
*Crassostrea virginica*

The eastern oyster is a type of bivalve. It has a soft body protected by two hard shells, which are held together by strong muscles. It eats tiny pieces of plant and animal food, which it filters from the water. The water is drawn into the partly opened shell and any food is caught on tiny sticky hairs on the oyster's gills.

# Common octopus
*Octopus vulgaris*

Size: up to 39½ in (100 cm) long

Range: worldwide except polar waters

Habitat: coastal waters

The octopus has eight long arms lined with suckers. It uses these to pull itself along, but it can also swim quickly by shooting jets of water out of its body. It spends much of its time hiding in crevices, then grabbing prey such as crabs, clams and shrimp.

# Lightning whelk
*Busycon contrarium*

Size: 15¾ in (40 cm) long

Range: Atlantic Ocean

Habitat: coastal waters

This large whelk has a beautiful spiral shell with brown markings. It lives on sandy or muddy seabeds in shallow water and feeds mostly on clams and other mollusks, which it digs out of the mud.

# Purple sea snail
*Janthina janthina*

This little snail cannot swim, but it drifts in the surface waters of the sea, clinging to a raft of bubbles. These are made from mucus the snail secretes, which hardens when it enters the water.

Size: 1 in (2.5 cm) long, including tentacles

Range: Atlantic, Indian and Pacific oceans

Habitat: oceanic

Size: body: 6 in (15 cm) long

Range: Indian Ocean, Red and Mediterranean seas

Habitat: coral reefs

# Chromodoris nudibranch
*Chromodoris annulata*

Nudibranches, or sea slugs, are related to snails, but they have no shells and are often brightly colored. This species has a pair of hornlike projections and a clump of feathery gills on its back. Sponges are its main food.

# Longfin inshore squid
*Doryteuthis pealeii*

Size: up to 30 in (76 cm) long, including tentacles

Range: northwest Atlantic Ocean

Habitat: oceanic

The squid has a long, torpedo-shaped body, four pairs of arms, and one pair of much longer tentacles. Suckers on the arms and the tips of the tentacles help the squid grasp its prey — mostly fish and crustaceans. A fast swimmer, the squid moves by a type of jet propulsion, shooting water out of its body to force itself backward through the water.

# ROCK CLINGERS

While most marine creatures swim or float freely in the water, some live firmly attached to rocks or other surfaces. This helps protect them from the waves that sweep over them twice a day as the tide comes in. Barnacles, one kind of rock clinger, are among the most common creatures on the shore. Huge colonies of them cover rocks and shore debris, and even attach themselves to other creatures such as mussels. Barnacles begin life as free-swimming larvae and spend a month or more floating in coastal waters, feeding on plankton. During its final larval stage, each barnacle finds somewhere to settle. It fixes itself to the surface with a cementlike substance that it makes in glands in its body. Once settled, it does not move again. Limpets, periwinkles and chitons can all cling to rocks by means of a suckerlike foot, which is so strong that they are almost impossible to move. But all these creatures can also move around on their own to graze on algae.

## ROUGH PERIWINKLE

There are many types of periwinkle, each adapted for life in different parts of the shore. The rough periwinkle lives on stones and rocks higher up the shore than most other species.

## CHITON

Unlike other molluscs, the chiton has a shell made up of eight sections held together by muscles. If in danger, the chiton can roll itself up like an armadillo.

## COMMON LIMPET

As limpets move over rocks feeding on algae, they leave a sticky trail of mucus behind them. This helps each limpet make its way back to the exact same place on the rock after each feeding trip.

## ACORN BARNACLE

When covered by water at high tide, the barnacle opens its shell at the top and puts out its feathery arms to gather plankton to eat. When the tide is out, the barnacle keeps its trapdoor top firmly closed.

# COMMON MUSSEL

The threads that hold the mussel on to rocks are made as a sticky fluid inside a gland in the mussel's body. This fluid hardens to keep the mussel firmly in place. The shell is in two halves. These are normally held tight together, but they can be partly opened so that the mussel can filter tiny pieces of food from the water.

# BLUE-RAYED LIMPET

Not all limpets cling to rocks. The blue-rayed limpet lives attached seaweed, which is anchored to rock or the seabed near the shore. The limpet grazes on the seaweed fronds, feeding on the seaweed itself and on small plants growing there, such as algae.

A colorful painted topshell clings to rocks on the seashore, surrounded by sea anemones and other creatures. The topshell, which is a cone-shaped kind of snail, feeds on tiny plants called algae growing on the rocks.

# WORMS AND ECHINODERMS

There are about 21,000 species of segmented, or annelid, worms. They include earthworms on land, as well as some freshwater worms such as leeches, but most live in the sea. All have a body that is divided into a number of segments. All 7,000 species of echinoderms live in the sea. There are four main groups — brittle stars, starfish, sea cucumbers, and sea urchins and sand dollars. Many have a body that is divided into five radiating parts with a mouth at one end and an anus at the other. Most echinoderms move around using tiny stilts called tube feet, each tipped with a sucking disk.

> Size: 7 in (18 cm) long
>
> Range: Atlantic and Mediterranean coasts
>
> Habitat: coast, coastal waters, deep sea

## Sea mouse
### Aphrodita aculeata

Despite its plump shape, the sea mouse is actually a kind of worm. Its upper side is covered with lots of grayish-brown bristles that give it a furry look and inspire its common name. The sea mouse spends much of its life under mud or sand in shallow water.

> Size: up to 5 ft (1.5 m), including stalk
>
> Range: worldwide
>
> Habitat: deep sea

## Sea lily
### Crinoidea spp.

This relative of the starfish lives attached to a rock by a stalk. Its branching arms are lined with tiny suckerlike tube feet. When feeding, the sea lily spreads its arms wide and traps plankton and other tiny particles with its tube feet. The food is then passed down grooves lined with hairs to the mouth, at the center of the body.

## Long-spined urchin
### Diadema antillarum

Sharp spines protect the urchin's rounded body from enemies. The urchin's mouth is on the underside of the body and has five teeth arranged in a circle for chewing food. By day these urchins stay hidden on the reef, but at night they come out to feed on algae.

> Size: body 4 in (10 cm) wide; spines: 4–15¾ in (10–40 cm) long
>
> Range: Atlantic Ocean and Caribbean Sea
>
> Habitat: coral reefs

> Size: body: 1 in (2.5 cm) long; arms: up to 4 in (10 cm) long
>
> Range: Atlantic Ocean
>
> Habitat: coast, coastal waters

## Common brittle star
### Ophiothrix fragilis

The brittle star has a central disklike body and five long spiny arms, each separate from the other. The animal's mouth is on the underside of the disk. The brittle star uses its long arms to catch small crustaceans and other creatures.

## Black sea cucumber
*Holothuria forskali*

Sea cucumbers are related to starfish, but they have long simple bodies. At one end is the anus and at the other is the mouth, surrounded by food-gathering tentacles. Rows of tiny tube feet run the length of the body. When disturbed, the sea cucumber ejects sticky white threads from its anus, which confuse predators.

Size: 5 in (12.5 cm)

Range: Atlantic Ocean and Caribbean Sea

Habitat: coral reefs

## Magnificent feather duster
*Sabellastarte magnifica*

The body of this spectacular worm usually stays hidden in a flexible tube attached to a reef or the seabed. The tube is made of fine sand stuck together with a gluey substance made in the worm's body. The worm catches food with its crown of feathery gills.

## Common sand dollar

*Echinarachnius parma*

The sand dollar has a flattened disklike body and a shell that is covered with short spines. On its underside are rows of tiny tubelike feet, which help the sand dollar gather tiny pieces of food from the water.

Size: 3 in (7.5 cm) wide

Range: North Atlantic and Pacific coasts, Arctic Ocean

Habitat: coast, coastal waters

Size: 4¾ in (12 cm) across

Range: western Atlantic Ocean and Caribbean Sea

Habitat: coral reefs

## Green paddle worm
*Eulalia viridis*

This worm lives under rocks among seaweed, both on the shore and in deeper water. It has four pairs of tentacles on its head and lots of tiny leaflike paddles down each side of its long body. It feeds mainly on other worms.

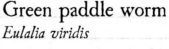

Size: up to 6 in (15 cm) long

Range: Northwest Atlantic coasts and Mediterranean

Habitat: coast

## Thorny starfish
*Echinaster sentus*

Large spines cover the body and five arms of this starfish. Two rows of special feet, called tube feet, extend down each arm. The tube feet work together, extending and contracting, to move the starfish around as it searches for prey.

# WHY DO ANIMALS BUILD NESTS?

While many animals manage without a nest or a home of any kind, others build structures that they use for shelter and for rearing their young in safety. This home may be specially built, like a bird's nest, or simply a natural hole or a sheltered spot. Homes may be made in trees, on the ground or in underground burrows. Birds generally use their nests only when breeding. They lay and incubate their eggs in nests and care for their young, but usually leave the nest once the young have gone. Some mammals, such as beavers and prairie dogs, spend much of their time in the homes they make. These may contain chambers for sleeping, caring for young and storing food. Insects such as bees, wasps, ants and termites also build elaborate homes.

The nest of the penduline tit hangs from the end of a slender twig, where it is hard for predators to reach. The nest is woven from plant fibres and has an entrance near the top.

Lodge

Beaver

Entrance

# SHELTER

The female harvest mouse builds a nest as a shelter for her young. She finds some sturdy cereal stems and starts by winding the leaves of one stem around another to make a platform about 19¾ in (50 cm) above the ground. She then takes lengths of grass or leaves and uses these to weave a ball-like structure, which measures about 4 in (10 cm) across.

Stumps of trees used by beavers to build lodge

Dam

# TERMITES

This large mound is made by a colony of small, soft-bodied insects called termites. The mound is made of soil mixed with the termites' faeces and inside is a complex nest. A maze of chambers and tunnels contains special areas for food storage and for eggs and young. Chimneys inside the mounds let air in and out and help keep the temperature in the nest comfortable.

# BEAVERS

Beavers dam a stream with branches and mud to create a lake in which to store a winter food supply. A shelter, or lodge, is then built of branches by the dam.

# INDEX

# ACKNOWLEDGMENTS

## PICTURE CREDITS
(t=top, b=bottom, l=left, r=right, c=center, fc=front cover)

### FLPA
6-7 Paul Sawer/FLPA, 64-65 Tim Fitzharris/Minden Pictures/FLPA, 110bl Paul Sawer/FLPA, 112-113 Frans Lanting/FLPA, 134-135 Chris Mattison/FLPA, 151tr Photo Researchers/FLPA, 152-153 Fronline/Fronline/FLPA, 194-195 Dave Pressland/FLPA

### OXFORD SCIENTIFIC FILMS
35tr Frank Schneidermeyer/Oxford Scientific Films, 38bl Rick Price/Oxford Scientific Films, 44tr Martyn Colbeck/Oxford Scientific Films, 62t Alastair Shay/Oxford Scientific Films, 63t Eyal Bartov/Oxford Scientific Films, 62-63 Stan Osolinski/Oxford Scientific Films, 85t Colin Monteath/Oxford Scientific Films, 99br Michael Fogden/Oxford Scientific Films, 108bc Hans Reinhard/Oxford Scientific Films, 110cr Alastair Shay/Oxford Scientific Films, 111tl Jorge Sierra/Oxford Scientific Films, 118tr David Cayless/Oxford Scientific Films, 129bl David Haring/Oxford Scientific Films, 148cl John Netherton/Oxford Scientific Films, 150bl Alastair Shay/Oxford Scientific Films, 151b Michael Fogden/Oxford Scientific Films, 158tr Gary Bell/Planet Earth Pictures, 179bl Richard Herrmann/Oxford Scientific Films, 192cr Anthony Bannister/Oxford Scientific Films, 192bl Andrew Plumptre/Oxford Scientific Films, 193b David B Fleetham/Oxford Scientific Films, 193tr Steve Turner/Oxford Scientific Films, 212tr Stephen Dalton/NHPA, 220tr Bob Fredrick/Oxford Scientific Films, 226br David Thompson/Oxford Scientific Films, 235cr Oxford Scientific Films, 247bl Paul Kay/Oxford Scientific Films, 250tr Roland Mayr/Oxford Scientific Films, 251cr Stan Osolinski/Oxford Scientific Films

### NHPA
18tr Haroldo Palo Jr./NHPA, 251tl Roger Hosking/NHPA

## ARTWORK CREDITS
MAMMALS: Graham Allen, John Francis, Elizabeth Gray, Bernard Robinson, Eric Robson, Simon Turvey, Dick Twinney, Michael Woods
BIRDS: Keith Brewer, Hilary Burn, Malcolm Ellis, Steve Kirk, Colin Newman, Denys Ovenden, Peter D. Scott, Ken Wood, Michael Woods
REPTILES AND AMPHIBIANS: John Francis, Elizabeth Gray, Steve Kirk, Alan Male, Colin Newman, Eric Robson, Peter D. Scott
FISH: Robin Boutell, John Francis, Elizabeth Gray, Elizabeth Kay, Colin Newman, Guy Smith, Michael Woods
INSECTS, SPIDERS AND OTHER INVERTEBRATES: Robin Boutell, Joanne Cowne, Sandra Doyle, Bridget James, Steve Kirk, Adrian Lascom, Alan Male, Colin Newman, Steve Roberts, Bernard Robinson, Roger Stewart, Colin Woolf